A Theory of Public Opinion

A Theory of Public Opinion

Francis Graham Wilson

With a new introduction by H. Lee Cheek, Jr.

Transaction Publishers
New Brunswick (U.S.A.) and London (U.K.)

First Transaction printing 2013

This book is printed on acid-free paper that meets the American National Standard for Permanence of Paper for Printed Library Materials.

Library of Congress Catalog Number: 2012006409
ISBN: 978-1-4128-1501-7
Printed in the United States of America

Library of Congress Cataloging-in-Publication Data

Wilson, Francis Graham, 1901-1976.
A theory of public opinion / Francis Graham Wilson ; with a new introduction by H. Lee Cheek, Jr.
p. cm.
Includes index.
Originally published: Chicago : H. Regnery Co., 1962, in series: Philosophical and historical studies ; v. 2.
ISBN 978-1-4128-1501-7
1. Public opinion. I. Title.
HM261.W55 2012
303.3'8--dc23

2012006409

CONTENTS

INTRODUCTION TO THE TRANSACTION EDITION

H. Lee Cheek, Jr.

Overview

Francis Graham Wilson (1901-1976), an eminent political scientist, a lifelong scholar of public opinion, and a central figure in the postwar American conservative intellectual movement, was born near Junction, Texas, to Horace Ernest and Stella Jane (Graham) Wilson. He graduated from the University of Texas in 1923, and earned a master's degree in political science the following year. He spent a year as a teaching fellow at the University of California, and a year as an instructor at Fresno State College, before pursuing doctoral studies at Stanford University. After earning his doctorate in political science at Stanford in 1928, he accepted a position at the University of Washington. While serving on the faculty, Wilson was a member of the Executive Committee of the American Political Science Association (1937-1940). During this period he was awarded a Social Science Research Council fellowship to study international labor relations. This research, which grew out of his dissertation, was published as *Labor in the League System* by Stanford University Press in 1934. His *The Elements of Modern Politics*, a theoretical introduction to the study of government directed against the pursuit of "political authoritarianism," appeared two years later.

In 1939 Wilson accepted a position at the University of Illinois, where he would remain until 1967. The transition marked the most significant period of his scholarship and teaching. During his tenure at Illinois, Wilson assumed a nationally prominent role in promoting the study of political philosophy and humane learning, while also mentoring many students. He would serve as department chairman from 1953-1957. His publications during this period include *The American Political Mind* (1949), a textbook that articulated many of Wilson's central arguments about the nature of the American regime; *The Case for Conservatism* (1951), one of the first defenses of the conservative mission in politics by a postwar writer, which appeared two years before Russell Kirk's *The Conservative Mind* (1953) and similarly defended a conservatism grounded in tradition rather than ideology; *A Theory of Public Opinion* (1962), a major critique of behaviorist methodologies in political science; and *Political Thought in National Spain* (1967), a work dedicated to reclaiming the enduring insights in the Spanish political tradition. Wilson also wrote two hundred scholarly articles and book reviews.

After retirement from the University of Illinois in 1967, Wilson taught at Long Island University from 1967-1970, before moving to Washington, D.C. In Washington, he was a member of the Cosmos Club and he became more involved in political activism, serving as president of Accuracy in Media, Inc., and the Committee on Constitutional Integrity, and as chair of the Catholic Commission on Intellectual and Cultural Affairs.

Since Wilson's death in 1976, three new or revised volumes of his scholarship have appeared as part of Transaction's ongoing series devoted to introducing Wilson to a new generation of scholars. These volumes include a new edition of *The Case for Conservatism* (1990); *Political Philosophy and Cultural Renewal* (2001), a collection of Wilson's scholarly articles; and, *Order and Legitimacy* (2004), a revised and extended version of his earlier work on Spanish political thought.

Challenging the Behavioral Ascendancy

Francis Graham Wilson was a leading student of American politics, political thought, and public opinion. While a major figure in American political science during the middle period of the twentieth century, he was reluctant to accept every alleged improvement or new methodology in the study of politics, even as he affirmed the need for the continued refinement and the advancement of knowledge.[1] Over time, Wilson increasingly questioned the drift of American political science away from what may be described as the discipline's inherited philosophical moorings into a distinctly behavioral-orientated academic enterprise. In no area, Wilson argued, had political science generally, and democratic theory in a more refined manner, become less reflective than in the study of public opinion. As both a witness to the "revolution," and as an erudite critic of the evolution of American political science, Wilson derided the new, uncritical reliance upon statistical methods and the lack of attention to the formal, institutional structures in the study of politics. Behavioralism possessed the capacity to advance the study of politics, but its limitations were becoming exceedingly apparent, according to Wilson:

> The study of public opinion has almost become in recent times a province of the behavioral scientists. Part of the revolution of the behavioral sciences has been the development of impressive techniques for the study of the public mind. The present writer has no quarrel except in detail with the quantitative study of public opinion. Still, there seem to be areas where there is little respect for the privacy of an individual, or for his status as a rational person with irrational tendencies. His right to know what use is to be made of the opinionative, attitudinal, or emotional material that is taken from him, it seems, is not always respected. Especially is this true where there are ideological and evaluative differences between the technician and the laboratized individual.[2]

In *A Theory of Public Opinion*, Wilson provides an enduring critique and refutation of the excesses of the behaviorist impulse, while affirming the historical and theoretical significance of the idea of public opinion for popular rule. Wilson was not opposed to the contributions of the prevailing behaviorist methodologies. However, he recommended the inclusion of all available sources of analysis in order to fully comprehend the relationship between public opinion and republican government. Wilson argued that the root of the problem lay in the inability of the "empirical technician" to "accept the idea of the legitimacy of philosophical inquiry."[3] In his endorsement of the combining of all approaches to public opinion—historical, philosophical, and empirical—to augment a more complete presentation and application of scholarship, Wilson urged a "reconciliation" among the advocates of classical and behavioral studies of public opinion.[4] A contemporary exponent of Wilson's approach to public opinion, Slavko Splichal, has accurately described Wilson as a "convergence" theorist of public opinion studies, who articulated a confluence of belief "based on different principles, interests, and methods of government adapting to public opinion—so that either public opinion actually supervises government and its policies or government supervises public opinion and monitors whether it enjoys the trust of the citizens."[5] In chapter seven, entitled "Systematic Techniques," Wilson articulates his theory of convergence, opining that "[p]ublic opinion by itself cannot be the only standard of political action. There is always a theory of human behavior behind it, and in the end public opinion is itself a technique by which such a conception shares in the creation of public policy."[6]

Wilson and the Recovery of Public Opinion

This volume represents the most complete introduction to Wilson's extensive scholarship on the evolution and role of public opinion in democratic political life. Part I surveys the historical development of public opinion and political institutions. Formal political participation preceded the concept of public opinion in almost all instances, Wilson argued. The idea of public opinion and the value of the idea come later. Public opinion is only conceivable when political opinion in theory becomes determinative for the actions of the involved public in practice. If public opinion is understood as a political force, Wilson urged that we must believe that opinion has value in itself, and that it is "a process operating within the public [that] is by definition to be distinguished from those who rule."[7]

Accordingly, the search for meaning becomes a central problem for the political scientist or political leader who wishes to understand public opinion. The contemporary student of the idea of public opinion must pursue such a clarification because, Wilson writes, "[t]he quest for meaning in the symbols associated with the study of public opinion is torn between those who believe it is somehow possible to say something *ought to be* and those who are mainly, if not exclusively, concerned with utilizing the vast modern array of quantitative techniques simply in order to find out what actually *is*."[8]

Wilson proceeds to assess the roles of consent, participation, and the historical elements in public opinion, including natural law and theological and political theories, and how the exclusion of these contributing elements to the idea of public opinion has immensely broadened the influence of contemporary behaviorist public opinion research. Wilson believed in the inclusion of values into the field of study, arguing that "[c]entral to any theory of public opinion is a conception of value formation," thereby aligning himself with the earlier contributions of Walter Lippmann and Jacques Maritain in opposition to the advocates of scientific theory as the only measure of public opinion, exemplified in the work of John Dewey and his epigones.[9] Wilson suggested that scientific valuations guided by scientific method would supersede moral and natural law valuations as a restriction upon the function of public opinion. Unfortunately, Wilson opined that if the seminal, consanguineous concepts of popular rule and institutions were not assimilated into all assessments, public opinion theory would concede that there was little absolute truth and moral value in the conduct of the state, placing governmental activity largely outside the realm of ethics.

Part II analyzes the development of what constitutes the public, the authentic sentiments of the citizenry, and the complexity of assessing the idea of public opinion. The delineation and elucidation of a definition of the public was essential to the idea of public opinion because "[t]he public is the locus where the drift of symbolism in mass attitudes is arrested by effective decision."[10] For Wilson, the public is a political and social concept involving groups and the state, but more fundamentally the citizenry.

In Part III, Wilson provides a theory for understanding the contributing elements to public opinion, and those sources of interpretation that might discourage a clearer understanding of the genuine views of citizens. One potential source of the current misunderstanding is the influence of psychology upon studies in public opinion research. Wilson suggested that psychology tended to view opinion as a neutral structure or emotional response with some reflective thinking. Instead, Wilson urged the revisiting of the formation of customary habits of thought, and to a limited extent, political tradition. Indeed, Wilson believed custom may be considered evidence of opinion. Opinion is essentially a matter of attitude, he suggested. First come feelings, then sentiments (feelings guided by rational analysis), and then attitudes or patterns of reaction. Attitudes are an organization of feeling and sentiment into consistent groups.

In the formation of public opinion, Wilson identified many key factors of influence that are certainly in accord with the tenor of present-day research in public opinion. He posited that the concept of opinion must be distinguished from the government itself, and that the evaluation of the role of government was even more central. The role of the idea of public opinion must flow from the citizenry, or the public, and when this transpires public opinion emerges. The public, with its opinion, becomes a factor in political control.

Part IV is a commentary on the future of public opinion in American politics. Wilson is most concerned about the nature of the American voting public; the incumbent lack of political participation; and, problems in the formation of opinion. The contemporary student of the idea of public opinion must acknowledge that majority opinion is not synonymous with public opinion. Public opinion, rightly understood, must incorporate both majority and minority opinion. On the other hand, democratic political life has a central problem in accurately detecting and interpreting dominant attitudes. As an advocate of majority rule, Wilson argued that although majority rule is not ethically superior, it is essential to deliberative decision-making.

The substantive importance of a convergentist view of public opinion to popular rule cannot be diminished, although this mode and concept of participation must be examined anew, given the continuing challenges to American politics. Framing his insight in a distinctly American manner, Wilson combined the most salient aspects of American political thought into a theory of public opinion that is both an endorsement of the role of public opinion, as well as an appraisal of the limitations of purely behaviorist interpretive models. In the process, Wilson helped refine our understanding of republican government, but more importantly, the limits of both mechanistic understandings of public opinion and excessively majoritarian, anti-deliberative notions of popular rule.

Works by Francis Graham Wilson on Public Opinion

Books, Manuscripts and Edited Volumes:

The Elements of Modern Politics. New York: McGraw-Hill Book Company, 1936.

A Theory of Public Opinion. Chicago: Henry Regnery Company, 1962; reprint, Westport, Connecticut: Greenwood Press, 1975; reprint, New Brunswick, New Jersey: Transaction Publishers, 2013 (with new introduction by H. Lee Cheek, Jr.).

Political Philosophy and Cultural Renewal: Collected Essays of Francis Graham Wilson. Edited by H. Lee Cheek, Jr., M. Susan Power, and Kathy B. Cheek. New Brunswick, New Jersey: Transaction Publishers, 2001.

"Tolerance and Consensus." Francis J. O' Malley Papers, University of Notre Dame Archives [Unpublished manuscript].

"The Christian Intellectual." Five Radio Lectures, Station WILL, University of Illinois, November 1958 [Excerpt published as "The Christian Intellectual," *Modern Age*, Volume 5, Number 4 (Fall 1961), pp. 361-372].

"Catholic Approaches to Public Opinion." Series of lectures delivered at Loyola University of Chicago, March 1962 [Revised and unpublished monograph-length manuscript "The Catholic and Public Opinion," in Francis Graham Wilson Papers, University of Illinois Archives].

Articles:

"The Pragmatic Electorate." *American Political Science Review*, Volume 24, Number I (February 1930), pp. 16-37.

"Concepts of Public Opinion." *American Political Science Review*, Volume 27, Number 3 (June 1933), pp. 371-391.

"The Inactive Electorate and Social Revolution." *Southwestern Social Science Quarterly*, Volume 16, Number 4 (March 1936), pp. 73-84.

"Peace and War Attitudes of the Authoritarian States." *Proceedings of the Institute of World Affairs*, Volume 15 (1938), pp. 37-42.

"James Bryce on Public Opinion: Fifty Years Later." *Public Opinion Quarterly*, Volume 3, Number 3 (July 1939), pp. 420-435.

"Political Suppression in the Modern State." *Journal of Politics*, Volume 1, Number 3 (August 1939), pp. 237-257.

Review of Robert C. Brooks, *Bryce's "American Commonwealth" Fiftieth Anniversary* (New York: MacMillan Company, 1939), in *Annals of the American Academy of Political and Social Science*, Volume 208 (March 1940), pp. 226-227.

"James Bryce: The Years of Reaction." *Journal of Social Philosophy*, Volume 5, Number 3 (April 1940), pp. 232-241.

Review of Harold D. Lasswell, *Democracy Through Public Opinion* (Menasha, Wisconsin: George Banta Publishing Company, 1941), in *Annals of the American Academy of Political and Social Science*, Volume 217 (September 1941), p. 174.

"*The Federalist* on Public Opinion." *Public Opinion Quarterly*, Volume 6, Number 4 (Winter 1942), pp. 563-575 [reprinted in *Communications and Public Opinion: A Public Opinion Quarterly Reader* (New York: Praeger, 1975), pp. 500-512; and as Chapter Twelve of *Political Philosophy and Cultural Renewal* (pp. 191-203)].

"Tradition and Propaganda." *Journal of Politics*, Volume 5, Number 4 (November 1943), pp. 391-406.

"Public Opinion in the Theory of Democracy." *Thought*, Volume 20, Number 77 (June 1945), pp. 235-252.

"Public Opinion and the Intellectuals." *American Political Science Review*, Volume 48, Number 2 (June 1954), pp. 382-339.

"Public Opinion: Theory for Tomorrow." *Journal of Politics*, Volume 16, Number 4 (November 1954), pp. 601-622.

"Public Opinion and the Middle Class." *Review of Politics*, Volume 17, Number 4 (October 1955), pp. 486-510.

Notes

1. For a succinct presentation of the myriad, interconnected scholarly controversies in American political science, see James Farr, "Political Science," *The Modern Social Sciences*, ed. Theodore M. Porter, and Dorothy Ross (Cambridge: Cambridge University Press, 2003), pp. 306-328; and, John G. Gunnell, *Imagining the American Polity: Political Science and the Discourse of Democracy* (University Park: Pennsylvania State University, 2004).
2. Francis Graham Wilson, *A Theory of Public Opinion* (New Brunswick, New Jersey: Transaction Publishers, 2013), p. xviii (hereafter cited as *Theory*).
3. *Theory*, Ibid., p. 17.
4. *Theory*, Ibid., p. 18.
5. Slavko Splichal, *Public Opinion: Developments and Controversies in the Twentieth Century* (Lanham, Maryland: Rowman and Littlefield Publishers, 1999), p. 97.
6. *Theory*, Ibid., p. 175.
7. *Theory*, Ibid., p. 8.
8. *Theory*, Ibid., pp. 15-16.
9. *Theory*, Ibid., pp. 37-38 (quotation from p. 38).
10. *Theory*, Ibid., p. 93.

ACKNOWLEDGMENTS

The author wishes to acknowledge the generous assistance he has received in the preparation of this manuscript. He is particularly indebted to the editors of Thought, The American Political Science Review, The Journal of Politics, and The Review of Politics for permission to republish material on the theory of public opinion which has already appeared in those journals. There is a lesser indebtedness to other journals which have published articles bearing only in part on public opinion, and from which numerous ideas have been taken. Librarians at the University of Illinois and Notre Dame University, as well as members of the staff of the Library of Congress, have been notably helpful in the extended but intermittent work of the author on this subject. The author has, of course, benefited from the criticisms of a number of readers who have offered suggestions for improvement, but more particularly he is appreciative of the assistance he has received from Dean J. W. Peltason of the University of Illinois, and the Reverend J. T. Durkin, S.J., of the Georgetown University Graduate School. Much of the work on the manuscript was done during a sabbatical leave granted by the University of Illinois, and the Graduate College of the University provided a grant at one stage in the preparation of the manuscript. Finally, it would be difficult to make an adequate statement of appreciation for the assistance and encouragement the author has received from Dr. David S. Collier, Executive Director of the Institute for Philosophical and Historical Studies, and from some of those associated with him.

F. G. W.

A PREFACE AND AN EXPLANATION

This volume is a study of some of the important aspects of the history and present situation of the idea, or concept, of public opinion. It is not a study of the history of public opinion itself, or of the changing content of the public mind. Except as incidental to the main interest of the study, the actual state of a public opinion at a particular moment is not directly discussed. In this sense, the volume is a phase of intellectual history, and a study of one of the many problems of political philosophy. It encroaches on philosophy itself to the extent that political speculation usually does.

The study of public opinion is more burdened than most social studies with diversity in the definition of terms and ambiguity in the modes of expression concerning the public mind. A theory of public opinion, as viewed here, is not necessarily associated with any particular form of government, such as political democracy. Whatever the form of government, there is certain to be, either explicitly or implicitly, some relation between what the masses of the people think and what the government does. The lasting tension between governor and subject is the matrix of the concept of public opinion. In principle, this volume is just as interested in ideas of public opinion in monarchical, aristocratic, or totalitarian systems of government, as in public opinion in the theory of democracy. For the purposes of this study, theory and practice that limit the force of public opinion are as important to the evolution of the concept as theory and practice which seek to expand the force or power of generally held ideas.

Furthermore, it is all but impossible to state immediately what is meant by public opinion. There are so many uses and definitions of public opinion that the subject must be approached with this confusion in mind. So many uses of the term public opinion are naturalized in the literature on the subject that they cannot, except by the most arbitrary choice, be excluded from scholarly acceptance.

The study of public opinion has almost become in recent times a province of the behavioral scientists. Part of the revolution of the behavioral sciences has been the development of impressive techniques for the study of the public mind. The present writer has no quarrel except in detail with the quantitative study of public opinion. Still, there seem to be areas where there is little respect for the privacy of an individual, or for his status as a rational person with irrational tendencies. His right to know what use is to be made of the opinionative, attitudinal, or emotional material that is taken from him, it seems, is not always respected. Especially is this true where there are ideological and evaluative differences between the technician and the laboratized individual. These are hard issues, and the "dangerous knowledge" of the depth manipulators and hidden persuaders, of those who control much of the content of the mass media, and of the subtle engineers of consensus (who but recently were "propagandists"), are all surely legitimately matters of public concern, for power—and today especially psychological power—must be subject to its responsibilities.

The behavioral sciences dealing with public opinion are pragmatic, statistical, calculative, and based on "models." In the nature of the case, the theoretical constructions reached are ideally to be held strictly to the immediate conclusions which may arise from empirical achievement. Whatever the value of the theoretical life, it is severely limited in the behavioral approach to public opinion, and it is limited because one of the continuing themes of "the commitment to science" is that other means of acquiring knowledge are limited in their possibilities of achievement. As a speculative and logical means of inquiry, philosophy would have then little to contribute to the study of the public mind. The imaginative and logical inquiry is not separated from facts, for a philosopher like Plato was remarkably empirical in his treatment of issues related to the individual, the city, and the cosmos. Though myth may be used to indicate the deeper and symbolic meaning of any level of existence, there should be a combination of fact and value in any significant intellectual inquiry into public opinion. This study is planned on the principle that speculative search is a legitimate mode of study, that it is not inconsistent with quantitative, psychological, or other techniques, if these other techniques are not used as a basis for drawing conclusions which legitimately belong to other areas.

Although the study of public opinion has become firmly a part of the behavioral sciences, it is the belief of this author that the propriety of historical, philosophical, and speculative social inquiry should not be questioned. In the full sense, public opinion must be viewed from a variety of angles, including speculative ideas about social classes and functional groups. The treatment offered here of quantitative and psychological techniques has in mind pointing out some of the theoretical implications of method, rather than attempting to study public opinion with those methods. One might say indeed that public opinion, like any decisive idea, has a history; it is subject to critical thought, and the study of it may have social goals in mind. Further, the study of an important idea such as public opinion is interactive, and no method of study of it should properly stand alone.

In organization, then, this study begins with the rise of interest in the subject as an "idea," not with the existential aspects of public opinion in any given human situation. The origin of intellectual interest in the examination of the theory or idea of public opinion is the first query, and the history with which we are concerned is primarily the history of the concept. Such an insight suggests the study of the notable ideas and institutions which, in the past, have been an incentive to an understanding of the idea of public opinion. Following this use of conceptual and historical data, we turn to a statement of the "modern inquiry" which leads into the realm of systematic techniques. Any extended treatment of this problem would reduce the significance of philosophical and speculative advances in the contemporary study of the public mind. Beyond this, social theory naturally suggests the issue of how public opinion is carried and expressed in the group structure of society. One is led to a treatment of intellectuals, of course, since they are the formulators and articulators of ideas and policies. Still, the issues of the middle and working classes can hardly be avoided in this age of struggle between conservative and revolutionary ideology. In the final aspect of the study, the value system, the obligatory quality of public opinion in relation to experts, and some general conclusions of the nature of free public opinion are offered.

PART I

THE HISTORICAL INQUIRY

CHAPTER 1

In Quest of a Public

I

The central ideas of a theory of public opinion seem already old wherever one encounters them in the history of thought. Even if the intensive cultivation of public opinion as a field of study has appeared only in the last hundred years, the materials for such study are present in all social systems. The arrangement of ideas, the focus of emphasis, and the techniques of authority may shift. Yet if we say that the relation of mass–thinking to the exercise of authority is the core of public opinion theory, such theory is present in all literate cultures. Public opinion has an evolutionary history, just as do the major concepts of legal systems, or the persistent issues of technical philosophy.

On the other hand, and like other problems in intellectual history, diverse ideas of public opinion have developed, especially as its intensive consideration emerged in the last century. Some of these conflicting ideas are very old, while others arise directly from the restatement of social issues in recent times. It is, of course, the more recent conflicting views which must occupy the present-day student of public opinion, though it is also necessary in a more complete interpretation to keep in mind the ancient formulations of the problem of generalized thinking in relation to the exercise of authority in society. If, by the early years of the nineteenth century public opinion had entered the main currents of political theory, what issues did its emergence raise? *

With various subdivisions, the focal issues in the theory of public opinion may be grouped into three classes. First, what is the historical, legal, and social nature of the public or of publics? Second, what is the nature of opinion? Is it something new or is it old? Is it permanent or changing? Is it associated with particular social developments, such as the middle class, mass communication, or urban society? May it be approached through legal, political, and philosophical study, or must it be considered wholly under psychological and sociological theory? Third, what is the quality of opinion? Under what conditions is it effective? What psychological forces govern its formation, and what is its relation to the means of social communication? How does public opinion express value judgments, and is a theory of correct value judgments necessarily a part of the theory of public opinion?

Obviously, these questions, and others which might be listed at this point, raise most of the ultimate issues in social theory. For us, as believers and practitioners of democracy, for example, must we say the public opinion is "real" only in a democratic movement? Since we accept the principle of majority rule in large areas of public decision, must we also say that the only proper political value judgments arise from the determinations of the majority, however we may decide who may belong in the majority? At the middle of the twentieth century we are in the midst of one of the great crises of the human spirit, and we have been forced to say that the opinions of our communist and fascist enemies have been completely erroneous and misled, while in turn we assert the justice of the predominant opinions of our own people. Can we say that there is here anything more than a decision of those who have been the more powerful in a universal conflict? Or, can we assert with any safety that whole areas of opinion have been entirely false, and that, on a basis of a proper principle of right, our own opinion and social symbolism are valid in science or philosophy?

* See Paul A. Palmer, "The Concept of Public Opinion in Political Theory," in *Essays in History and Political Theory* (1936), 230 ff.

II

The formal means of participation of the masses in making political decisions is one of the fundamental interests in the study of public opinion. Unless the formal means of participation reach to the center of power, democracy must remain institutionally incomplete.* Yet this institutional imperfection is just what we must assume, and we must interpret the development of participation as an effort to bring the shared symbolism of individuals and groups into closer and closer relationship with the formal means of making decisions for a whole society. The expansion of the idea of the "people," the growth of the idea of "popular sovereignty," the principle of majority rule, and the formality of constitutional procedures all fit into this general scheme. It is an age-long effort to make the individual personality mean more in the slow and often clumsy operation of the larger community. However, the evolution of participation, that is, the growth of the idea of the people, must be distinguished from the parallel but differential growth of the concept of freedom of opinion. Historically, formal participation has run far ahead of the idea of free opinion, and free opinion is logically perfect only when there is no mechanism of political censorship or coercion. Probably only the anarchists can say that they really believe in a completely free opinion, while believers in government and its attendant coercion can be forceful supporters of mass participation in decision-making.†

Similar distinctions should be made in connection with majority rule. Majority rule theory goes back to classical times, but even today it is not coupled with the completely free expression of any opinion. In support of public decisions, the majority is ready to deny the right of expression to certain opinions, especially when it is believed they contradict the principle of the continued existence of the community itself. But majority

* Cf. Paul W. Ward, *Sovereignty* (1928), 82 ff.

† Thus, William Godwin's *Enquiry Concerning Political Justice* (1793), is probably one of the first works to advocate a generally free opinion.

rule has always been an incomplete and formal means of reaching decisions in accordance with generally held opinions. In the early ideas of popular sovereignty, "the people" referred to limited groups such as the secular nobility, or the action of the people had to be taken through their magistrates, as in sixteenth and seventeenth century Calvinistic thought. Sometime during the eighteenth century the people began to mean the mass of human beings, to whom the classical doctrine of majority rule was applied. The political individual came to be clearly defined along with the definition of the modern territorial state. The absolute state and the absolute individual, argued Ward, emerged together.* But the medieval defense of majority rule through Church institutions and natural law philosophy became in the eighteenth century the foundation on which arithmetical utilitarianism was built. Aside from intellectual discussion in which numbers had no bearing, it became possible with James Mill and Jeremy Bentham to defend public decision through the formalities of political parties and electoral procedures.†

To construct a "model" of the citizen which measures the influences that are effective in decision, is to depict the power process. It implies no justification of participation, consent, or democracy in general, since the same method might be applied in any form of political grouping. Ultimately, political theory must demand some justification of the structure of participation, or the justification of some reformed or altered society. The

* Ward, *op. cit.,* 50.

† See Ladislas Konopczynski, "Majority Rule," *Encyclopaedia of the Social Sciences,* X, 55 ff. See also Harold F. Gosnell, *Democracy, The Threshold of Freedom* (1948); Alfred de Grazia, *Public and Republic* (1951); Josiah C. Wedgewood, "A History of Parliament and of Public Opinion," *The Political Quarterly,* V (1934), 506-516; M. B. Ogle, *Public Opinion and Political Dynamics* (1951). See John D. Lewis, "Some New Forms of Democratic Participation in American Government," in *The Study of Comparative Government; Essays Written in Honor of Frederic Austin Ogg,* ed. by Jasper B. Shannon (1949), 147-176, for an examination of participation in the administrative process. Democracy is defined as popular participation in the political process, and not as any particular governmental form.

formal definitions of public opinion may simply state facts, and they may not be in any case a defense of a right of general popular participation either in private or public groups. Participation is, clearly, the proper avenue of approach to the study of public opinion, for, in various senses, public opinion is participating opinion. But the legitimation of participation rests on the older, broader, and more philosophical proposition that just governments are governments to which, in some sense, the subjects have given their consent. Like participation, consent is never perfect, and like it also there are variations in forms of consent. Since we can hardly say that non-existent opinion can be public opinion, we can hardly say that a primitive and inarticulate acceptance of a governing order is really consent. But the conscious consent of the subject, validated in some formal manner, either tacitly through custom or through some more formal system of ratification of a form of government and of public policy, has long been an ideal of Western tradition. Just as some have insisted that public opinion implies a degree of uniformity or unanimity, so consent at the fundamental levels of social organization must imply some degree of consensus.

The uniformity implied must extend at least to the continued existence of the community, and, short of revolution, it seems to involve the formal continuity of the political system, or of the constitution whether written or unwritten. In this sense, consent suggests an agreement on the essential symbols of political integration, such as the common social institutions, the constitution, established practices in the use of power, the support of the nation, the ethnic group, the language, religion, or the outward trappings of loyalty. These might be regarded as the deeper reaches of the general will. Hearnshaw, thus, concludes that "public opinion and communal conscience find their outlet into action by means of the general will." * The organicity of a society, if any, can be found only in the areas of general agree-

* F. J. C. Hearnshaw, *Democracy and Labour* (1924), 44-46. Also, Willmoore Kendall, "The Two Majorities," *Midwest Journal of Political Science,* IV (November, 1960), 317-345.

ment on what is proper, true, or suitable to the common good. Here, at the deeper level of public opinion, as the level of consent in a legitimate society, we can find unanimity, and there, then, we may find, perhaps, the public opinion of the general will.

In the discussion of public opinion there is a distinction of profound importance to be remembered. Participating opinion, reflecting as it does uniformity in consent to some things about the community, is, nevertheless, outside of the government; the public is never the government, although the public does influence, approach, or even control the government, or the makers of decision. But however close the opinion of the influencing groups may come to controlling the government, it is still not the government. Opinion as a process operating within the public is by definition to be distinguished from those who rule. The importance of this proposition may easily be perceived, and it is as significant in modern as in ancient societies. And when it is forgotten in the revolutionary assumption that the general mass of the people are the government—and that there is no distinction between the rulers and the national sovereignty of the people—then both freedom and democracy, and both consent and participation can be destroyed, in any meaningful sense.

In the French Revolution, the people and government were identified in a common national sovereignty. But this was a denial of the older principle that the people are not the government, though they may share in it and control it. It was this idea of the French Revolution which so profoundly aroused men like Burke, and which served as a prime cause in awakening the conscious political conservatism of modern times. It became understood that to regard the people—and in turn public opinion—as identical with the government eliminates as enemies of the people the individual or group—together with individual and group rights against authority. In other words, this false identification results inevitably in suppression at home and aggressive imperialism abroad; it becomes a "democratic tyranny." Ever since the French Revolution, some such process has been at the base of totalitarian regimes, whether Italian fascism, German National Socialism, or communism. Such regimes consider that there can be no rights against the "unanimity" of the "people" either at home or abroad.

Therefore, a theory of public opinion in any true democratic sense must respect the fact that the people and their governors are distinct, that the governors do indeed draw their power from a basic level of consent to social structure and institutions but that, beyond the area of common agreement or general will, the governors must also seek consent by respecting the group and individual rights which form the effective pattern of opinion in any free society.*

It is a central proposition in Western political philosophy that a just government arises from the consent of the community.† This idea has been intermingled, however, with opposing principles which minimize the importance of popular participation. For aside from minor religious or proletarian movements, it has not been assumed that the people could decide there is to be no government at all. Thus, while the form of government arises legitimately from the consent of the community, it is inconceivable that the people should refuse to be governed or that they should consent to be governed by tyranny or a despotism, *i.e.*, without regard to the recognized principles of justice or law.‡ It is between these antithetical impossibilities of consent to tyranny and consent to the chaos of anarchy, that the true theory of functioning public opinion must be found.

* See Alfred Cobban, "An Age of Revolutionary Wars: An Historical Parallel," *The Review of Politics,* XIII (1951), 131-140.

† The remaining material in this section is taken by revision from my article, "Public Opinion in the Theory of Democracy," in *Thought,* XX (1945), 236-242.

‡ The most elaborate tracing of community consent in the West is, probably, to be found in R. W. and A. J. Carlyle, *A History of Medieval Political Theory in the West* (6 vols., 1903-1936). But see also Charles H. McIlwain, *The Growth of Political Thought in the West* (1932); Ewart Lewis, *Medieval Political Ideas* (2 vols., 1956); John B. Morrall, *Political Thought in Medieval Times* (1960).

The notion that legitimate government arises from a community consent does not of itself imply democracy, since consent may be given to any of a number of forms of government. The consent of which we speak is clearly popular sovereignty, but this means that popular sovereignty and democracy must be distinguished, otherwise any government however lacking in immediate political participation might be called a democracy. Tyranny itself might slip in under democratic coverage. To say that ultimately all just governments are validated by community consent, without asserting that participation must be continuous, is to make a distinction between constituent and governing activity. In the first case, the opinion of the community (however organized) has a range of choice limited to the forms and ends of government. Such a consent could not imply consent to any government—such as totalitarian regimes—whose policy is inherently contrary to the moral order or to the social nature of man.

The historic distinction between the community as a constituent force and a governing force is a logical starting point for any theory of public opinion, whether in a democracy or in some other form of government. Under this distinction, public opinion must be in action at least once: namely, at the founding of the state or at the beginning of each major change or new regime; but the theory also implies that men may not consent to have no organized society, and they may not consent to moral slavery. In theory the form of the participation in constitution-making is not important; it must, however, be effective. Historically, this consent may be through coronation oaths—*i.e.*, a governmental contract between the ruler and the people through tacit or customary consent—or through the more modern formality of the constitutional convention and constitutional referendum. In theory, likewise, it may arise through individuals alone or through groups. It may be modern individualism, Rousseau-like, or it may be corporate as through medieval estates, as emergent parliamentary institutions would show. Such a view remains valid whether Catholic or seventeenth-century Protestant theory (as represented, for example, by Althusius) is considered.*

Alternatively, under this conception it is said that all government comes from the community, that the ruler or the governing order is representative of the community, and that government itself must be for the common good. Within such a range, which includes both procedural and substantive limitations, the opinion of the community has a right and even a duty to function. Western political theory has illustrations to offer of thinkers who would ignore the moral principles associated with the common good, but it does not offer us examples of thinkers who, in order to increase the *power* of the people, would have the common good ignored. Machiavelli spoke to the prince and urged that morality might be ignored for the common good; Nietzsche ignored both the historic conceptions of morality and the common good—but in Nietzschean thinking the people were the rabble.

Another historical point may be urged. Medieval theory assumed there was no choice as to the existence of the organized community. It was this belief which in part made possible the scholastic integration of Aristotle with Christian thought. God ordained the state—though in Christian thought it might have been from the fall, as St. Augustine suggested, or in addition from the social nature of man as St. Thomas insisted. The modern doctrine of social contract, as distinguished from the ancient theory of governmental contract, implied at least that there was some choice as to whether the state should be created. Yet one does not assume that Hooker, Althusius, Pufendorf, Hobbes, Locke or Rousseau really meant that men might agree not to have an organized community at all. Thus the theory of the social contract being avowedly a mere useful fiction or "reasonable" idea, in no way actually enlarged the function of public opinion.

* See Wilfrid Parsons, "St. Thomas Aquinas and Popular Sovereignty," *Thought*, XVI (1941), 473 ff; *The Politica Methodice Digesta of Johannes Althusius*, ed. by Carl J. Friedrich (1932); Otto von Gierke, *The Development of Political Theory*, trans. by Bernard Freyd (1939); Ives Simon, *Philosophy of Democratic Government* (1951).

The historic principle of popular sovereignty has not been Procrustean, rather it has been Promethean. Its very ambiguity when removed from historical context gave it power; it might be used in a thousand different ways; it has been a misty halo which could be summoned to surround all revolutions and every reaction. To the extent that the limitation upon man's right to consent to either tyranny or chaos was ignored or rejected in particular circumstances, it became associated with the dream of all the discontented and unfortunate. It has been a symbol which might be invoked by all who have sought power with the support of the people. Popular sovereignty almost, but never quite, became the principle that work-a-day political justice is merely what the people want.

The transition from historic popular sovereignty to Western democracy was a product of an age of confusion which began in the sixteenth century. On the one hand, there were specific things which it was considered that the power of the people should do, and therewith emerged the whole problem of what practical techniques the people might use. On the other hand, the basic divisions in modern theory of the function of public opinion appeared as the problem's philosophical counterpart.

In each period the sovereignty of the people has meant different things; it has been the focus of political conflict. For those resisting established order, protest in the name of the rights of the people has been the easiest rallying point. The sovereignty of the people has meant historically the rights of the many against the one or the few—against a tyrant or an oligarchy of optimates. The tyrant is, of course, one of the simplest of political symbols, and the principle of tyrannicide always slumbers in the hearts of the people. The divine right of the people was placed against the divine right of the monarch in seventeenth-century England, and this opposition resulted in the formal, legal execution of the king, and then in parliamentary control of the succession to the throne. The sovereignty of the people has meant the dominance of the majority over the minority, and here the counting of votes has become the symbol of legitimate power.

In more recent times, democratic idealists have seen in the dogma of popular sovereignty the expression, at least ultimately, of a higher social will, though such a will might be expressed either in representative or executive leadership.

In modern times, it is the continuous effort of the leaders of the lower classes to do away with the economic advantages of the rich which has given widest scope to the concept of popular sovereignty. The story of the class struggle does not imply, however, that mere opinion is a measure of justice. It is the function of the people against whom injustice is practiced to do justice through popular action. Central to the discussion of course is the proposition that the possession of wealth is an injustice, rather than any idea that poverty is wrong. The leader makes his claim to popular allegiance by promising to right evil by dividing the wealth, and pledges thus to eliminate unjust distinctions. The implicit promise is made whether or not the technical political situation warrants such assurance to the masses. The statement of truth is a function of leadership; the acceptance of truth is the function of those who are the people. Conservative thinkers insist there is little difference between the struggles of democrats against oligarchs in the ancient world and the struggles of the masses against plutocrats in the modern world. In all such cases, however, it has not been assumed that there is to be either active or frequent participation of the people in the work of government. Even in revolutions the function of the people is largely to obey. Milton and Locke did not go as far as the theorists of direct democracy, whether in Switzerland or in the Progressive movement in the United States.*

III

In any case, the vague and theoretical conception of public opinion as it emerged from the historic principle of popular sovereignty did bring about the invention of devices for the

* Cf. A. R. Lord, *The Principles of Politics* (1926), 120-121; Robert Shafer, *Paul Elmer More and American Criticism* (1935).

expression and enforcement of the will of the people. Naturally, the expression of the will of the people has been much easier than the enforcement of policies which may be, or seem to be, approved by the participating public. This process of invention is still going on—although in the fifty years since the initiative, referendum, recall, and the system of primaries, there has been little development.* Some political thinkers today are laboring for the increased power or efficiency of representative institutions,† but to others the real perfection of political technique is in the area of public administration. On the side of public participation in administration is the decision of the Supreme Court in 1947 which interpreted the unlisted natural rights of the Ninth Amendment to include the right of political participation; while on the side of administrative power is the increasingly vigorous insistence upon the right of the scientific administrator to speak publicly and to share in the shaping of policy. In defense of the scientific policy-making autonomy of the civil servants, an influential political scholar, C. J. Friedrich, holds that we can no longer accept without qualification the "mythology" of the will of the people.‡

While some may have asserted that the participation of the people in the governing processes has become increasingly im-

* Walter Lippmann, *A Preface to Politics* (1914), 17, urged that democracy has an unfounded faith in automatic political contrivances. Lippmann has continued his examination of democracy in his *The Public Philosophy* (1955). See H. F. Gosnell, "The Polls and Other Mechanisms of Democracy," *The Public Opinion Quarterly,* IV (1940), 224-228, where the polls are listed as another device to make popular government work.

Ellis P. Oberholtzer, *The Referendum in America* (new ed., 1911), offers a critical view of the techniques of direct legislation. Cf. the speech of Senator Henry Cabot Lodge in 1907 in Senate Document, No. 114, Sixtieth Congress, First Session.

† George B. Galloway and others, "Congress-Problem, Diagnosis, Proposals," *The American Political Science Review,* XXXVI (1942), 1091 ff; Galloway, *The Reorganization of Congress* (1945); Ernest S. Griffith, *Congress: Its Contemporary Role* (2nd rev. ed., 1956).

‡ See C. J. Friedrich, "Public Policy and the Nature of Administrative Responsibility," in *Public Policy,* ed. by C. J. Friedrich and Edward S. Mason, Vol. I (1940), pp. 3-24.

possible in practice, the crisis in democratic institutions has shown the danger of regarding the right to participation too lightly. Further, the growth of the civil service has led to some insight into the dangers of too great a bureaucratic organization.*

Democracy as a form of government must be judged by the political devices it uses in the management of public power. It is difficult, if not impossible, to determine at what particular point in constitutional history a government has become democratic. It is equally difficult to determine when a particular political system has ceased to be democratic, since formal political devices spread so easily from one system to another. For like any theoretical system, the democratic has never attained what may be called technical perfection. Generally, the adherents of "democracy" accept as "democratic" the historical system as developed and practiced by certain countries of the West. In these countries the diffused conception of popular sovereignty has come closest to realization.

IV

It has become increasingly difficult for the average member of the public at large to determine the facts of the matter and the status of the controversy, as the studies of social scientists have become more complicated in divergent postulates, concepts, and theories—and in the techniques which may be used to indicate "truth" about social relations. The facts regarding the functioning of a society become meaningful of course in the light of postulates and devices for the correlation of data; but the theory of a just or legitimate society is perennial, and the individual must finally be committed to some theory of what social justice in political institutions is—meaning he must be committed to some conception of an ethical order. The quest for meaning in the symbols associated with the study of public opinion is torn between those who believe it is somehow possible to say that something *ought to be* and those who are mainly, if not exclusively,

* See Cyril N. Parkinson, *Parkinson's Law* (1957).

concerned with utilizing the vast modern array of quantitative techniques simply in order to find out what actually *is*.

During the nineteenth century, as the study of opinion began to develop, the early writers on the subject formed several modes of approach. A man might draw ideas from his own ideology—a liberal, for example, might extrapolate the conceptions of liberalism to the interpretation of the concepts of public opinion. Another writer might employ historical data, such as the study of laws or the speeches of political leaders. Still others developed a manner of inquiry into the meaning and trend of events. Such speculative studies might often arrive at the same conclusions as would have been reached by applying later techniques of statistical and survey data, but the modern empiricist and quantitative student would say that only the latter approach furnishes proof—although an exponent of the classical and traditional approach might reply that proof on a broad and permanent basis could well be more significant as it emerged from historical inquiry than as it issues narrowly from the time-limited focus of interviews and surveys. It is clear, however, that the energetic and able devotees of the current statistical techniques regard all efforts which came before them as old-fashioned and of little value, from a methodological point of view. Such at least has been the case from the time of World War I to the present—when many students of public opinion now seem to be concluding that their empiricism has approached the limits of its development as a useful tool of analysis.

There are today indications of a reconciliation between what might be called the classical and speculative mode of study and the statistical and survey techniques. To the person who believes in the validity of the traditional philosophical approach, that is the attainment of knowledge through intuition and logic culminating in a natural metaphysics geared to the existence of a transcendental order and revelation, there is still a question. And the question arises because the acceptance of speculation seems to have been limited to epistemology—an epistemology which is compatible with the survey-quantitative-statistical techniques.

Since the struggle between the empiricist and the philosopher has gone on at least since the days of the Greeks, there is no chance, of course, that an immediate reconciliation between the two modes of seeking knowledge will be or can be brought about. Nevertheless, if the empiricist can be brought to admit that values and ethical judgments about a just political order may be valid, even though they are not demonstrated by statistical techniques, there is, indeed, the possibility of a new era.

The unfortunate aspect of the situation is that the speculative and philosophical mind can accept the use of empirical techniques more easily than the empirical technician can accept the idea of the legitimacy of philosophical inquiry. At one extreme, a behaviorist may say that a statement of value is just so many words which derive meaning from the fact that they are related to behavior. At the other extreme, a philosopher may say with Plato that a true idea has reality in the mind of God, and that the behavior or the object is merely an imperfect reflection of the absolute reality. One may place, in the middle, it seems, a position related to the Aristotelian—namely, that the idea as true and rational is related to the nature of an object or situation. To the behaviorist, concerned as he is with the study of interests and groups, theory has utility because it is readily applicable to concrete or factual situations. But theory at a high level of abstraction is not a suitable tool for use in the quest for the true nature of public opinion. Thus, concepts and speculation are regarded by the empiricist as true as they are concerned with ideas which fit into empirical techniques, but not as they are concerned with philosophical inquiry in general. However, as Voegelin said: "The attack on metaphysics can be undertaken with a good conscience only from the safe distance of imperfect knowledge." *

But, granting the behavioral conception of speculation and philosophy, it has been argued there is no conflict between empirical data and theory building. Lasswell has stated that the newer developments of techniques and instruments of study have

* Eric Voegelin, *The New Science of Politics* (1952), 20.

added no new theories or concepts to those developed in the nineteenth century.* Or, in another sense, the empirical methods are regarded as supplementary to the speculative. And Lazarsfeld has suggested that such ideas as the "climate of opinion," or the notion of a "public opinion system," form bridges between the speculative and the quantitative method in the search for the reality of public opinion.† Moreover, the classical systems developed ideas which the statistical methods have confirmed by their own quantitative techniques. Albert V. Dicey noted on the basis of historical information and analytical observation that laws foster or create opinion. The quantifiers have called it the "feed-back" effect of a law, and Lazarsfeld has noted that neither method—classical or quantitative—seems to offer a convincing explanation for this fact.‡

It is obvious that a reconciliation between the classical inquiry and the survey techniques promises a deeper and broader meaning for the quest of definition and understanding of the ideas associated with public opinion. While the quantifier is committed to a method in the study of the public, the philosopher seeks a larger truth; although the philosopher has no objection to facts or to the mathematical consideration of them, he would go beyond epistemology to the order of meaning and the nature of the public itself.§

* Harold D. Lasswell, "The Impact of Public Opinion Research on our Society," *The Public Opinion Quarterly*, XXI (Spring, 1957), 32 ff; Herbert H. Hyman, "Toward a Theory of Public Opinion," *ibid.*, 54 ff; Paul F. Lazarsfeld, "Public Opinion and the Classical Tradition," *ibid.*, 39 ff.

† Lazarsfeld, *ibid.*, 44, is quoting MacIver, *Academic Freedom in the United States* (1954). The public opinion system would include the alignment of opinion, the structure of communication, and the ground of consensus. Combined with newer methods of study, public opinion becomes an analyzed distribution of attitudes.

‡ Lazarsfeld, *op. cit.*, p. 47. Frederick F. Stephan, "Advances in Survey Methods and Measurement Techniques," *ibid.*, 79 ff, gives a bibliography covering in detail the last twenty years of quantitative public opinion research.

§ S. M. Lipset, *Political Man: The Social Bases of Politics* (1960), Part II, in which participation through voting behavior is discussed may be considered an example, though the empirical is obviously of more interest to the author than speculative or interpretative considerations.

CHAPTER 2

The Great Ideas: A Converging Stream

I

Many theories of public opinion have germinated within Western culture, and many of these ideas have shown remarkable power of survival, so that in the process of the development of modern political thought, it may be said that present theories of public opinion are built on the enduring conceptions of the past. But they have been built on the basis of new combinations of old ideas, which induced developments and the resurgence of concepts which were not always important, such as the modern systems of techniques for the expression of opinion. Consent, legitimacy, and technique must be seen as primal ideas in formation of a "public opinion democracy." It is the purpose of this chapter to bring together in brief discussion the most important ideas which have helped in the formation of the modern conception of the public mind. In the matured political society, the ideas which seem most important are (1) the nature of the citizen, (2) the supremacy of the law, (3) the medieval re-emergence of the classical notion of the possibility of sound opinion, (4) the mixed constitution as the proper context for the expression of opinion, (5) the direction and control of communication, (6) the wisdom or lack of wisdom of opinion, (7) the issue of legitimacy and the obligation of opinion, and (8) the statement of philosophical views in relation to the proper expression of opinion.

The first pre-condition of a theory of public opinion is the development of a clear discrimination between those who are ruled and those who rule. Ruler and subject must be reasonably separate and ascertainable in a community, and the community must be ordered in such a way that there is some code or set of norms to which both rulers and subjects may appeal. In some sense at least the community must be aware of morality; it must have a moral consciousness in which individuals share as members of the community. Essentially, also, it must be a morality for all men, and some on this basis will say that the voice of the people is the voice of God.* Breasted has referred to the "dawn of conscience." Moral discernment in Egypt gradually descended from the aristocrats of the royal court and the temple priesthoods to the provincial nobles and then to the masses.†

The emergence of "form" in rulership, the sense of a community in existence, and a code for the operation of the community—these are the pre-conditions of the existence of public opinion, as well as for the intellectual formulation of the problem. Morality has been embodied in the historic and customary codes—the Egyptian, the Hebrew, and the great systems of customary law such as the Chinese. But as the code has impinged on the man, the man in turn could insist that others ought to obey, even though he might not have power to enforce obedience. Conscience would insist that the general custom or opinion of the community has generated obligations for those who have official or governmental positions. The theory of public opinion in its long and complicated history has differed profoundly on what the role of opinion should be in the "proper" society; but that law and conscience should coincide is one of the great and early ideas of Western man.

* One of the earliest uses of *Vox populi, Vox Dei* is found in a letter by Alcuin to Charlemagne near 798: "Populus iuxta sanctiones divinas ducendus est, non sequendus; et ad testimonium persone magis eliguntur honeste. Nec audiendi qui solent dicere: 'Vox populi, Vox Dei,' cum tumultuositas vulgo semper insanie proxima sit." *Monumenta Germaniae Historica*, Epistolarum, Tomus IV (1895), 199.

† James Henry Breasted, *The Dawn of Conscience* (1935), 19-20.

II

In the more mature societies of Classical civilization, the concept of order and obligation merged into the brilliant conception of the Greeks on the nature of the citizen. A citizen was one who shared in the government of the community, even though the shares might vary in different forms of government. In primitive societies, these shares might be merely an unbreakable system of common sentiment in which all agreed; however, for Classical Man the idea of citizenship was refined until it became embedded in the systems of public law in both the Greek city-states and in Rome.* The citizen, the bearer of the virtue, order, and law of a society, became the member of a public. He was thereby a public law participant in the control of the society in which he lived. There are many conceptions of "the public," but the most common and, indeed, the most durable notion of it focuses on popular participation in government. The Greeks in their great ages knew many different forms of government, but the Greek democracy is a suitable beginning point. For the Greek intellectuals formulated the main issues of public opinion: the nature of participation, the qualities of opinion, and the political structures which would express it most effectively. Since the representative system was not highly developed among the Greeks, election meant in general the election of magistrates and not representatives. It was natural, therefore, that Greek attention to public opinion should center on the qualities of the judgment of the common man, rather than on the public techniques of political control.†

* Lewis H. Morgan, *League of the Ho-De'-No-San-Nee or Iroquois,* new ed. by H. M. Lloyd, 2 vols. in one (1904), p. 71. Speaking of the Iroquois Confederation, Morgan said: "Running through their whole system of administration, was a public sentiment which gave its own tendency to affairs, and illustrated to a remarkable degree, that the government rested upon the popular will, and not upon the arbitrary sway of chiefs."

† Naturally, the classics of Greek political writing are to be consulted on this problem—Plato, Aristotle, Thucydides, Plutarch and others. Among recent contributions of interest is Ernest Barker's "Elections in the Ancient

Hesiod and Pericles, for example, extol the virtues of the common man. Hesiod admired the farmer, and Pericles—in the funeral oration reported by Thucydides—praised the soldier who was willing to die for his country. But the critics of democracy valued more highly the man of skill as against the common man, whose virtues were primarily obedience to moral standards, willingness to work, and capacity to make prudent judgments. It was an expression of the historic conflict between the "man in the house," the expert and bureaucrat, and "the man in the street," with his Greek and New Testament claim to common sense and morality. Pericles' oration praised the capacity of the Athenian to form good judgments on political questions, while at the same time he was a brave soldier and a man who could support himself. The *Old Oligarch* * pointed to the perennial weaknesses of the common man's judgment and the consequent aberrations of the democracy; but Aristotle said that the ordinary man might form good judgments on common political problems. Yet, Thucydides' description of the class struggle in *The Peloponnesian War* shows public opinion to be savage and absurd; and it will remain so, he said, as long as human nature is not changed. Plato could show the incompetence of general opinion, which surely was not knowledge; and Vergil in the *Aeneid* spoke of the ugly force of Fama—rumor and report.†

On one thing at least most of the Greeks were agreed: a citizen is one who participates in the government of his community. Plato and Aristotle both accepted this idea, though their beliefs in regard to the quality of the judgment, or the mind of the

---

World," *Diogenes*, No. 8 (Autumn, 1954), pp. 1 ff. A. H. M. Jones, "The Athenian Democracy and its Critics," *The Cambridge Historical Journal*, XI (1953), 1 ff, has shown impressively the small amount of pro-democratic literature among the Greeks, or at least the pro-democratic literature that has been preserved. Likewise, G. C. Field, *Political Theory* (1957), 275 ff. J. A. O. Larsen has shown there were significant developments in representation in the Classical world. See his *Representative Government in Greek and Roman History* (1955).

* This is a work falsely attributed to Xenophon. It is part of the *Pseudo-Xenophon*. The author is unknown.

† See Vergil's *Aeneid*, Bk. IV, 174 ff.

citizen, might differ. A Greek citizen contributed his opinion on particular problems either in the assemblies or on the juries; and if the occasion were present he served as a magistrate or as an officer in the armed forces. But in the *Republic,* Plato's description of "democratic man" is one of the most savage criticisms of democracy ever written. In addition, Plato thought of the common man as sitting in his cave, with his back to the light, unable to acquire true knowledge of reality. Although Aristotle considered the common man to have potentially a good judgment on matters concerning his personal experience, and the harsh description of democratic man in Plato's *Republic* is not repeated in Aristotle's *Politics,* even Aristotle would concede readily enough that such men and such conditions can exist in popular governments. To Plato the remedy was government by the philosopher, who had some understanding of truth as it existed objectively in the archtypes, which according to Platonic philosophy were the higher reality. But Aristotle, and the more moderate or less revolutionary minds of Classical times, would rely on political rather than philosophical remedies to correct the weakness of public opinion. Granted that popular assemblies were institutions of popular sovereignty, and in turn the agents of the sovereignty based upon the will of the masses, it was still possible to mix and blend oligarchy and democracy in such a way that polity might be produced. And polity was not a democracy, though public opinion would have its legitimate place in such an organization of government. Thus, the long Western debate on the nature of public judgment and its proper share in government was begun.

III

It has been suggested that the root idea of public opinion is some conception of what constitutes a public; and that the central significance of public opinion is that it participates in the ruling of the community. But there are many modalities involved, quite aside from the mechanical question of a public and the precise means by which its system of participation is realized. Certainly, one of the oldest of the ideas associated with public opinion is that a public in projecting its opinion is acting, and must act, under the law. In other words, legitimate public opinion is always an orderly force; its formalities are predictable, and it operates under an exterior standard. This standard is the law or *jus* in the sense of a legal system. It is not law which opinion makes at a certain moment, nor is it the positive law of any governmental agency. For opinion to act within the law, of course, suggests a means of enforcing standards; it suggests the ultimate effort to create some kind of a rule of law in all of society; it is the quest for constitutional society. Like the ruler, opinion has a *jurisdictio,* a legitimate function in making public decisions. Probably also the most effective means of directing opinion has been the legal custom of a society. In Roman law, the fiction of the *lex regia,* or the idea that the will of the prince has the force of law, stands against the *digna vox,* or the idea that majesty must obey the law.

One of the ideas on which the freedom of public opinion is based is the notion of a higher law, a natural law or the existence of a moral order which extends beyond the immediate judgment of magistrates or people. Until the rise of modern legal positivism, it was assumed that both kings and people stood under the higher law—the natural and divine law. Greeks and Romans made a partial identification between the natural law and the existing man-made law, and some such relationship rather generally has been accepted by most systems of law. Though one might say that the identification between the moral law and the customary law has been closer than in the formalized and codified systems, still the identification has existed. And it has been based, finally, on the proposition that man can by reason discover the moral nature of the world, and thus the will of its Creator. The action of the people must take place within the principles laid down by the law, and the legitimacy of opinion itself must be judged within the standards of the legal system. Natural law, or moral law, gives public opinion its basic content, though it does not directly furnish many of the immediate and prudential judgments which must be made. According to Professor Corwin, natural law has been in fact enforced against rulers, or perhaps on occasion even against the people.* Moslem law, Chinese law, and all the Western systems, including canon law, may therefore present fruitful suggestions as to the nature and function of public opinion.

In the modern tension between intellectuals and common men, there has been a rejection both of custom and of natural law as the context for the legitimate action of the public. Rather than law and the moral order, the intellectuals have often suggested that science should be the standard for the judgment of the quality of public opinion, its right to be heard in public decision, and the obligation such opinion can impose on the community at large. There are times when the intellectuals and the masses move together, accepting in general the same system of philosophy and the same system of moral obligation. In a Western, Christian-leavened society, the intellectual is not often at war with the common man, though the level of statement may be very different. The moral wisdom of the masses, as St. Paul saw it, should not be in contradiction with the philosophical understanding achieved by intellectuals. In the seventeenth century a collection of proverbs reported:

> The People's voice, the voice of God we call,
> And what are *Proverbs* but the people's voice? †

Custom, as the proverb would indicate, is a valid formulation of the judgment of the participating public, and for the Neapolitan philosopher Vico ‡ it might even be a formulation of an emergent, developing law of nature. It would be the duty of the intellectuals to see the opinions of the masses in such a context, and thus to bear them respect in the decisions of a government. Vico was suggesting, in effect, a doctrine of progress; and through the stages of

* See Edward S. Corwin, *The "Higher Law" Background of American Constitutional Law*, reprinted 1955, from *Harvard Law Review*, XLII (1928-1929), 149 ff, 365 ff; Ewart Lewis, "The Contribution of Medieval Thought to the American Political Tradition," *The American Political Science Review*, L (June, 1956), 462 ff.

† See *The Newberry Library Bulletin*, III (July, 1954), 183.

‡ *The New Science of Giambattista Vico*, trans. from third edition (1744) by T. G. Bergin and M. H. Fisch (1948).

human evolution to the free society, there would be a basis for optimism as to the quality of the judgment of the masses. Yet what one never finds, whatever the standard of judgment of public opinion, is the principle that any and all judgments of either rulers or subjects are correct, valid, or obligatory.

In the Christian view of the state, for example, it is never a mere rubber stamp for a statistical majority, for the state has its own proper authority and function in the attainment of the common good. The state has a duty to attain justice in human society in so far as it is possible, in accordance with prudential judgments of particular situations. Yet, it is the modern intellectual of a certain type who has insisted that all social judgments are relative or cultural and not subject to proof. Hence, it is the relativism inherent in all judgment which gives the common man the right to participate in political affairs. In concrete detail, however, such a position has not resulted in accepting an unrestricted liberty of judgment of those who vote or assist in making decisions. Rather, it has meant that the elected representatives and the civil servants are to be the guide of the whole democracy. Public opinion would thus remain under the law of science.

Much of the medieval controversy over the nature of popular opinion centers therefore on the kind of "law" under which opinion is to function. If a "public" exists, it exists within some level of society, and there are modes and standards by which opinion may be given its position of authority. Public opinion signifies participation, through the law, in the decisions which are made in the community. The long conversation on the power of public opinion concerns the proper scope of opinion under a given political system. If one seeks justice in the community, then the political system must be a means whereby power is made responsible. One of the causes for the richness of the Middle Ages in political thought is the discussion, direct and otherwise, of this right of the community to consent to its government. But consent was always under the law, the higher law, and in accordance with the rational and moral principles which should govern human behavior. "In England," said George L. Haskins, "the rule of law was chiefly a means of putting a bridle upon government at a time when the king was not subject to popular control. In the United States—in the hands of such men as Marshall, Story, and Taft—it was turned into an instrument to control the action of popularly chosen officials and legislators, as well as to limit the power of governmental agencies to determine for themselves the scope of their lawful powers. In both countries, therefore, the rule of law has been an instrument to give the citizen a check upon government and the officials, and for that reason it remains an enduring heritage of our legacy from the Middle Ages." *

In medieval thought Aristotelian philosophy has a more complicated relationship to ideas about public opinion than in Classical times. Aristotle discussed opinion at a rather concrete and behavioral level, and it was a discussion short, in any case, of the application of his metaphysical principles. He seems more interested in describing institutions and in the virtues of the citizen than in a general and theoretical approach, which would inquire whether, on philosophical grounds, the common judgment may be trusted. Aristotle begins his *Metaphysics* with the statement that "All men by nature desire to know." It was in the Middle Ages that some of the implications of this statement for politics were sought. The Scholastics said, generally, that natural desire cannot be in vain. Siger of Brabant, Averroes, Albert, and Thomas held that desires were capable of being fulfilled as in the perfection of the sciences. Albert and Thomas held that pleasures and other influences may prevent the achievement of the desire for knowledge, while John of Jandun said it was fulfilled collectively in men, though distributively as in each individual. Thus, philos-

* George L. Haskins, "Executive Justice and the Rule of Law; Some Reflections on Thirteenth-Century England," *Speculum*, XXX (October, 1955), 537-538. See also Barnaby C. Keeney, "The Medieval Idea of the State: The Great Cause 1291-2," *The University of Toronto Law Journal*, VIII (Lent Term, 1949), 48 ff; "Military Service and the Development of Nationalism in England, 1272-1327," *Speculum*, XXII (October, 1947), 534 ff.

ophy and the sciences are perfect in the majority of men. Both John of Jandun and Marsilius of Padua seem to be optimistic, if not utopian, about mankind in its totality.

As a doctrine bearing on the theory of public opinion, therefore, one may consider the non-futility of natural desire, the Averroistic doctrine of the unity of the intellect in all mankind, and the application of these principles by Marsilius of Padua to the civil community. Averroes and Siger contended there was a single active intellect for all mankind, and Marsilius seems to project such an intellect to the corporate will of the city. In consequence, when individuals think and desire as parts of the whole they do so in a superior way. According to Professor Alan Gewirth, the University of Chicago medievalist, Marsilius makes the first political application of the premise of the non-futility of natural desire. People desire and do achieve a knowledge of political life, and the citizen has good and specific political desires. One arrives, thus, at the philosophical, though not practical, proposition that a corporate, medieval majoritarism which considers both number and quality in men has a sanction that others do not have. For as Nicolas of Cusa held, the majority will achieve what is right and useful. In such a system, Marsilius saw that unordered desires would not prevent the attainment of proper goals in his Aristotelian and republican system. Moreover, under the Aristotelian principle of the natural impulses of men toward the good life, it would be impossible that a majority should turn against the maintenance of the civil community. "From this it clearly follows, of necessity," says Marsilius, "that the whole body of the citizens, or the weightier multitude thereof, which must be taken for the same thing, can better discern what must be elected and what rejected than any part of it taken separately." The good that men naturally desire is to be fulfilled in the *universitas civium.**

* See Alan Gewirth, *Marsilius of Padua: The Defender of Peace;* Vol. II, *The Defensor Pacis* (1956), Appendix II, pp. 435 ff. And *Defensor,* I.xiii.2.

IV

On the one hand, popular opinion is to be governed by the law, and on the other, opinion becomes the enforcer of the law against those who have power. The theory of public opinion suggests, therefore, the central question of what controls opinion should have, and how control should be exercised. In the Greek and Roman struggles between oligarchy and democracy, one can sense a pattern of arrangements that might either constrict or expand the power of opinion under changing conditions of politics. It is true, apparently, that practically all students of governments have assumed that some role is to be given to popular opinion in the organization of a just government. If one considers the Classical answer to the query of the proper control of opinion over the affairs of the community, the answer is clear. Opinion is part of the balance of forces that may be embodied in the mixed constitution, as depicted by Aristotle, Polybius, Cicero, and on through St. Thomas to the eighteenth-century admiration for the British Constitution. Public opinion has a share in governing, but the problem is to find that proper share and install it in public law. Under the mixed constitution, the power of opinion would be balanced against the aristocratic and super-aristocratic or monarchic-executive powers which provide a formal unity to the state.*

Still, the extension of the rights of the people was consistent with the mixed constitution. For instance, the struggle over the extension of the suffrage, which culminated in popular victory in the last century, was conducted within the structure of the mixed and balanced system of government. The victory of democracy meant the effort—though not a very successful one—of vesting an effective, sustained sovereignty in the masses of the voters. It has meant the loss of interest in the mixed constitution, and the affirmation of the ultra-democratic conception that nothing in

* See Kurt von Fritz, *The Theory of the Mixed Constitution in Antiquity* (1954).

the political system should stand in the way of control through popular opinion. Beyond the right to vote, the democratic leaders demanded a program of direct legislation, the abolition of judicial review, and the legal regulation of political parties. Yet the plain fact was that the formal democratization of the state did not subject the government to the control of public opinion, at least in the sense contemplated by those who developed the modern democratic system. The maxim of the iron law of oligarchy, as argued by Alexander Hamilton in *The Federalist*, seemed to hold: the larger the number of participants in a system, the fewer the number who control. As the modern state became more complicated in its functions, it developed many devices for the control of public opinion. The operating state—the political class as a whole—began the long process of establishing controls over the masses, which we have been able to observe in dictatorship, and in fascist and communist regimes.

Here, then, is one aspect of the deeper dialectic of public opinion. One idea is that opinion should control the government, or at least some aspects of community decision-making; against this stands the idea that the expert, the man in the office, or the psychological expert, must control opinion when it is unsuited to govern because of a lack of prudence, sound judgment, or common sense. The standards governing opinion are, among others, the standards of the civil servants, the lawyers, and the judges.

Those who operate and control mass communication, whether in advertising or in politics, are the heirs of those who in the past have wished to limit the directive power of popular judgment. Mass communication is a kind of appeal to the people, though appeal to the people is found in all societies, including forceful examples in the Classical world. The struggle over the suffrage, the techniques of the free election, and the effort of the civil service to be autonomous, merge into the issue of the private organization of propaganda against a politically dominated means of mass communication.* In the extreme, the modern suc-

* E. Colin Cherry, "The Communication of Information (An Historical Survey)," *American Scientist*, 40 (October, 1952), 640 ff, gives a survey

cesses of totalitarian governments, fascist and communist, have demonstrated an irrationality that political rationalists had thought impossible. Moreover, propaganda has not been directed solely against the uneducated, but also with success against the educated. Those most educated, though not always the most rational, have not been immune to the force of the propaganda of a revolutionary class, or to that of any government of the more democratic type, for that matter. Orwell's *1984* is based on significant empirical data concerning the power accumulated by the control of mass communication.

In another sense, such a control over minds should not surprise the student of opinion. In part it is a question of what power over minds it is possible to have, and for the rest it is a question of the moral right of any institution to shape the minds of young and old. In a democracy it should be said that the government has only a limited right to govern the content of minds, being limited in its power by the freedoms of the family, the church, and other groups to shape the opinion of those who accept their membership. The power to control the thought of men has been increased by the techniques of mass communication, including propaganda, censorship, and suppression, as well as by the overall power of education. But we do know that the power of the most absolute of governments—that is, the modern communist and fascist ones—is limited to some extent, even after years of intensive propaganda. Such was dramatically the case in the Hungarian revolt in 1956.

Many devices have been employed to control the minds of those who participate in some degree in the government of the community. Communication in the ancient world may have been slower, but it was effective nonetheless. Sea lanes were controlled, and the roads of Rome were efficient means of communication. Oracles in Greece, auguries in Rome, divination everywhere, including the ancient Orient, all played their part. The Pythoness

---

of the more technical and scientific aspects of modern mass communication. On some of the earlier traditions of the American civil service, see H. J. Ford, *The Rise and Growth of American Politics* (1898).

might speak in parables, but attitudes were shaped by what the divinities said through her. In a more violent manner, insurrection will be suppressed by the sword and not merely with words. In our day we sometimes fear the power of mass communication, and "Big Brother" government has become a reality in the totalitarian state.

It is apparent that the most powerful directive and control of opinions is tradition. Among the powers of the world are the great traditions which have borne value and judgment into the heart of man from time immemorial. The Confucian tradition has been a shaper of the opinions of both subjects and rulers from the days of the legendary sage emperors; tradition might be used to direct the course of government, since the Confucians said that "Heaven sees as the people see; Heaven hears as the people hear." But government could also use it with power in the restriction of ideas that were not favored officially, and it could use the traditional literature in the training of the public servants. In contrast to the Confucians, the Chinese legalist school ironically allowed the people a share in decisions already made, but there was no consultation in a new matter. Every great cultural tradition has served some such function, though clearly the Chinese tradition, including its penetration into Southeast Asia, has endured longer and exercised a greater power over more individuals than others, whether we consider the Hindu, Moslem, Buddhist, or the Classical tradition of Western man.*
Even in the mobile society of industrial-urban man, tradition plays its powerful role, for tradition is the source of values, both religious and political, economic and social.

V

The theory of opinion includes another profoundly important issue: what is the rational quality of a given opinion? Or, in

* On Indian problems, see Donald M. Brown, *The White Umbrella* (1953); Richard A. Gard, "Ideological Problems in Southeast Asia," *Philosophy East and West*, II (January, 1953), 292 ff.

more general terms, it has been asked whether the opinions of the public are good, elevated, sound, obligation-creating, or rational in sentiment and idea. Indeed, aside from the debate on the extent to which the masses should be allowed to participate in government—with which this argument of quality is closely related—the judgment of the quality of common opinion is the central issue in the theory of public opinion. Participation in the community and the quality of common judgment are the two perennial inquiries of the student of public opinion. Moreover, such inquiries become a question of philosophy, or, as Walter Lippmann argued it in 1955, *The Public Philosophy*. Ultimately, the judgment of public opinion is a judgment of its truth.

The Classical outlines of the argument are clear. It is the argument of Plato, the lover of wisdom, against the Sophist, the Machiavellian man, and the practitioner of an art of public success. It is the Ciceronic argument for Stoic moderation that one finds in *De Officiis*. It is the Aristotelian defense of a balanced polity against democracy, which is the unrestrained and direct government of the masses in their own interest. The man in the house knows technique and philosophy, while the man in the street knows honesty and morality. Which is the proper method of estimating the rationality of a particular judgment, whether of the man in the street or the man in the office? A rational judgment is one that fulfills the requirements of a specific philosophical viewpoint; it is knowledge, let us say, in a logical and systematic manner. Broadly, intellectuals have insisted, as did Spinoza and Kant, that the liberty of the philosopher is more significant than that of the common man, and that the philosopher comes closer to truth than common men. Whatever may have been his philosophy, the philosopher has welcomed the chance to advise rulers. Under Augustus it is recorded that the talents of men of letters were at the service of the government, and notably among them were Vergil and Horace. Augustus, and other rulers in other times, favored the use of the literary arts in the revival of civil spirit and in the restoration of religion.

The theory of the quality of opinion is torn between ideas

which assert as a fact the rationality of a particular body of opinion, and those trends of thought which insist on the rationality of the expert and the philosopher. In a democracy neither position is generally acceptable in its extreme form. Some kind of middle statement is essential. Thus, in a democracy it may be argued that the quality of some opinion is rational, or that men may be taught virtue and brought up to a level that is compatible with the technical necessities of modern government. If one exalts ethics one becomes utopian, and if one lets all decision become an art then pure Machiavellianism is the result. The democratic insistence seems to be that there is a practical wisdom, a system of prudence, that falls between the extremes of utopianism and Machiavellian irresponsibility. As the ancients, men like Cicero in *De Officiis,* taught, it is possible to transmit the virtues to men in general. And that sterling political virtue, moderation, with the balancing of institutions, can be spread through society. It can be embodied in a national tradition, and it can be taught in the whole pedagogic system. The quality of public opinion is, then, worth being considered by those who formally make the last political decisions.

VI

Since the revival of democracy a little over a century ago, one of the converging ideas in the theory of public opinion has been that public opinion creates an obligation for public servants to follow. Such an obligation is seldom stated without reservation, and the question becomes one of the specific circumstances in which public opinion is to be observed as a matter of duty. In the emergence of the idea of public opinion it seems to have been held that public opinion creates as public truth an obligation of obedience on those who govern, as well as upon those who live under government and themselves help to shape the content of public judgment. Consent to government has in theory served both those who wanted and those who rejected a democratic system of government.

In a strict sense, the social contract was constitutive of society; it did not create government but a society in which government might operate. There might or might not be, then, a governmental contract, for the two could be combined into one.* The issue for public opinion is how and under what conditions did contractualism encourage the belief that the political class is obligated to follow the mandate of public opinion? If liberty is expressed in social and governmental contracts, one may also say that liberty is not merely the right to control government. Though natural law theory generally provided standards for the control of government, it was also a criterion of history and events for the unmarked member of the public. Consent has never meant, it seems, that men are free to decide for or against anything and everything that might come to mind. Nor has liberty meant that an individual has a completely arbitrary will in the conduct of social life. There could be no society, in fact, if such were the case. There could only be anarchy in the most deplorable sense of that unhappy word.

But contractualism does stand for the proposition that a legitimate government is founded on the consent of the governed, and that part of the freedom and equality of men is to give such consent. Of course, a legitimate government is one that is just, for consent alone is not enough. Consent is constituent, that is, it creates legitimate political society and its government, but essentially the theory of public opinion is not concerned with such consent, since public opinion theory assumes the existence of the government in the first place. Public-opinion consent is properly consent to particular policies or decisions. In principle contractualism must lend an impulse to day-to-day consent to governmental acts. One can see in John Locke how this impulse operated. It means for Locke the acceptance of the monarchy and the parliamentary system, the election of representatives, and a majority rule within the proper ends for which government exists. But in Locke's Whig conception of government, including

* Heinrich Rommen, *The State in Catholic Thought* (1945), 245.

the prerogative of the Crown, there was no strong demand for the expansion of the suffrage. Such a demand had been made, however, before Locke wrote. The Levellers had developed, probably for the first time in Western thought, a full conception of consent to government on an almost day-to-day basis. Their "Agreement of the People" was, no doubt, more of a governmental than a social contract. It involved the right of individuals to consent to the form of government and to vote for those who were members of Parliament.

For Locke as well as the Levellers, participation, or actual consent, was not enough. There must also be a standard of justice or rights which will protect the liberty of the subject both as an individual and as a participant in politics. Under natural law and rights, it could be pleaded that public opinion will be of high rational quality, and that it will create an obligation for both citizen and ruler. Kendall has insisted that part of Locke's argument is the latent premise that public opinion will be rational.* The latent premise is the foundation for the obligation generated by public opinion. It is easy and appropriate to conclude that the social and governmental contract theories helped provide a basis on which public opinion has a right to bind the government.

Let us say that one strong current in consent theory has carried with it the idea that a person in authority has to obey those who give consent, for consent to government is given for specific purposes. When such purposes or ends are not sought, consent may be withdrawn. From the *lex regia* on, it has been held that power may be withdrawn by the people. St. Thomas, for example, said: "If to provide itself with a king belongs to the right of a given multitude, it is not unjust that the king be deposed or have his power restricted by that same multitude if, becoming a tyrant, he abuses the royal power." †

It is clear, however, that the theory of obligation to obey public opinion is not based on mere consent, or massive con-

* Willmoore Kendall, *John Locke and the Doctrine of Majority Rule* (1959), *passim.*

† St. Thomas Aquinas, *On Kingship,* Ch. VI, 49.

sent generating power enough to sustain or destroy rulers. It is based on consent plus legitimacy in the character of public acts. The standards have varied with the changing teachers of a society, who have formulated "the public philosophy" of a community. From the ancient world on, one of the central themes has been *libertas* or equality, or some such formulation of the eternal aspiration toward justice. Liberty is one way of formulating the context of obligation; public judgment must stand for and seek to attain liberty, which is and always has been the liberty of an individual first, and then organizations to which he is committed. Both citizen and government have an obligation to obey public opinion when it stands for liberty and justice.

There is a striking similarity between the Christian conception of the moral capacity of the common man and the Greek defense of democracy in Pericles' oration. The obligation drawn from public opinion is both wisdom and art; it is prudence at its noblest dimension. Pericles stressed the technical capacity of the ordinary citizen as well as his understanding of social life; but St. Paul saw more the moral wisdom of the many, the God-like glory of the poor. In both cases, it is not said that any particular person is either wise or an expert on a phase of public business. But it is assumed that by education a very considerable number of the adult population of a state can be brought to this level. To Pericles, it was within the capacity of any man to be a good servant of the state, as well as an apt pupil of Athens, the cultural and pedagogic mistress of Hellas.

VII

Two great streams of ideas in the theory of public opinion may be observed. There are those who would trust public opinion, because they trust the moral judgments of the common man. But such people do not say they trust all men. Historical experience must be judged and criticized, but the common man has the possibility and often attains a sound moral evaluation of men who have power. Against this position are found mainly those who mistrust the *techne,* or the art and skill, of the ordinary citizen. Public opinion is to be trusted as it follows the civil servants and philosophers, who labor always to form the values of a society. But it is seldom if ever said that all public opinion is to be trusted. Democracy, indeed, is defended more than public opinion is trusted. And the reason is simple, since democracy is often defined, not as the government of public opinion, but as the implementation of a certain system of policy. In one case, some public opinion may be mistrusted because of its moral imperfections, and in the other it is to be mistrusted because of scientific and technical deficiencies. One can trace to the Classical world both of these major views. Even in a democratic age such as ours, it is important to discriminate between the bases upon which the government may direct or control the formation of public opinion.

Central in any theory of public opinion is a conception of value formation. It is clear that the establishment of values comes from traditions of teaching, in which the intellectuals are the more powerful force. "Intellectuals" means teachers at nearly all levels and in all kinds of institutions, writers journalistic and otherwise, scientific and technical people, professional men, and management, all of whom defend their group interests with a traditional rhetoric.* Intellectuals become marked as groups largely because of traditions in learning, religion, judgment and philosophy. To observe the formation and reformation of the value system is the chief reason for the study of intellectual history. But the value system is handed on to the citizen with his plurality of obligations and allegiances, and it becomes, in the realm of public discussion, the various aspects of public opinion.

In our own day those who seek to "manage" public opinion by shaping values are engaging in public discussion. Jacques Maritain and Walter Lippmann, for example, plead for a return to belief in an objective moral order or a system of natural law that may be applied to political decision. Others, like John Dewey

* See Richard M. Weaver, *The Ethics of Rhetoric* (1953).

and those who have followed him, plead for a secular conception of authoritative opinion. They follow the intellectuals who have urged the scientific method. The scientific method is to become the source of authority and the standard of public opinion; and it is to build on the optimism of the eighteenth century in the crisis of the twentieth.

Public opinion is usually, it seems, a slightly embarrassing notion. It is easier to talk about "democracy" or "socialism," for instance, than to indicate the conditions under which public opinion creates obligations for a government to follow.

CHAPTER 3

The Necessary Institutions of Public Opinion

I

The creation of the necessary institutions of public opinion has not been a steady historical process. It varies between periods and between societies, between eras when the democratic tide runs high and those in which a faith in expertise demands a diminution of the power of common opinion. But central at all times is the establishment in public law of the means by which the opinion of the citizen can be brought to bear on government. To create such institutions in public law is a test of fidelity to the idea of public opinion—one of whose most important sources was the axiom, formulated as early as medieval times, that what touches all should be the concern of all. But there are also institutions in public law which retard or prevent the expression of public opinion. Indirect election, long terms of office, the control of the means of mass communication, the reservation of decisions to a small administrative group, and the traditional restrictions on suffrage are all well-attested devices. Yet it hardly needs to be observed that the growth of the technical and scientific functions of the state, and the great tasks of war and diplomacy, have also drawn the power of decision into few hands and into secret discussion.

II

It is the purpose of this chapter to present an account of the more impressive developments in the institutions of public opinion. It is the problem, more specifically, of the generation of the public. One begins, quite naturally, with the arrangements of the Classical world. The Classical assembly, both in the Greek cities and in Rome, is the prototype of means by which the citizen speaks to his government with authority and command. Generally, it has been said that there were few, if any, representative institutions in the ancient world, and that this explains the political frailty of Classical democracy. Our own experience with democratic failure should make us modest in making judgments. Curiously, little was written in the ancient world in defense of democracy, but A. H. M. Jones in an article on "The Athenian Democracy and its Critics," has concluded that Greek democracy was much better than its critics report. It appears that the slaves and metics were reasonably well treated, and the rich were probably not robbed as much as is commonly said.* A democratic election in a Greek city was, first of all, not an election to a representative assembly; an election was held usually for those who were in some kind of executive position. Only after the development of representative government could the modern notion of an election be understood.† But it has been indicated in recent studies that representative systems were the common pattern in Greek federalism, and certainly the choice of representatives would involve some election, however indirect. J. A. O. Larsen believes that the Greek term *synedriake politeia* means representative government—an institution for which it is commonly thought that the Greeks had no name—and points

* A. H. M. Jones, "The Athenian Democracy and its Critics," *The Cambridge Historical Journal,* XI (1953), 1 ff.

† Ernest Barker, "Elections in the Ancient World," *Diogenes,* No. 8, Autumn, 1954, pp. 1 ff. See also J. A. O. Larsen, "Cleisthenes and the Development of the Theory of Democracy at Athens," *Essays in Political Theory* (1948).

out that Polybius implied that representative government was normal in the Greek federal states.*

Democracy came to mean in Roman times, according to Larsen, the absence of monarchy. Hence, any non-monarchical government was democratic; and, in Latin, democracy was translated as *libertas*. Liberty or freedom thus had, for a time at least, an anti-monarchic connotation.† Democracy was not associated with representative institutions in the federal organizations of the Hellenic world. True, it was associated with forms of government, but the primary and lasting association was with the assembly of citizens, with the popular jury system, and with the rotating executive functions a citizen might engage in. One of the Classical period's greatest contributions to political tradition is the concept of the citizen as a participant in government. In addition, the system of assemblies in the Greek cities and in Rome was sufficiently formalized to be a constitutional public, and it injected into public law the institutions of participation. Obviously, the extent of popular power varied, but voting was a fact—a fact of which the citizen of the *polis* was fully aware.

Yet one thing should be clear: such participation did not mean recognition that all law is a product of the will of the people. Then and now the law has tended to be a limiting factor on the scope and force of popular participation, though it is true, of course, that customary law is a form of legislation. It should be asked, indeed, just what were the institutions of the Classical world which restricted the participation of public opinion in the control of the state. Oligarchy, the oracles, and respect for tradition all played a part. Oligarchy, as lauded by the *Old Oligarch*,

* J. A. O. Larsen, "Representation and Democracy in Hellenistic Federalism," *Classical Philology*, XL (April, 1945), 65 ff; *Representative Government in Greek and Roman History* (1955).

† Chester G. Starr, "The Perfect Democracy of the Roman Empire," *American Historical Review*, LVIII (October, 1952), 1 ff. Liberty was later associated with discord. "The concept that the Roman Empire is the perfect democracy because it gives each what is his due is one of the most original in the political thought of the Empire, and appears to be a direct reaction to imperial conditions." See Starr's *Civilization and the Caesars; the Intellectual Revolution in the Roman Empire* (1954).

was regarded as having more wisdom than the people, and to many thinkers of Classical times it seemed the ideal form of government. The advice of the oracles was sought in times of crisis, and even the most learned consulted them to discover the proper course of conduct—as Xenophon frequently reminds us. One of the most striking of the supercessions of the people's own power to determine national action, however, was the lawgiver and the tradition of the lawgiver. Solon and Lycurgus stand out as almost mythical figures in the ancient world, and there is the story of how Lycurgus left Sparta after being given the promise that the laws would not be changed until his return. The cultivated respect for the lawgiver in Greece is beyond the comprehension of the irreverent in our century. Yet we can understand better, it would seem, the Roman respect for the civil law, which in fact stood clearly above the assemblies of the people. Among the Greeks the codification of the law did not reach the creative stage attained by the Romans; law was customary, but decisions did not become formal precedent, since popular juries decided cases; nor was there a class of lawyers and judges with the power reached in technical law by the Roman jurisconsult. Roman jurists were clear that custom was a source of law, but they were also clear that the jurists must determine the exact legislative effect of custom.

III

With the achievement of the *libertas* of the Empire, the ancient Greek and Roman assemblies were pushed aside. Municipal life, where some vitality in such institutions might be expected, withered away in the Hellenistic age, and government by emperors, soldiers, and civil servants took the place of the more ancient system of popular participation. Thereafter, only in the notion of *lex regia* did the Roman civil law carry forward the petrified remnants of a theory of popular sovereignty. The will of the prince has the force of law because the people have given him this power, according to the *Institutes* of Justinian and the observations of jurists like Ulpian. One of the nagging questions in Western intellectual history is whether the civil law has been an agency for the expansion of freedom or for the confirmation of the powers of government. Did not the Roman law confirm authority in the empire? In the course of time did it not overturn the customary laws of Western nations, except England where the common law survived? These are questions that are answered in part from chauvinistic considerations. However, civil law became the foundation of most of Western law; it became identified with the *ius commune* and as such it fostered specific rights which must be listed ultimately among the natural rights of men under the rule of law. The *ius commune* even contended with the rising *ius gentium* in the sixteenth century for the right to govern the relations between nations.* On one occasion Alexis de Tocqueville observed that when any ruler wanted to seize additional power, it would be strange if a lawyer were not at his side to tell him that under the civil law he had a perfect right to increase his power. Roman Law, he said, has perfected civil society, but it has degraded political society, because it was primarily the work of a highly civilized and very servile people. Throughout Europe the interpreters of the civil law became the principal ministers and agents of kings.†

While the *lex regia* thus in effect operated to strengthen the ruler, it also kept in the memory of men the Classical system of participation and the idea that one basis of legitimacy is the consent of the governed. Civil law served both to restrict and to encourage the expression and the power of public opinion. As law, it was remote from the people, being a technical law known only by the experts; but if it supported the ruler, it also suggested that the state was governed by law, that there was a natural law and a law of nations which is discoverable by reason, that legis-

*Alfonso Garcia Gallo, "El Derecho Común ante el Nuevo Mundo," *Revista de Estudios Políticos*, No. 80 (March-April, 1955), 133 ff; Alvaro D'Ors, *Las Romanistas ante la Actual Crisis de la Ley* (Madrid, Ateneo, 1956).

† Alexis de Tocqueville, *L'Ancien Régime et la Révolution* (8th ed., 1877), 331-332.

lative custom is generated by the people, and that there were rulers who accepted the great counter statement to the *lex regia*, the *digna vox*. That principle of the "worthysaying" was that rulers should be under the law, and that in turn all government officials were subject to the law in their public acts.

It is difficult to evaluate the importance of legislative custom as a means of expressing opinion. Custom in the Middle Ages was, indeed, the law of the land. Custom was, for the most part, the law of the *leges barbarorum*, though much of Roman law was incorporated into the customary codes of Western Europe. It was, perhaps, in this way that Roman civil law developed into the *ius commune* of the West. From the standpoint of opinion expression, it seems that the content and extent of custom were a matter for official interpretation. No matter how popular a custom might be, no one went to a common man to find out its meaning or how it should operate. But from the time of Classical law to the present, it has been considered that custom can be a legitimate source of law, and that it may both make and repeal more explicitly formulated law. It is reasonable to assume that so long as legislative custom arises from the sentiments and behavior of the masses, the law is likely to that extent to be in harmony with the general opinion of a society. So long as the ruler accepts the obligations of the law, noting that part of the law is the custom of the realm, long-run opinion has at least some negative control over what is done by a government. An additional force of public opinion in custom came from the medieval and traditional identification of the customs of the realm with the law of nature —an identification commonly made by both lawyers and philosophers, such as St. Thomas and William of Occam. The enforcement of the right of nature was translated into the rights of an individual under the law of nature. Enforcement of the law of nature was the enforcement of custom, and the enforcement of the custom of the realm made it necessary to call upon all who were in the realm. There is, therefore, some connection between great documents like Magna Carta and the idea of the sovereignty of the people. Indeed, the Classical civil law doctrines of custom extended into the Middle Ages, and influenced the customary systems, such as English law.

There are other and informal or customary means by which a determined opinion of the people can be made influential on government. Some students of Asiatic societies and of Mohammedan polity have insisted on the ability of ordinary people to press their ideas with effectiveness on the doings of their rulers. Chinese villagers could protest to their rulers; the threat of non-co-operation has long been a weapon with oriental peoples. Mahatma Gandhi's non-violent non-co-operation had deep roots in the efforts of Asiatic people to express public opinion. The effectiveness of this expression was not through representation, but rather through protest—including such relatively minor manifestations as songs and poems critical of the government. The secret brotherhood and the boycott of officials have, it is pointed out, brought about changes in public policy. Such opinion was, of course, of the traditional kind; it would not in any case be a proposal for new policies, nor opinion on technical solutions for immediate questions. In the extreme, a revolutionary movement could be organized, though unarmed people have seldom been able to win. Probably the richest experience in the negative expression of public opinion is the long life and leadership of Mahatma Gandhi. Certainly, if an Indian agreed with Gandhi, he could turn to his leadership with some hope of success in the conflict with the British. The devices and the experiences of common men in resisting their rulers are varied indeed. No regime has yet reached the power depicted by Orwell in his prophetic novel, *1984*, in controlling what people think; but it would seem that propaganda and other devices make the power of the modern state over opinion far greater than the corresponding powers enjoyed by earlier tyrants.

IV

The contemporary student is not concerned generally with Classical systems of public opinion expression, nor with Asiatic or more primitive types of regimes in which custom has been a predominant social force. The issue for the modern man is the "state" which somehow rose from the medieval epoch into the Renaissance and Baroque periods. Obviously, the modern state began to emerge in medieval times—indeed, the Middle Ages may be called "the restoration of the state," following the disintegration of the Classical political system.

There can hardly be a simple explanation of the rise of what we know today as the state, "the country state" or "the nation state," and it is certainly not fully continuous with the Roman Empire. Among the great continuities, however, one can observe the revival of the study of the Roman law toward the end of the high or early Middle Ages approximately in the twelfth century, and the restoration of the study of the Greek city state, through the rediscovery of Aristotle. These were added to the memories of the *populus Romanus* as it existed then in Western Europe, the ideas of the Scriptures, and the extremely variant practices in municipal and diocesan government. There was, thus, a deep foundation on which to build a theory of the people's participation in politics. The tradition of the ancient world in regard to participation was carried over into the literature and intellectual traditions of the day. "It is very important to observe that the State, in the modern sense of the word, has two independent origins," said C. N. S. Woolf, "that it is both the Empire on a reduced scale and the older, self-sufficient, non-universal *polis*. Clearly the way was now open to a great advance in political thought. It was with great difficulty and against even their own will that the lawyers had raised up the *civitas* and *regnum*, from their original and dependent position, to an independent and equal position with the one original world state, the empire. But, starting from Aristotle's *Politics*, the recognition of the *polis* (whether translated by *civitas* or *regnum*) as the 'state,' so far from presenting difficulty, would seem a necessary conclusion." *

* C. N. S. Woolf, *Bartolus of Sassoferrato; His Position in the History of Medieval Political Thought* (1913), 267.

Both Aristotle and Roman law carried forward the principle of citizen participation, the idea of the citizen's consent to government, and by implication the duty of the citizen to see that the higher law—the divine and natural law—was observed by the government. But it is not so clear that participation, as in the estates of the realm or in local assemblies, had the purposes of injecting new opinion into government. It was clear that opinion was to enforce "the law" through the means of participation, but not even the formal rulers were considered to be legislators.

Another institutional concept was carried forward at the time of the restoration of the state in medieval times. This was the concept of the continuity of the Roman people, the *populus Romanus*. It was real to Vergil at the beginning of the empire, for it was the great overshadowing fact whose existence had been prophesied from the time of the fall of Troy. No doubt the extraordinary vitality of the *Aeneid* in the literature and thought of the Western world is one of the great reasons for continuity of belief in the existence of the Roman people; and in the Middle Ages Dante could still build the political philosophy of his *Monarchy* on it. The concept of the Roman people was a reality to the civil lawyers, such as Bartolus in the fourteenth century and his successors; and they incorporated in it the virtues of the Greeks. At the same time the Roman people in any age would have all the rights they had in the past, and it would thus be their right to participate in government, or to establish through the *lex regia* the right of a ruler to be in office. We must conclude that one of the foundations of modern participation in government and the right of opinion to be heard is the long-enduring concept of the Roman people. It is a concept of great significance in the formation of the institutions which characterize the West.

The study of the Middle Ages in recent times not only has demonstrated historical and cultural continuities which the eighteenth century refused to see, but it has also shown that the Middle Ages were a period of singular political inventiveness. It was, indeed, during that period that the primary institutions for the expression of public opinion came into being. Parallel with the creation of institutions necessary in the modern state, there was also a growing sense of the community. The idea of "community of the realm" acquired a broadened meaning, and its application grew beyond the baronage to embrace the whole community. One may associate such growth with nationalism—and such association is quite correct—but the "community of the realm" implied as well that the duties of all men toward the state were in process of widening definition. "By the end of the reign of Edward II, the phrase 'community of the realm' sometimes identified the union of all individuals and subordinate communities, of which the baronage was one; in other texts it excluded the baronage and the Church, and meant the commons in Parliament, who represented most of the free population. There is evidence that peasants were loyal to the community long before they became an active part of it." *

As already noted, the medieval maxim *quod omnes tangit ab omnibus approbetur* became, no doubt, one of the foundations for the development of representative institutions, the primary ones for the expression of public opinion.† According to Hoyt, "this maxim at first implies a consent which is merely individualistic. Three developments are necessary to transform it into a principle of representation: the growth of majority rule in the corporation (and the community); association of *quod omnes tangit* with judicial procedure and due process of law in the courts; and subordination of consent to the idea of the common welfare." Ewart Lewis has appropriately indicated that medieval consent was consent to a common good.‡ With these develop-

* Barnaby C. Keeney, "Military Service and the Development of Nationalism in England, 1272-1327," *Speculum,* XXII (October, 1947), 549; see also, "The Medieval Idea of the State: The Great Cause, 1291-2," *The University of Toronto Law Journal,* VIII (Lent Term, 1949), 48 ff.

† This statement comes from the Roman law, *Codex* 5, 59, 5, dealing with the testamentary rights of co-heirs.

‡ Ewart Lewis, "The Contribution of Medieval Thought to the American Tradition," *The American Political Science Review,* L (June, 1956), 470. But see *Medieval Political Ideas* (2 vols., 1954). Cecil S. Emden's *The People and the Constitution* (1933, 2nd ed., 1956), is a useful work on this question.

ments, a conception of public law began to emerge from the private law of the medieval period. Public law was being built on the maxims and procedural rules of Roman private law; and a valid concept of public law had been constructed by the end of the thirteenth century.*

But those who have investigated medieval practice have been struck with the great variety of the institutions of participation, and the inventiveness of the medieval mind. It is virtually impossible to bring together all the illustrations of practical participation in the government of various medieval corporate bodies, as well as the community of the realm. The origins of modern practices in regard to methods of voting, elections, and systems of tenure in office are to be found in the communes, and in a great variety of religious and corporate organizations, including economic corporations. Léon Moulin believes the electoral system first developed in the Mediterranean communes in medieval times, though "majority" had no precise meaning in the Middle Ages. Indeed, it did not until the nineteenth century. In the development of electoral techniques, according to Moulin, the religious orders and especially the Church had priority over the emergent state.†

* Robert S. Hoyt, "Recent Publications in the United States and Canada on the History of Representative Institutions Before the French Revolution," *Speculum,* XXIX (April, 1954), Part 2, 369-370, which is a symposium on "Medieval Representation in Theory and Practice." J. S. Roskell, "The Social Composition of the Commons in a Fifteenth Century Parliament," *Bulletin of the Institute of Historical Research,* XXIV (November, 1951), 151-172, argues that Parliament became representative in the mid-fifteenth century, with the growth of strength in the third estate. Professor Corwin suggests that the baronage discovered that maintaining Magna Carta required the support and the participation of all classes; there was, thus, in Magna Carta a democratic impulse as part of its principle of growth, that is, the extension of rights to others than the previously privileged ones. See Edward S. Corwin, "The 'Higher Law' Background of American Constitutional Law," reprinted 1955 from *Harvard Law Review,* XLII (1928-1929), 149-185; 365-409. See M. V. Clarke, *Medieval Representation and Consent* (1936); J. Russell Major, *Representative Institutions in Renaissance France, 1421-1559* (1960).

† Léon Moulin, "Les Origines Religieuses des Techniques Electorales et Deliberatives Modernes," *Revue Internationale d'Histoire Politique et Constitutionnelle,* New Series No. 10, April-June, 1953, pp. 106 ff.

C. H. McIlwain in his essay on "Medieval Estates" has observed that the law books of Justinian had made known in England the Roman concept of the populus as the ultimate source of authority, and ideas found in Glanville and Bracton may be used as illustrations. The barons were, indeed, the only estate of the realm. Representation in the later constitutional sense hardly can be said to have developed. Still, the barons alone paid taxes, and their decisions in a direct sense affected only themselves. In their political functions they probably had a vague sense that they were acting also for all other classes in society.* In time, however, the magnates began to doubt that they could act for others, and it was proposed that the estate of the knights should be summoned. The lords spiritual became less certain of their capacity to act and bind the whole clergy. It is this broadening of the basis of political decision, combined with the idea of the ultimate authority of the people, that led to the establishment of the House of Commons. The extension of representation was, no doubt, motivated both by the desire for additional monies and for the purpose of controlling the local administration of justice. Those sent to Parliament were assumed to have in their hands a delegated authority, and they were supposed to act for the class from which they were selected.

In the thirteenth century Parliament was really several bodies representing different interests, though separation into different houses and estates did not go as far as in some Continental countries. The lower clergy and the merchants were brought into the Commons. By the fourteenth century, however, Parliament had become one organization, though in deliberation it was separated into different functional groups. The knights and burghers had become the body of the realm.†

While documents on the origin of parliament as an institution are best preserved in England, it is clear that at the same time

* Charles H. McIlwain, "Medieval Estates," *The Cambridge Medieval History* (1932), Vol. VII, Ch. XXIII, and pp. 665-666, 675.

† *Ibid.*, 680-681. See W. Roscher, *Politik* (2 Auf., 1893), 275 n, for a discussion of the division of medieval people into political groups and classes.

there were, in the thirteenth century, similar developments from similar situations over much of the Continent. Under Philip the Fair in France, the national estates were assembled for the first time, and the bourgeoisie were represented, owing to the enfranchisement of the communes. The struggle with Boniface VIII demanded larger revenues than the feudal system in a more unorganized condition could provide. The estates in France were, in practice, concerned with all of the important affairs of the kingdom, and the States General did represent the whole community in some degree.* But in contrast with the English Parliament, the French estates were without a regular time of meeting, and their power did not develop as in England. However, the Third Estate in the fifteenth century, for example, pleaded the cause of all non-noble people in the realm, and it represented limitations on royal authority. Since the duty to send delegates was established, in practice the inhabitants of the French *villes* assembled to elect to the estates. The nobles elected their delegates, and the non-nobles did the same. Moreover, the franchise was wide, and decisions were sometimes taken by a majority vote.†

Representative institutions developed with some maturity in Spain during the thirteenth century, though they declined later during the fifteenth and sixteenth centuries. According to McIlwain, the claims of the people to a share in government were more fully recognized in Spain than in England—particularly during the time of the strength of the Spanish Cortes. It has been suggested that the Cortes of Catalonia, of all the Spanish estates, most resembled a modern legislative body. There were three estates in Catalonia: the clergy, the nobles and the knights, and

* R. W. Carlyle and A. J. Carlyle, *A History of Medieval Political Theory in the West* (6 vols., 1903-1936), VI, 206 ff; McIlwain, *op. cit.*, 683 ff.

† The Carlyles stress especially the representative character of the medieval estates. In Vol. VI, p. 101, they note that in 1381, the regent in France, in the name of Charles VI, abolished earlier aids of taxes as contrary to pre-existing liberties and customs, and the ordinance was issued by an assembly in Paris. Whether or not it was a States General, it had a representative character.

the proctors for the towns. And in Spain the estate representation of cities and towns was probably more highly developed than elsewhere. The Third Estate of Catalonia, however, was more similar to the Third Estate in France than to the Commons in England, for "no Spanish *procuradores* represented such a body of constituents as we find in the English County Court." * In Spain all the delegates were deputed by the *universitates* of cities and villes, and none came, as in England, from a rural county. The failure of medieval representative institutions outside of England occurred because as in Spain they were unable to make the Crown dependent upon them for its revenue. Still, in the fifteenth-century Spanish Cortes, the king agreed not to interfere with the choice of delegates, and to leave their selection to the control of custom. But this was a point which was not easily or permanently settled.† If the powers of the Spanish Cortes were short-lived, nevertheless while they existed they enforcd more genuine popular rights in Spain than in England. Laws were valid only with the consent of the delegates, but taxes were placed on the cities alone, while the nobles were expected to render personal service. When permanent taxes were laid, the king was able to get along without regular meetings of the estates.

In Italy under Frederick II, we find what is often called the "first example of the modern representative system." For in 1232, two representatives from each city and *castello* were called to treat of the utility and the common good of the realm. In Italy during the fourteenth century it became common for estates to meet in many parts of the country. In Germany, however, because of the decentralization of authority and the power of sep-

* McIlwain, *op. cit.*, 695 ff, 700.

† Carlyle and Carlyle, *op. cit.*, VI, 206 ff; Marie R. Madden, *Political Theory and Law in Medieval Spain* (1930), 59, notes that the first Cortes of Barcelona was held in 1064 at Gerona in which the Count and his wife confirmed the *Ustages*. They agreed they would hold to the constitutions of peace and truce among Christians, and give protection to the Jews. The Cortes was held in the Cathedral church, and it was attended by bishops, abbots, magnates, and good men. The good men were probably free men with some property.

arate princes, the formation of a national representative system was delayed. Nevertheless there are many indications in the Middle Ages of the principle of representation in the *Landstände* and *Reichstag;* but it was not until Lewis of Bavaria was engaged in his struggle with Pope John XXII that the Third Estate was called upon to give support to the imperial claims, and even so it was after the Middle Ages that the German estates were fully established. Estates came into being more or less contemporaneously in the late Middle Ages in Sweden, Iceland, the Isle of Man or the "States" of Jersey, and in the Irish and Scottish parliaments. In Scotland, the kings never were able to control the nobility, and they could not be called to attend.*

V

Let us assume that the modern state has emerged. Parliament in the Baroque state was generally a recessive institution, and the great institution of modern European monarchy had been created. The monarch had power, but he was the symbol of the unity of the state, and in theory he stood above public opinion and partisan organization. He was supported by a newly created bureaucracy, which had pushed the old aristocrats aside—as Tocqueville demonstrated—because they had not learned soon enough how to function efficiently in the modern state. Newly refurbished and powerful institutional ideas supported the state; Roman Law had come to its own in Europe, and it was jostling canon law into the background. Moreover, Bodin, Grotius, and Hobbes contributed to the modern world the conception of political sovereignty—a concept which seemed materially to help in the organization and the unleashing of the centralized power over the citizen-subject. With the modern conception of the state, an art which would allow governments to protect themselves against opinion began to develop. The secret of state, *ragion di stato,* and the *arcana imperii* armed the holder of po-

* McIlwain, *op. cit.,* 704 ff. It is observed here that in Scotland the first real organ of nationalism was not the parliament but the Kirk.

litical authority against the opinion of the man in the street.

Spengler has described the process by saying that with the Spanish-Gothic spirit of the Baroque, a stronger and more severe style of life spread over Western Europe. The Spaniard felt in himself a great mission, not "I" but simply "It is." According to Spengler, the Spaniard of that period saw himself as a priest or a soldier; he served either God or the King. Only the Prussian style of life called into being a similar ideal of such severity and self-renunciation, which was seen in the sense of the fulfillment of duty in Count Alba, the famous commander who served Charles V and Philip II. Only the Spanish and Prussian peoples stood up against Napoleon. And here, in the Escorial, the modern state was made. From Madrid came the great system of interest politics of dynasties and nations, cabinet diplomacy, and war as a planned and executed move in the midst of far-reaching political combinations.* In such a state the ruler and the civil servant were the servants of the people, but the people were not to be consulted on the intricate and difficult problems of the state. Rather it might be said that the function of government in the Baroque period resembled the function of Baroque architecture—it was to persuade the people.

The new state was not favorable to the power of public opinion, even though Frederick the Great might consider the basis of authority the social contract. Now the concept of the "public" as the general community subject to government had been created. (Did not Louis XIV say, in effect, "I am the government?") And what was rediscovered in the Baroque era, after its loss in the fall of the Classical state, was a renewed system of techniques for control over thought and behavior which seem to be inherent in any strong state. Now a state is supposed to serve the rational needs of men. A state's power is for the service of justice and the common good, which in itself does not specify that the major trends in popular opinion are to be followed. What those who defended government against opinion—Bodin, Gortius, Hobbes,

* Oswald Spengler, *Preussentum und Sozialismus* (1921), 27.

Hooker, James I, and Richelieu, among many others—discovered was the unused potential of political persuasion in a properly organized government. And their discoveries were not limited to methods of crude coercion, or police technics in uncovering sedition, but developed also means of controlling the mind by propaganda. The state as propagandist began to be understood in its role as efficient teacher of the public mind. Like many thinkers of the ancient world, the men of this period did not stress the importance of the *truth* of religion. What was important for them in regard to religion was the power of state-supported religion to serve the state—rather than to have the state serve the purposes of God. St. Louis and his holy adviser and kinsman, St. Thomas Aquinas, were indeed remote from the concentrated military and bureaucratic power of the new state. Among its most persuasive symbols was the institution of permanent or continuous taxation to support the civil service trained in the Roman law and the armies trained in the newer weapons of the age.

The Baroque state was not friendly to the Classical conception of the citizen as one who participates in making public decisions. The public was not a participating group of citizens, but was—as Bodin insisted in the spirit of his time—a group of subjects whose opinions on political matters were irrelevant or even dangerous to the public interest. Still, it was understood generally that there was an explosive quality in the public mind. Machiavelli warned new rulers to be careful about the subject, especially his family and his property; Botero, one of the more ambitious of the exponents of *ragion di stato,* sometimes saw the public with a friendly glance, and then he feared the tumult and disorder implicit in ordinary people thinking about the state.* Such an ambiguous attitude toward common men is quite common among the intellectuals of the Renaissance and the Baroque. When the people attempted to resist government, they became turbulent—but when they agreed with the large objectives of public policy, they shared in the wisdom of their prince.

* See Gionvanni Botero, *Practical Politics* (Ragion di Stato), trans. by G. A. Moore (1949).

Absolutism was in effect a defense of government against opinion; and it developed institutions which were effective in controlling public opinion. The Renaissance and Baroque states were not believers in popular sovereignty; the predominant idea was the sovereignty of the ruler, though it might be conceded that originally the people had determined the form of government under which they lived. If the social contract were stressed by some as a democratic device, it was soon turned the other way. Hobbes' social contract is no foundation for liberty; and powerful rulers, if they did not claim divine right, could claim a traditional and prescriptive consent of the people to their sovereignty. Two primary institutions which expressed the Baroque mind were the "good prince" and the confessional state. Neither served the right of the people to direct the government, for government depended on the prince and not upon opinion; and the religion of the state was determined by circumstance and international agreement. The individual did not have a right to select his faith or to educate his children in his own beliefs. With obsolescent estates and the immaturity of the urge to create parliaments, there were few means of expressing public judgment. The "election" did not decide public personalities or public questions. No doubt the good prince in the confessional state—the exponent of *cujus regio ejus religio*—may be defended as a means of terminating the religious wars, but such a political system had to be overcome before the modern conception of public opinion was possible.

VI

The defense of public opinion is associated with other ideas, such as liberty. Its defense is related to constitutions, to legal systems which protect private right, and ultimately protect the rights of free speech, press, religion, and others. Among the more obvious political developments which helped forward the idea of public opinion was the Classical conception of the mixed constitution.* But the resurgence of the Classical conception of balance took another form in the eighteenth century. For here one encounters "the Gothic constitution," or the ancestral constitution (in Britain especially) under which liberty was realized. Such a system provided, as did the Classical theory, a formal share of popular participation in government, and it was appropriate in a time when modern parliamentary forms were becoming fixed. The Gothic constitution may have begun in the period of the "estates," but it flowered in the modern period when the theory of representation was formulated. Indeed, the model for the Gothic constitution was the British system of the eighteenth century before the age of revolutions. It was associated with the Teutonic, or Anglo-Saxon theory of virtue; and thus it was part of a once significant association between race and politics. Gothic institutions were a reflection of Teutonic virtue; among the Anglo-Saxons, Gothic institutions bespoke the decadence of the Normans among the English-speaking peoples. In other words, such a theory was related to the various ideas which had been included in the mixed constitution. The Gothic myth of the seventeenth century was, therefore, related to republican as well as to monarchical theory.†

The great modern surge toward a theory of public opinion is associated with British constitutional theory and practice. This statement is correct for both the more proletarian and the more conservative political movements, for both in their way turned toward the British political system. The British Constitution epitomized a kind of natural constitutional law, which all free societies might copy in degree and in so far as their own institutions would permit. It provided a model for both revolutionary and conservative versions of representative government. It was the "parliamentary system" which other countries tried to copy;

* In Aristotle the mixed constitution was a balance between democracy and oligarchy; in Polybius, the Roman constitution was a balance between the executive, the Senate, and the assemblies of the people.

† See Samuel Kliger, *The Goths in England: A Study in Seventeenth Century Thought* (1952); "Emerson and the Usable Anglo-Saxon Past," *Journal of the History of Ideas*, XVI (October, 1955), 476 ff.

and it has been just about the only form of government in the West which has been exported to other countries. The British Constitution might come into being from the constituent consent involved in a social contract; it may have come from a kind of theory of divine or providential cause; or it may have been a kind of necessary and inevitable expression of the Gothic virtues —its importance in any case for the theory of public opinion rests on the fact that it provided a share of participation for the people in the day-to-day operations of their government. There was, in other words, a role for public opinion in the British exemplification of the mixed, balanced, or Gothic constitution.

Those who praised the British Constitution in the eighteenth century, both before and after the French Revolution, recognized that British institutions provided a legitimate function for popular opinion in government. There might be argument over the proper extent of the power of public opinion, and there were theories, such as the middle class view, which would restrict the rights of the masses to share in power. But those who wished in the name of democracy to expand the right of opinion turned naturally to British institutions as the model of their hoped-for systems. Perhaps no other political form has been so much at the same time the model of the conservatives and the revolutionaries, as was the British Constitution during the nineteenth century.

The British Constitution has continued its role of model for both conservatives and their opponents down to the present time. For some it is the monarchy, for others the system of parliamentary representation, for others the responsibility of the ministry, and for still others it is the system of political parties which seems to be a model of stability. From Montesquieu, De Lolme, Blackstone, Donoso Cortés on to our own time, the story is the same. Not only did British experience in the middle of the seventeenth century show the rise of public opinion to the first rank of political power, but public opinion seemed to have attained in the Constitution a stable legality. It is out of this experience that many have reached the conclusion that it is only under a parliamentary system of responsible cabinet government that public opinion can attain its full and legitimate power.

However, the conservative view has stressed the "share" of the people, not the complete dominance of public opinion. The traditional mixed constitution historically provided a balance in which other powers—such as the monarchy, the courts, the civil service, the aristocracy, even the upper middle class—might serve as modulating forces in political decision.* Conservatives were attracted to the social stability of the British—their monarchy, aristocracy, the power of their courts, the high quality of the English civil service, and the position in parliament of the House of Lords. In this complex of powers the people had their share; in this complex public opinion was powerful but it was also responsible, and the balance of the constituent powers prevented the historic aberrations and hysteria which intellectuals foresaw and feared in the early days of popular participation. Indeed, the role of public opinion in England has seemed to many to reflect the ideal of Classical moderation which was praised in Cicero.

It is under the complex set of circumstances found in British experience that the most widely accepted theory of the function of public opinion has emerged. It was brought together and fused into a single theory in the brilliant perception of Edmund Burke at the time—the only time—he was elected to a public office, a seat in the House of Commons. And what Burke said in his now classic statement came directly from the theory of the British Constitution. Yet, it may well be considered a kind of confused body of statements which has resulted in a mixture of contradictions—a fragmentation whose constituent ideas were consistent but were never properly blended. As a classical theory of public opinion, it has little to do with the theory of different forms of government, including the historically important British system of balanced powers. Its contribution to the theory of the proper function of public opinion, however, came to be widely accepted.

* On the trends in French conservatism, see René Rémond, *La Droite en France de 1815 à Nos Jours* (1954).

It held that in the relation of the citizen to his rulers, the subject had a right to be heard, but only when he was responsible and informed, and only within the participation allowed by the law, assuming that the law observed the canons of justice. The ruler, whatever may be the quality of his personality, has the right to govern—even against the will of the people—provided he too obeys the law which limits or extends popular participation, that he is informed, technically competent, that he has a sense of the practical—such as the necessity of observing the tradition of a people—and that he is honest, a man of good conscience, and knows and observes the regulations of justice.

The most effective and the most classic statement of a theory of public opinion which clarifies the right of the common man to say "no" to the government, and the government to say "no" to the common judgment of the citizens, is stated by Burke in his Letters to the Electors and Sheriffs of Bristol. In modern democracy, as in other systems of government, some things cannot be said; and while almost any public official follows in his conscience and behavior the Burkean theory, he is not at liberty as a matter of good politics to say so. But it may perhaps be agreed that there are few, if any, members of the United States Congress today who would not in practice agree with Burke's observation to the fortunate electors of Bristol that an elected officer's primary duty is to give his voters suitable attention, the sincere benefit of his knowledge, and his informed judgment concerning the general welfare. Likewise, there are few modern public men capable of thinking about the problem, who would deny that our natural rights are embedded in our prescriptive and conventional constitutional order.* No doubt these same people would agree with Burke that most of mankind are not excessively curious about political theories, as long as they are really happy; "and one sure symptom of an ill-conducted state, is the propensity of the people to resort to them." Moreover, the public happiness may well de-

* See Burke's *Speech to the Electors of Bristol,* 3 Nov. 1774; *Speech Previous to the Election,* 6 Sept. 1780; *Letter to the Sheriffs of Bristol* (1777).

pend on the effectiveness and integrity of the virtual representation accorded the people by those representatives who give their full attention and knowledge to the attainment of the public good. The public good in America, or elsewhere, is hardly to be attained—according to the classical and Burkean theory—by an exact proportion of one representative to a specified number of voters in a carefully defined electoral district.

The wishes of constituents, thought Burke, should have great weight, "their opinion high respect; their business unremitted attention." In any clash between their interests and his own, the representative must prefer the interest of the constituents. But in contrast, the representative should never sacrifice "his unbiased opinion, his mature judgment, his enlightened conscience" to any man or set of men. The representative does not derive these qualities of character from the pleasure of the voter, nor from the law and the Constitution. "They are a trust of Providence, for the abuse of which he is deeply answerable. Your representative owes you, not his industry only, but his judgment; and he betrays, instead of serving you, if he sacrifices it to your opinion." Burke continued by condemning in eloquent language instructions or mandates of an authoritative character issued by the electorate to the member of Parliament. The mandate to the representative is utterly unknown to the laws and Constitution of England. "Parliament," he said, "is not a *congress* of ambassadors from different and hostile interests . . . but Parliament is a *deliberative* assembly of *one* nation, with *one* interest, that of the whole." When an election is over, the electors have not chosen a member from Bristol, but a member of *Parliament* of the English nation.

In 1780 when Burke returned to Bristol to canvass for his re-election, he found his opposition too strong and he withdrew his name from the poll. But it was only after he had given a lengthy and ringing defense of his conduct in Parliament, his defense of the real interests, the future interests, of the people of Bristol. He had been too busy in Parliament defending the real interests of Bristol to spend much time in the city; he had given the people virtual representation because he had defended the interests of the nation. He had favored freedom of trade for Ireland, which was resented by the Bristol merchants; he had supported a bill for relieving debtors of imprisonment; and he had voted for the repeal of the penal provisions against Catholics in the law of 1699. His courageous attempt to defend his voting record was sufficient to convince some of his constituents, but not enough to win him another term as an elected member of Parliament.

Burke's theory was at war, even as he formulated it, with the late eighteenth-century demand for a more effective expression of public opinion in the "unreformed House of Commons." Virtual representation was, likewise, clashing with the new breed of arithmeticians and calculators of electoral and representational reform. In both England and Ireland the mode in which extra-Parliamentary opinion could operate on government was becoming well-nigh a revolutionary question. But in spite of democratic arithmetic and the more complicated mathematics of majority rule, we still have in our theory of democracy the proposition that the representative owes his voters just what Burke said he did: attention, knowledge, and informed judgment; in the end the public man must be a leader, which means he has a conscience, and the people must follow the man of wisdom, courage and technical competence.*

Nineteenth-century monarchy and the restrained parliamentary system were, to European conservatives, the proper system for the expression of public opinion. Hegel's theory of civil society as separate and distinct from the state may be cited, for public opinion was found in society and it was controlled in degree by the sublime detachment of the monarch. German constitutional monarchy, the *Rechtsstaat,* was a set of institutions somewhat

* See C. P. Ives, in *Modern Age,* 4 (Winter, 1959-60), 90. The right of the common man to resist the decisions of government is especially acute in the United States since the judges, not responsible to the electorate, have been making revolutionary public policy on racial and civil rights matters.

similar to the traditional theory of British monarchy, and it could be regarded as well as an annotation on the ideal of mixture and balance. Like the British Constitution, the German constitutional system was truly a "Gothic institution." * Public opinion would be expressed in the Parliament, but the German Parliament would not be sovereign. Nor did the German system before the Weimar Republic have any fully evolved mode of cabinet responsibility.

Democrats have said, of course, that such a system of mixture and balance does not give the people their rightful sovereignty, and that the only popular sovereignty worthy of the name is one in which there is no check on majority will. As one of the great institutions of Western Europe, monarchy provided both for an expression of popular will and for a check on the force of public opinion. Monarchy has been an extraordinarily popular institution. It symbolizes the ideas of the popular mind, and power shared with the representatives of the people is both an authorization and a check on public opinion. Such a role was played by German constitutional monarchy, and in part it is still played by the other constitutional monarchies of Western Europe.

VII

We come to the essential question of the necessary institutions of public opinion. What are the proper means, the best means, of giving expression *and* power to public opinion? Broadly, it is said that the power of public opinion is greatest, and it is also most free, in a republican system which is at the same time democratic. For surely one of the elements of the power of public opinion is an approach to political or institutional democracy. Democracy may mean many things, but it must at the least allow the common man the right of expressing his judgment effectively about the conduct of the public official. What agency, then, should represent popular opinion? It may be the monarch; it may be the

* See Guido de Ruggiero, *The History of European Liberalism*, trans. by R. G. Collingwood (1927), 211 ff.

parliament or congress; it may be the civil service, or some kind of trained ruling class; or it may be the judiciary. Yet, in another sense, it is generally held that the representative system is the highest agency for the effective expression of the popular mind.

Historic republicanism appealed to the public for its support, but it did not take a stand in principle for the continuous, effective expression of popular judgment on current political questions. In the seventeenth century discussion of English republicanism, the principle of popular sovereignty was modeled on that of the Classical world. The people gave consent to a legitimate government, and such consent might involve the social contract as the ultimate and remote foundation. Government was furthermore subordinate to the moral foundations of all governments —the divine and natural law; and the people in all their political activity were subject to the same law. In their versions of republican theory, Sidney, Milton, and Harrington took such a position, though the fundamental laws of politics might be different for each of them. Locke was no republican, but his theory became the foundation for much American republicanism, and his insistence on the supremacy of the natural law helped to transmit to Americans from Europe the Great Tradition of political morality. Locke declared that when men emerged from a state of nature into a community, they "must be understood to give up all the power necessary to the ends for which they unite into society to the majority of the community. . . ." But the ends of the community would be determined by the natural law and the rights of the members.* Public opinion was not free to repeal the law or the rights of nature, but it was free and, indeed, had the duty to enforce in the state these high standards. Its freedom arose within the boundaries of the higher law.

Republicanism was, moreover, associated with the principle of the mixture and balance of the constitution, very much on the model of the Classical polity in Aristotle or of the Polybian theory of the Roman Constitution. The republicanism of men like Milton

* John Locke, *Second Treatise*, Sec. 99.

turned out to be aristocratic in tone, just as Roman republicanism had been. But it can hardly be said that modern American democracy is different, since our democracy resembles the Aristotelian polity more than the Greek democracy. American democracy has some of the qualities of the aristocratic republicanism of the seventeenth century.

The period from the end of the eighteenth century until well into the nineteenth century can be termed a time of invention which increased the participation and power of public opinion. At first there was an argument for the extension of the suffrage within a context of the rule of law. The organization of political propaganda groups became effective early in the nineteenth century, and the pressure group and the political party eventually became standard devices of democratic politics. In America the argument that almost all public officials should be elected, led even to the election of technical state officials and judges. The culmination of effort to give public opinion power was the invention and installation of direct democracy, the plebiscite on laws, in Switzerland and the United States.

Montesquieu once said that the failure to define the electorate was one of the principal causes of the ruin of Rome.* Yet the concern for definition of the right to vote, the primary discrimination in the definition of the general political public, came rather late. One of the first political thinkers to be concerned with formal definition was Francisco Suárez, who was led to his inquiry by attempting to outline the idea of majority rule: who should be included in computing the greater number? "There is a general agreement on this point, that there should be reckoned in this number only persons who can give consent to consuetudinary law. All infants and all persons mentally defective are therefore excluded. Some would also entirely exclude women on the ground that they can exercise no legislative authority. Among men, they exclude all below the age of twenty-five years. However, I can-

* Charles de Montesquieu, *The Spirit of the Laws*, Bk. II, Ch. 2.

not find any basis in law or any justification in reason for the exclusion of the last two groups." *

It is clear that the great drive to expand the power of public opinion has in degree receded, and for fairly noticeable causes. The chief reasons for hesitation in trusting public opinion in our century are the observable process of disintegration of parliamentary government, the uncertain operation of the party systems, the lack of mass restraint in demands made on the political system, the impossibility of recovering a "stolen" election, and the overall question about the rationality of men. This latter query was instigated primarily because of the discovery of psychological investigation, after which the infra-rational became the first concern of many students of politics. Ideas held by Graham Wallas are, no doubt, relatively harmless since they are largely cautionary; but the impact of Freudian theory upon political thought is profound, and the subconscious mind is held to be a vast and unpredictable force. It may be used to explain the madness of either leaders or the docile masses who follow them. But it has all added up to the crisis in European life foretold by Nietzsche, Amiel, Burckhardt, Tocqueville, and others. The crisis denies the more pleasant assumptions of those who felt that some kind of progress was inevitable. To say that the common man should have a directing power in government is a specific proposition of limited content: it does not in fact imply any content to the opinions of those who are given directive power. In the extreme it could be said that whatever the public might decide should be accepted as the standard of political justice.

Yet the breaking-up of nineteenth-century institutions, the alternative form of state—the Soviet regime, the strong fascist type, and its mild form under Mussolini, or the even milder one in Spain—the madness of the rank and file, the emergence of the mass man, as well as the propagandist intellectual, have all led

* Francisco Suárez, *Selections from Three Works*, trans. by G. L. Williams and others (Carnegie Classics of International Law, 1944), 529 [*On Laws and God the Lawgiver*, Bk. VII, Ch. 9].

to the proposition that the ascendency of public opinion cannot be justified simply in a formal sense. Moreover, there are other institutional developments which suggest that deference to public opinion has passed its peak of influence. One may note the emergence in the democratic state of a civil service relatively independent of the legislative body, the military services able to demand whatever they consider necessary for defense, the development of a vast system of governmental secrecy, the *arcana imperii* all over again—all of these developments show the growing power of even democratic government in relation to the opinions of ordinary men. Civil servants of whatever kind naturally turn to the executive for protection, and in turn the strong executive of the modern warlike state turns to the bureaucracy for support against whatever part of the public might be critical.

One way to state the issue is to ask: what kind of political force will take the place of a vigorous, driving public opinion, such as functioned in the time of the fullest development of parliamentary government? First, there is the new administrative organization of the state; and second, there is the vast organization of groups —functional, professional, and otherwise—which in most instances hardly allows for popular control. Obviously, the great alternative to the sovereignty of public opinion is the sovereignty of some elite, the men in the house against the men in the street, a mandarin or samurai class, or more specifically the sovereignty of a trained ruling order. The democrats used to say they wished to restore jurisdiction to the citizen, and not to destroy him. The critic of popular opinion has been concerned with the education of a ruling class on the theory that the masses cannot possibly be educated to the complicated tasks of government.

VIII

From ancient times, interest in training the ruling class has been fairly continuous. Plato's concern with the best training for rulers is present in all his writings, together with his insistence on control over widely held opinions. Book Six of the *Laws* might be regarded as a treatise on administration.* Aristotle seems to be balancing the merits of different forms of elites in power. One might trace such interest through a great variety of thinkers who wrote on the formation and the duties of princes. Sir Thomas Elyot in *The Boke Named the Gouvernour,* first published in 1531, was concerned with the education of the ruling class. He took from the Classical writers the assumption that men in general may be educated in the virtues, but he did not assume that all may govern as in a democracy. Education is always a tool for the "formation" of rulers, but it is not always the necessity of the masses.

It was the same motive that led Sir Henry Taylor in 1836 to plead for the study of public administration in his forgotten classic *The Statesman.* Through administrative study and organization the "best wisdom in the country contained shall be perpetually forming itself in deposit." And without creating "Administrative Government" there will be only "government of fetches, shifts, and hand-to-mouth expedients." Education and examination in the recruitment of the ruling order were his first considerations; he gives only incidental reference to public opinion and majority control in Parliament.†

* Jerome Hall, "Plato's Legal Philosophy," *Indiana Law Journal,* 31 (Winter, 1956), 171 ff; cf. Andrew Hacker, "Dostoevsky's Disciples: Man and Sheep in Political Society," *The Journal of Politics,* 17 (November, 1955), 590-613.

† *The Works of Sir Henry Taylor* (London, 1878), Vol. IV, "The Statesman." Especially, 331.

PART II

THE MODERN INQUIRY

CHAPTER 4

The Emergence and Shaping of the Study of Public Opinion

I

The conditions under which the study of public opinion emerged need to be examined, since much of the contemporary concern with opinion is the development of methods and techniques. The rise of the study of opinion was an obvious result of troubled times during the last century. It was the result of an era when the masses of people were becoming organized to express their political demands, and mass opinion became recognized as a powerful force on government. Around the middle of the nineteenth century, inquiry into the nature of public opinion became the plaything of newspaper writers, of political leaders in their speeches, and of scholars and intellectuals who sensed, if vaguely, that a new discipline was taking shape. But the dialectical tension between the educated and the mass was not resolved either by new study or by political reform. The sudden view of masses on the march was a troubling and fearsome sight.

It was a time in which the universities began the systematic study of society; a time in which the social sciences were making their appearance, led by the triumphs of that most dismal science, political economy. It was a time in which almost every leading thinker held that the doctrine of progress must inevitably be attached to the idea of the advancement of the people who, as James Mill urged, were to grow in wisdom and power by learning to read and by having the right to vote at a mature age for members of parliament. It was a time, also, in which the liberal mentality believed that the people could be weaned easily from their traditional loyalties. The student of society was led to deal with public opinion, already a well-established term, as one of the concepts of social and political theory.

It has been doubted whether there should be one agreed-upon definition of public opinion,* but in fact there is little chance of such a situation arising. From the beginning of modern social science, there has been sharp disagreement on most of the questions it has considered.

In 1852 Joseph Moseley declared that "there is no word that has played so important and conspicuous a role in the political events of recent times as Public Opinion." † The public, he thought, was really the people at large, but their wants or political desires are reflected either in custom or in legislation, especially reforms such as Catholic Emancipation, the Parliamentary Reform Bill of 1832, and the repeal of the Corn Laws. Laws arise from public opinion and legislative science, which is an art for the experts and for the informed when there is no public opinion on a given question. While it was Lord Chatham (1708-1778) and Wilkes who first organized public opinion to control the government, English political leaders had long since recognized the possibility. A statute of the time of Edward VI (1547-1553) forbade under pain of treason all assemblies of more than twelve persons in order to change the laws of the kingdom. Moseley thought this was necessary in order to effect the change in English religion. While petitions have been recognized in England as a means of expressing opinion, the writ summoning Parliament from the time of the thirteenth century and Edward II stressed consent to action by the government. Such ancient consent was

* See the remark of Paul F. Lazarsfeld in *The Public Opinion Quarterly,* XII (1948), 497, in his review of L. W. Doob, *Public Opinion and Propaganda* (1948).

† See Joseph Moseley, *Political Elements; or, the Progress of Modern Legislation* (1852), 119. Moseley is surely a neglected author in the history of the idea of public opinion.

asked both for the member of Parliament and for those whom he might represent.*

Since the word "public" includes all members of the community, public opinion is therefore the opinion of all. All may be present in public meetings, join associations or clubs, and all may sign petitions, for the meeting and the petition are two of the chief means of expressing opinion. In action, public opinion may be direct or indirect. Direct action is in effect revolutionary and dangerous, while indirect action, the more common and persistent form, is a great power in society. What is the evidence for the existence of public opinion? Moseley noted in 1852 that widespread public meetings were an indication that a majority of the public may have reached a certain idea of truth; petitions to the Crown are also evidence of opinion; and likewise the opinions found in "the haunts of business and pleasure." Groups in society—orders, classes, interests—often believe themselves to be evidential of public opinion in general. Moreover, the press as the interpreter of opinion gives further evidence of its existence. But the best evidence of public opinion, according to Moseley, is the general election, where the opinion expressed constitutes in all probability a fair representation of the community. The political parties accept the results of a general election as representative of all of the community—especially since, at the time Moseley was making his observations, the electorate still represented property, and consequently education and intelligence.

In spite of his sanguine approach to opinion, Moseley was aware of the power of organized and energetic minorities who are able to convince the public that they are representative of opinion in general. Moseley concluded that more definite means of ascertaining general opinion was therefore needed, and until we can be sure we have become able to discover what is really majority opinion, it would be just as well if the term, "public opinion" were less often used as a guide, "or as an instrument of power." The term "public opinion" is too often misapplied or even

* *Ibid.*, 259 ff. On English development, see Cecil S. Emden, *The People and the Constitution* (1933, 2nd ed., 1956), *passim*.

fraudulently applied. Thus, we come to an essential proposition: public opinion has no absolute right against the government, that is, those who are the exponents of the science of legislation. The people of England have a limited right to govern, and they have a duty to govern properly. Moseley believed that the people in general often lacked sufficient knowledge to discern the truth. He says that though everyone now claims the right to have absolute opinions, he doubted the wisdom of the masses in the towns. Even in the clubs and among the intelligent classes, prejudice and private interest vitiate opinion. On the contrary, even the commonest intellects can form sound opinions about fairness and integrity, and general opinion may often correctly distinguish the needs of the people. Nevertheless, the government has a far greater capacity than public opinion to gather correct information, though Parliament itself is relatively faithful to public opinion. Public opinion at best is but the raw material of legislation, and investigation must be the basis of lawmaking.

In the end, however, according to Moseley, consent or participation can never be coextensive with the duty of obedience. The elector has his right as one who belongs to the public; the right to vote does not inhere in him as a person, nor in him as a member of a class or of an interest group. A voter is the trustee of the people, for the whole community has the right of consent, not the single individual; a member of Parliament represents the whole community first and his own electors second. He must be loyal first of all to the "One Great Public." *

* *Ibid.*, 287. In his savage attack on public opinion, Urquhart proposed in 1855 that if we could get rid of the organs of opinion (the press, such as the London *Times*) we would have no public opinion, and we might get men in government again. The supremacy of opinion in England has meant the pre-eminence of evil, the prostration of mental faculties, and life in the herd. Ministers like Lord Palmerston now manufacture opinion, and the press is working for its own extinction, since it has become a public nuisance. See David Urquhart, *Public Opinion and Its Organs* (1855). The discussion of William A. Mackinnon, *On the Rise, Progress and Present State of Public Opinion in Great Britain and Other Parts of the World* (2nd ed., 1828), will be left to the chapter on "Public Opinion and the Middle Class."

II

The German discussion of public opinion began, as in other countries of Western Europe, fairly early in the nineteenth century, but systematic discussion of it came several decades later. J. K. Bluntschli in his *Staatswörterbuch* in 1862, noted that public opinion had been a great power in the previous century and just before the French Revolution. To him, public opinion was primarily the opinion of the great middle class, and that opinion was like the chorus of the ancient tragedy, for it was an expression of the *Zeitgeist.* Moreover, religion was in conflict with the development of genuine public opinion, for public opinion could not exist without the free development of the power of thought and judgment. Writing a little later, in 1880, Franz von Holtzendorff,* because of the German emphasis on the folk spirit, and because he recognized a total European cultural context for opinion, regarded public opinion as a vast and traditional confluence of the currents of human judgment. But at the same time, he saw that the organization and effectiveness of public opinion had been closely associated with the development of finance and credit in the modern world, and this again has been associated with the rise of the middle class.† Holtzendorff believed that it was late in the eighteenth century that public opinion began to resist censorship and political secrecy. The establishment of the

* Franz von Holtzendorff, *Wesen und Werth der Öffentlichen Meinung* (2nd ed., 1880), 1 ff, for this material.

† Hans Speier, "Historical Development of Public Opinion," *The American Journal of Sociology,* LV (1950), 376 ff, suggests with Lord Acton, *Essays on Freedom and Power,* ed. by Gertrude Himmelfarb (1948), 267, the influence in France on the rise of public opinion of the growth of the public debt and the increasing importance of the opinion of creditors. Both Jacques Necker and Alexander Hamilton saw the close connection between public finance and public opinion; they were both important in the use of publicity in connection with governmental finance. Sir William Temple's essay, *On the Origin and Nature of Government* (1672), is often cited as an early discussion of opinion, the authority of government being derived from opinion. Speier also emphasized the importance of the middle class in public opinion, connected as it was with the spread of literacy and the cheapening of mass communication in the eighteenth century.

open public which was set against the *arcana imperii* became the foundation of the power of opinion in modern times. Naturally, the press under these conditions became a center of interest as the first great organ of mass communication.

German thought on public opinion from the outset refused to identify the sovereignty of the people with the government, and, in contrast with French revolutionary doctrines of national sovereignty, Germany regarded public opinion as being outside the government. But if one adds the bureaucracy with its secrecy, and one remembers that the modern bureaucracy became an effective political force in the state of Frederick the Great, public opinion is quite clearly something outside the government and distinguished from governmental opinion. The bureaucracy in part stands over against the press.

However, Holtzendorff, as a student of government, was able to see that public opinion must be studied in close connection with the existence of the state. It is a counseling or judging in relation to political power. While it operates traditionally in the same manner as the customary law, limiting and affecting governmental decision, public opinion is still concerned with the application of tradition to immediate issues. In any case, in recent times the evolution of society has made significant the distinction between private and public opinion. England was to the nineteenth-century student of opinion the classic ground of its development. But to our German author, the modern English free press had grown out of older rights of public opinion, that is, a general right of the people to be concerned with the activity of government. In England, public opinion has meant "common opinion," for the public was an undivided mass of subjects. Thus, public opinion was for the English something more than the sum of all publicly expressed opinions, and it was not to be identified merely with the ideas of political parties and the party press. Like the common opinion of doctors of the law, public opinion must be regarded as unified opinion, for from this unity comes its power over its opposite the government, or in England the Parliament and the Ministry.

The meaning of public opinion as drawn from English experience is, to Holtzendorff, the contrast between secret, parliamentary procedure and the open or public discussion of government in the world of common opinion, particularly the press. Therefore, there could be no identity between public opinion and a parliamentary majority, the formal opinion of party leaders, or the actual decisions of the government. German thought thus regarded public opinion as representing an insistent but unwelcome participation of the mass of citizens in government business, and the general German tendency has been to minimize the organized participation of the people in governmental decision. Holtzendorff believed, however, that there has been a growing cleavage between the effective range of public discussion through general communication and the ideas of the folk in all modern nations, for the people often have no opinion on what governmental circles consider to be significant public issues. And often, as Saverio Scolari said, public opinion is the opinion of all and the opinion of none.* Holtzendorff concluded that public opinion may be expressed best when a few speak with spiritual power, as the ancient Hebrew prophets spoke against the kings in the name of the people.

Holtzendorff attempted by distinctions or oppositions to clarify the nature of public opinion. Public opinion stands against private opinion; as Tom Harrisson has said in our own time, it is "what you will say out loud to anyone." † Holtzendorff distinguishes public opinion from the opinion of government organs, for even

* Holtzendorff, *op. cit.*, 54.

† Tom Harrisson, "What is Public Opinion?" *The Political Quarterly*, XI (1940), 374. Edward L. Bernays has developed a similar idea. In his article "Preview of American Public Opinion," *American Mercury*, March, 1944, he sought to explain private opinion in the United States in order to predict what people will talk about out loud. See his *Public Relations* (1952), 253 ff. Congressman Hugh D. Scott defined public opinion as follows: "Public opinion is private opinion on the loose. It is what you think multiplied by all the other people who are thinking about the same thing." He quoted T. H. Huxley to this effect: "That mysterious independent variable of political calculation, Public Opinion." No reference given. See Hugh D. Scott, *How to Go into Politics* (1949), 60.

in a free state, expert opinion must often stand against folk opinion. Opinion may assist, but it cannot claim the right to govern.* Further, public opinion stands against the opinion of political parties as more narrow and restricted groups. In England, parties are primarily associated with majorities in Parliament, while on the Continent, Holtzendorff argued, the parties hold their views as dogmas, and they insist on the duty of public opinion to follow them. Public opinion is to be distinguished in general from expert or specialized opinion, as well as from the opinion of particular social classes.†

To place public opinion outside government poses a problem which public leaders hesitate to discuss in a democracy—that is, the necessity for the government itself to judge the quality of opinion, and the decision by the government that it will or will not follow the general currents of common, mass, or traditional opinion in its own view of public events. To Holtzendorff, public opinion ceased to be public when there was a lack of civic spirit; when private interests became supreme over the general welfare; and when opinion, perhaps as in revolutions, became anarchic, despotic and terroristic, seeking individual advantage through the tyranny of the mass. Though public opinion shows considerable competence in its support of public morality and in the judgment of criminal matters, Holtzendorff holds that the government must still assume a responsibility toward public opinion, and the statesman, following the prescription of Hegel, must try to bring about the development of an informed public opinion

* Holtzendorff, *op. cit.*, 59, says: *Die Grundforderung des modernen Verfassungstaates bleibt zwar dass mit Hilfe der öffentlichen Meinung der Staat regiert werden soll.* Speier, *op. cit.*, 376, defines public opinion as "opinions on matters of concern to the nation freely and publicly expressed by men outside the government who claim a right that their opinions should influence or determine the actions, personnel, or structure of their government." Public opinion is, then, a kind of communication between the citizen who speaks openly and the government which publicizes just what it wants to.

† Holtzendorff, *op. cit.*, 58 ff.

which can arrive at the truth and stand against the errors and contradictions of the opinion of party and press.*

III

Two of the more significant writers of recent times who have, no doubt, been of great influence in developing present attitudes toward public opinion, are A. L. Lowell and Walter Lippmann. Both regard the concept of the public as correlative to opinion; they have—let us say—an "adjective theory" of opinion. In their thinking the public has been related to the fact of political participation, but as a kind of group—perhaps larger than the sociological view prescribes—but nevertheless still fundamentally an addendum to the group process. Lowell believed the public to be those who are willing to abide by the decision of the majority. He believed that the primary condition necessary to the existence of a public, however, was a certain homogeneity of view in the treatment of questions where decision by political action was possible. Lippmann agreed with Lowell in making the essential problem of the public its participation in making decisions,† but he insisted on the ineffectiveness of the masses in dealing with the

* The control of the press in the interest of a healthy public opinion is not an idea alone associated with the Germany of the last century. See Edward Cary Hayes, "The Formation of Public Opinion," *Journal of Applied Sociology*, X (1925-1926), 6-9. Hayes argued that the government must provide for the formation of public opinion, just as we have pure food laws. Newspapers, which represent the power of wealth, must give way to the power of ideas freely derived from free discussion; each newspaper should be compelled by law to give an equal amount of space to each of the four leading political parties in the last election.

† See A. L. Lowell, *Public Opinion and Popular Government* (1913), and Walter Lippmann, *The Phantom Public* (1925). See E. M. Sait, *Political Institutions,* A Preface (1938), 501-502, 506, for a critical view of the theory of "publics." The "public" has never meant simply an interest group. Ludwig Freund, "Power and the Democratic Process," *Social Research,* XV (September, 1948), 341, observes that "public" involves anything that concerns a large enough number of people to warrant attention by the government or by those who attempt to influence or direct govern-

"unseen environment." In line with this idea, Lippmann proposed a set of canons to be used in weighing the activity of the public or publics. A public consists of those who are spectators, who are not judges of the merits of a question, and who are interested chiefly in making certain "rules of the game" which must be obeyed by the parties to a dispute.*

But "rules of the game" are, let us say, decisions of a formal nature which should give rise to the environment or context in which other more specialized decisions are made. In a democracy the assumption must be made that individuals or groups are helping to make the rules and immediate decisions of society; otherwise public opinion is a purely negative principle, for it is then merely the recognition of the fact that people must submit to government. The conditions under which "effectiveness" arises are the conditions of participation, and in turn this leads to emphasis on the nature of the public, as well as on the ideas or opinions that become components of a political decision. One may readily admit that much democratic theory oversimplifies participation by understating the inertia of the people and the difficulties of setting up proper procedures by which any group of people can make its voice heard. Likewise, participation can be viewed in a purely formal light by limiting it to voting for candidates on election day, rather than by including in it the informal pressures which are brought to bear when decisions are about to be made. Lobbies as well as ballots are important in democratic decisions, and any effective participation may well be raised to a power by the modern system of mass communication through which latent opinions are crystallized and organized. Participation, thus, includes the expression of opinion, though the conditioning of

---

ment, that is, the politicians. Cf. R. M. MacIver, *The Modern State* (1926), 342; W. Brooke Graves (ed.), *Readings in Public Opinion* (1928); R. M. Christenson and R. O. McWilliams (ed.), *Voice of the People; Readings in Public Opinion and Propaganda* (1962).

* See Lippmann's *Public Opinion* (1922). This volume has been one of the great stimulants to the recent development of the study of public opinion. Lippmann's work has also been highly influential in establishing the idea of "publics" in the terminology of public opinion study.

participation may involve interest, influence, or political subjection and mental conditioning, as in the modern dictatorship.

When the effort to make a sharp analysis of the idea of public opinion began, it was apparent that a loose discussion of popular sentiment or widely held prejudices would not be sufficient to advance the discourse. There has been, therefore, a far-ranging treatment of the public, and the processes of opinion, as a foundation on which to build a theory of public opinion. Sociological, legal, and constitutional interpretations have been tried, but in more recent years the sociological view has more or less carried the argument. Here, the definition of public is deliberately kept flexible in order to clear the way for a more rigorous consideration of opinion. In general, the sociologist has given the term "public" a vague or broad interpretation in order to be able to direct his study of public opinion specifically to the opinion of any group on immediate or controversial issues.

In contrast, many students of opinion primarily interested in politics have been willing to regard public opinion as the whole stream of community thought, whether related to impending decisions or to values which have long been accepted as tradition. The public could not, however, be regarded as any social group, since it had to be that particular kind of group whose action—however organized—was related to effective policy decisions. Such decisions might in fact be those that sustained already adopted principles of action and thus be out of the field of controversy, or they might be decisions growing out of public debate on relatively new or newly-presented issues.

The crucial point in theories of the public should be a consideration of the nature of what the public does. If one says the public is just "any group" there is no suggestion of why, functionally speaking, the public has to be mentioned at all. When we speak of the effectiveness of public opinion, we speak both for the effectiveness of opinion and the public. The political view of the public arises from the context of public decision, even though we might define the public, as Lippmann does, as those who are spectators to the context of power.* The public involves some concept of "the decision," but it concerns also the mechanics of decision in relation to those who do not actually make it—that is, to those outside "the government." In the evolution toward democracy, therefore, it is peculiarly important to observe the means by which the members of the political community have been able to relate their opinions to whatever decisions are made; that is, the development of the means of political participation becomes in effect the keystone in the history of the public. The public is, indeed, a group which participates in the making of public decisions, though the effectiveness of such participation must vary historically and under different social conditions. Thus, the history of the public is the history of participation, whether we deal with the East or the West, or with the practices of Classical or modern civilization.

In contrast, many questions arise when we consider the public as an effective and organized group in the making of public decisions. What about oligarchies and elites? If in reality a decision is oligarchical in nature, does it mean that the public is the oligarchy? If the fundamental division as to power is elite versus masses, as Lasswell suggested two decades ago,† and if the reality of large-group participation fades, then what about the public? Or, if pressure groups are thought to make the controlling decisions in politics, is the public merely those who participate through such groups? The perennial fact of non-voting, the pervasive conditioning of the political party, or situations in constitutional government where important officials, like judges, are appointed and the general population has only a limited effectiveness, must all be considered.‡

* Walter Lippmann, *The Phantom Public* (1925).

† H. D. Lasswell, *Politics, Who Gets What, When, How* (1936).

‡ *The New English Dictionary* traces "public" to early Latin usage, from *poplicus*, *populus*, and *publicus*, where finally the adult male population was involved. Public is, in general, the opposite of private; it pertains to the people of a country or locality; the people as a whole. In fifteenth-century England the "public thing" (from *res publica*) was spoken of. The public is open to all members of the community; it is not private to any;

Since the results of public opinion polls have been considered in our time a common measurement of public opinion, the implicit theory used by the directors of the modern polling institutes has become, therefore, of crucial importance in conceptions of public and opinion as they are developing today. In the first issue of *The Public Opinion Quarterly* in 1937, Floyd H. Allport defined public opinion in these words: "The term 'public opinion' is given its meaning with reference to a multi-individual situation in which individuals are expressing themselves, or can be called upon to express themselves, as favoring or supporting (or else disfavoring or opposing) some definite condition, person, or proposal of widespread importance, in such a proportion of number, intensity, and constancy, as to give rise to the probability of affecting action, directly or indirectly, toward the object concerned." *

Allport argued that his definition attempts to incorporate all the elements on which there is agreement among scholars. In constructing his definition, he rejected what he deemed to be either historical or then current fallacies in the concept of public opinion. The personification of public opinion he considered a blind alley, as well as the personification of the public. He rejected: the group fallacy; the fallacy of partial inclusion in the term public, *i.e.*, the abstraction of a specific interest, as saying that all who have a common interest are the public; the fiction of an Ideational entity, such as a Platonic idea; and the group-product or emergent theory that public opinion is the product of

---

it is the community or people as an organized body, nation, state or commonwealth; the community as an aggregate, but not in an organized capacity. It is also spoken of as the world at large or mankind; or a particular portion of a community. John Ruskin, *Arrows of Chace* (1880), I, 21: "There is a separate public for every picture and for every book." Ruskin's use of "publics," as quoted by NED, is one of the early statements of the present sociological view that there are many publics. The NED speaks of opinion as distinguished from knowledge or certainty, which is, of course, one of the oldest views. In reference to the United States, see Harriet Martineau, *Society in America* (1837), III, 7: "the worship of opinion is, at this day, the established religion of the United States."

* *The Public Opinion Quarterly*, I (1937), 7 ff, 23.

group discussion. In a similar manner Allport rejected the "eulogistic theory" that a group-product in opinion is superior to individual opinion, and finally he objected to the confusion of public opinion with the public presentation of opinion. In general, one might say that his approach to the theory of public opinion was based on the idea that we face a new historical situation in which there are no longer small "publics," but rather mass opinion through the processes of education and the modern systems of mass communication.

With a similar technique of study, another distinguished student of public opinion, William Albig, has said that "publics are simply large groups." The opinion process, Albig argued, "is the interaction occurring within a group on a controversial issue." Public opinion, thus, deals with matters of controversy where no opinion is at the moment commonly accepted. The sociologist devotes his effort to a study of the public opinion process, granting the inchoate nature of publics as large groups produced by mass communication and the techniques of the modern systems of communication. Accepting these central assumptions, the student of public opinion does not concern himself with the content of opinion at a given moment, nor with its truth or falsity, but with the situations and issues and the techniques which continually operate to give rise to public opinion polarities.* There is no public opinion when there is consensus and no discussion; and consensus is, thus, distinguished from opinion, even though consensus may produce decisions if it is the standard by which secondary matters may be judged. However, popular systems of thought or ideologies suggest further

* William Albig, *Public Opinion* (1939), 1 ff. See also Albig's *Modern Public Opinion* (1956). Kimball Young, *Social Psychology* (1946), 430-431, has said: "Opinions are really beliefs about a controversial topic or with respect to the valuative interpretation or moral meaning of certain facts. An opinion is not quite so certain as a conviction." See W. P. Davison, "The Public Opinion Process," *The Public Opinion Quarterly*, XXII (Summer, 1958), 91 ff. Cf. Clarence Schettler, *Public Opinion in American Society* (1960), Part I. Schettler stresses interaction and conflict, and the contribution of the minority to the formation of public opinion. He does not stress participation.

conclusions, for though modern man as a member of large publics has a vast amount of information, most of it is shallow, and unrelated to any deep roots in integrated thought systems. It is often predigested, simplified and served to the citizen through catchwords, slogans and other forms of symbol. In contrast with modern times, public opinion played some part in ancient civilizations, but in Albig's view the publics then were "limited in number and size," the mechanisms for the expression of opinion were rudimentary and communication was limited." *

If one looks primarily at opinion and observes conflicting trends of thought, as well as the diverse levels on which any opinion is held, from the sheerest neurotic reaction to the most careful and rational defense of an idea, the term "public" becomes an adjective describing opinion. "Public" must be an idea which can follow opinion through any level and in any direction. In this case, public must be as diverse as opinion, and the proper solution is to say there are many publics, for there is no organic entity which can be called public opinion. A person is inevitably a member of several or many publics. In 1909, for example, Walter J. Shepard defined a public as "any unorganized association of individuals bound together by common opinions, sentiments, or desires, and too numerous for each to maintain personal relations with others. . . ." † In line with this reasoning, he distinguished

* Albig, *Public Opinion,* 19. In speaking of a discussion of public opinion in the New Guinea tribes, Albig believes that "in these primitive groups there is no opinion process, no interaction with resultant group opinion, comparable to the process in modern publics." There would be no public opinion in the sense of discussion on a controversial point as it occurs in the large modern public under systems of mass communication. (*Loc. cit.*) The critic might raise the question of when quantitative differences in communication become qualitative to such an extent as to control the meaning of the concept. Likewise, it can be said that the word "controversy" is extraordinarily vague. When is a controversy a controversy? Or, when is a group large enough to be a public?

† Walter J. Shepard, "Public Opinion," *The American Journal of Sociology,* XV (1909), 36. E. P. Herring has defined the public as "the populace viewed as a great undifferentiated mass." *The Annals of the American Academy of Political and Social Science,* 179 (1935), 167-175, "Official Publicity under the New Deal." R. E. Park distinguished a public from a

between public opinion, public sentiment, and public will, and further between public opinion and the organs of public opinion, including the newspaper as its primary organ.*

Because the student of behavior is vitally interested in the group process in society, it is not illogical that the idea of the public should have become integrated with the general modern examination of group behavior. Public opinion, for the behaviorist, must be viewed as a whole series of reactions involved in collective deliberation—that is, the communication essential and preliminary to participation in decisions. It is a form of group thinking, implying that differences may be settled by the deliberative social process. This argument leads to the position, already noted in Albig, which is characteristic of much modern inquiry—that public opinion involves live or controversial issues. Public opinion is more than the judgments involved in custom or the mores, though social opinion which is embodied in the mores may be the force or the system of attitudes holding society together. A public arises, therefore, when we go beyond traditional controls, as for instance in the market place. "In short," Carroll D. Clark said, "when current events rather than arbitrary standards became the controlling factor in directing activities, and when interests began to be organized functionally, the public was born." † Clark con-

---

mass by saying that a mass is unorganized, while a public is a social grouping in which all members communicate. See Park's *Masse und Publikum* (1904), cited by A. M. Rose, "Public Opinion Research Techniques Suggested by Sociological Theory," *The Public Opinion Quarterly*, XIV (1950), 206. C. W. Smith, *Public Opinion in a Democracy* (1939), 13, defines the public simply as all people capable of thought in a particular area or group. Smaller groups, however, he considers as only parts of the public.

* A similar theme was stressed by *The Outlook*, 96 (1919), 379-381, when it argued that there is no big public that includes the entire body of men and women, for there are a dozen publics. There is a public interested in the revolting spectacle at Reno, but there is a far larger public that hates it. In general, the article attempts to refute the idea that the purveyers of pornography can defend themselves on the ground that the public demands it.

† See Carroll D. Clark, "The Concept of the Public," *The Southwestern Social Science Quarterly*, XIII (1933), 311-20, 316. Clark cites especially in support of his view George A. Lundberg, "Public Opinion from a

tinues by saying that there are special publics as well as a general public, the special public being the organized group interest. But the general public in its political capacity is functioning in a realm which is largely magical, traditional, and unsecularized. This is to say simply that the general public acts more in the manner of social opinion than public opinion.*

We have seen how the identification of the public with groups, in the study of group process, has led to vagueness in the notion of the public. Publics are large groups, as Albig said, and the characteristic of modern times is the "large public." Thus, there are as many publics as there are large groups. Likewise, Harwood L. Childs has argued that "a public is simply any collection of individuals." Publics are both organized and unorganized, and opinion is simply "a verbal expression of attitude." Public opinion means, thus, "any collection of individual opinions designated." † In accordance with the contemporary emphasis on the study of communications, Childs observed that technical improvements in the means of communication have greatly enlarged the size of publics. Without suggesting that public opinion must be unanimous to be so, he argued that "public interest" in the United States is and can be only what the public, what mass opinion, says it is; and by mass opinion he meant the collective

---

Behavioristic Viewpoint," *The American Journal of Sociology*, XXXVI (1930), 387-405; R. E. Park and E. W. Burgess, *Introduction to the Science of Sociology* (1921), 831-833, for the distinction between the mores and public opinion. For further statements by Clark, see Norman C. Meier and H. W. Saunders, *The Polls and Public Opinion* (1949), 115 ff.

* See Francis G. Merrill and Carroll D. Clark, "The Money Market as a Special Public," *The American Journal of Sociology*, XXXIX (1934), 626-36. The argument here is that segmental interest groups function as special publics, and that the money market reveals the nature and functioning of special publics. "It is only when its interests or policies collide with those of other groups that they attract the attention of the general public and provide an issue for public opinion."

W. I. Thomas and Florian Znaniecki in *The Polish Peasant in Europe and America* (1918), are recognized by sociologists as having fixed the concept of "attitude" in the study of the social process. The concept of attitude has been used as a basis for the distinction between social or traditional opinion and public or controversial opinion.

† Harwood L. Childs, *An Introduction to Public Opinion* (1940), 41-42.

opinions of the American people as a whole. As one of the founders of *The Public Opinion Quarterly*, as one associated with the development of public opinion polling techniques, and the study of mass communication, Childs' interest is clearly not in the concept of the public but in the process of opinion formation. What we read, see, and hear through mass communication helps to shape our opinions, and thus the control of propaganda is one of the central problems of democracy. He believed, for example, that there should be a permanent government commission to investigate, report on, and control propaganda in order that fair competitive practices should prevail. The race for the support of opinion, especially of mass opinion, should be in the open.*

IV

The varied fortunes of public opinion polling have renewed with insistence the problem of the definition of the terms, "public" and "opinion." Do the polls deal with public opinion? No, the answer has been, because the polls, with their foggy notions of the public, have been unable to isolate public opinion as a coherent object of study. In other words, the polls do not examine the process of decision in a society, for it is from the process of decision that understanding of the public will be reached. In a discussion which sharpens the notion of the public, Herbert Blumer in 1948 insisted that 1) public opinion is a function of a society in operation, 2) society is organized in functioning groups, 3) these groups must act through such channels as are available, 4) key individuals, that is, decision-making personalities, must assess popular influences as they know them, 5) public opinion is formed and expressed through existing modes of social operation, and it occurs as a function of a society in operation,

* *Ibid.*, 125. Childs argues that in general the polls of opinion show the competence of the masses and that by them our faith in democracy has been restored. See also Harwood L. Childs (ed.), *Propaganda and Dictatorship, A Collection of Papers* (1936).

in which the interaction of groups and individuals results in very unequal shares of influence, and 6) in a realistic sense public opinion is a collective product of the pattern of diverse views and positions on the issues that come from the public to the individuals who have to act in response to public opinion. Thus, public opinion which is unknown to those who make decisions is not really public opinion because it is ineffective. The decision-makers must judge of the public opinion that counts, in so far as they can understand the structure of the society they are governing.*

Sampling procedures cannot get public opinion, therefore, because they consider society as composed of disparate individuals, and one cannot know if a sample includes those who participate or the influence they may have in the participation process. Blumer stressed participation, because in effect there is no public opinion without effective participation. The polls cannot find public opinion because they ignore the framework and functional operation of public opinion. The pollers may believe that public opinion ought to be a kind of average cross-section of the population, but the issue is whether in other than an accidental sense the cross-section can predict what the voters or the decision-makers will do. Blumer contended that the election process is fatally incapable of really giving expression to public opinion as it exists in a social structure. A model of the opinion process might be attained by working back from those who act on behalf of public opinion, through the existing channels of participation to the original and organized group sources of public opinion. It is the structure of a society that determines in large measure what private opinion becomes public, and thus starts through the process toward the social or political decision.†

* Herbert Blumer, "Public Opinion and Public Opinion Polling," *American Sociological Review*, XIII (1948), 542 ff.

† *Ibid.*, 546 ff. It is this problem that the British Institute of Public Opinion worked on. See Harrisson, *op. cit.* Public opinion is articulate top-level opinion, and not that of the general public, many of whom have no opinions or information on essential political matters. The public opinion process is that by which private opinions become matters of open expression, that is, respectable opinion. Harrisson contends that private opinion gradually

Investigations of public opinion lead from the analysis of attitudes and opinions to the process of group life and the effectiveness of group action in the shaping of policy, particularly and ultimately the policy of political society. Group analysis is thus closely related to the principle of participation as the clue to the nature of the public. The clue to the public becomes the general problem of the effectiveness of that participation. In terms of social psychology it is an issue of the group process, but in terms of political theory it is an issue of consent as the validation of legitimate government. Participation in a functional sense has as its validating idea consent to authority.* Consent from the official's point of view may be simply acceptance of a decision: that is, there is no revolt or refusal to obey. But consent from the individual or group point of view, means bringing about a desired decision. And here a group has at its disposal many of the same means of pressure and communication the government itself is bound to use. It will be readily admitted, however, that in the long pull the power of the government to gain acceptance of a decision is far greater than the power of a group to reverse it. But the effectiveness of participation is a recurring theme. After studying the leadership of Lord Palmerston, Kingsley Martin declared that "public opinion is a col-

builds up a pressure which breaks into the open. Thus, from private opinion today one can predict what public opinion will be tomorrow. Public opinion, being what anyone will say out loud to anyone, is only a part of a vast body of private opinion. Published, or mass-communicated opinion, is often remote from public opinion and more so from private opinion. Press campaigns are successful only when they express already existing public or private opinions.

See A. M. C. Lee (ed.), *New Outline of the Principles of Sociology* (1946), which contains an article by Blumer. Gabriel Almond, *The American People and Foreign Policy* (1950), 680, suggests the need of research to discover "models of social structure" which will, especially, indicate the structure and functional history of elite groups. Somewhat similar trends of thought are found in William Albig and others, "Process of Opinion Formation: A Symposim," *The Public Opinion Quarterly*, XIV (1950-1951), 667 ff.

* On the nature of consent, note C. W. Cassinelli, "The 'Consent' of the Governed," *The Western Political Quarterly*, XII (June, 1959), 391 ff.

lective term which can be accurately used only to denote a common opinion relative to some one defined issue held by an effective majority in a certain group of persons." *

Whatever one's idea of public opinion may be, we can agree with Robert C. Binkley upon the basic fact that things of the mind, whether rational or not, are shared; it is the sharing of opinion under certain conditions that makes it public.† The sharing of the mind, its attitudes and opinions or polarities, is the broader foundation of community and the emergence of communities into the larger society; but public opinion, and more particularly the public, is a mode or a specific means of sharing.‡ Probably no two people have exactly the same shading or background of opinion on anything, and even the process of interaction or sharing must change the nature of an opinion itself. How is opinion shared so that it becomes public opinion? It may be shared in expression and in action that leads to decisions. Opinion then becomes a verbal fact or a formulation for action. Thus in action the formality of expression is of fundamental importance. In one sense, therefore, the public is the context of popular participation, and the formal opinion it represents may in degree be unlike the particular opinion of any single individual. The public is the locus where the drift of symbolism in mass attitudes is arrested by effective decision. The public then implies the system of formal means of participation whereby a symbol is shared with personalities who are making effective

* Kingsley Martin, *The Triumph of Lord Palmerston, A Study of Public Opinion in England before the Crimean War* (1924), 27. Lasswell states that attention aggregates are not publics. "An individual passes from an attention aggregate to the public when he begins to expect that what he wants can affect public policy." See Wilbur Schramm (ed.), *Mass Communications* (1949), 112.

† Robert C. Binkley, "The Concept of Public Opinion in the Social Sciences," *Social Forces,* VI (1927), 396.

‡ Doob suggests that "public opinion refers to people's attitudes on an issue when they are members of the same social group." But "an attitude is an internal response which the individual has learned as a result of past rewards and punishments." See L. W. Doob, *Public Opinion and Propaganda* (1948), 27, 35.

decisions. Participation implies a decisional conception of the public, assuming, of course, that the decision reached has only a formal relation to the symbolic polarity used in the communication of ideas. The validity cluster in each individual cannot itself be either completely transferred to another or embodied in a formal political decision.*

* See Harold D. Lasswell, "Technique of Decision Seminars," *Midwest Journal of Political Science*, IV (August, 1960), 213-236; R. O. Nafziger and D. M. White (ed.), *Introduction to Mass Communications Research* (1958); L. Festinger and D. Katz, *Research Methods in Behavioral Sciences* (1953); S. S. Ulmer (ed.), *Introductory Readings in Political Behavior* (1961).

CHAPTER 5

Controversy, Tradition, and Culture

I

At this point in our inquiry, it is appropriate to study public opinion in a series of widening contexts. Is public opinion concerned only with controversial issues? Is it related to customary modes of thought which have a far greater stability than the changing boundaries of public controversy, or, indeed, can tradition be regarded as a mode of expression of public opinion at all? Beyond this, one encounters the cultural pattern, its interpretation by social scientists, and the question arises concerning the relation of public opinion to the encasement or the envelope of culture which must surround any particular expression of opinion. The material then in this chapter relates primarily to sociological questions, though behind sociological analysis one is certainly touching upon a philosophical anthropology. We are dealing with the social context of the expression of the mind of man, and with some of the contours of his freedom. Thus it must be asked whether public opinion is permanent, as is the force of tradition, or whether it is fluid, as all controversy is fluid. The obvious answer is that it is both. But the modern attempt to broaden the public into the interactive social process, combined with the insistence that opinion must be narrowed to the immediate system of controversy, requires further discussion.*

* It is necessary to observe that any definition of opinion as an "atti-

Every nation which has lost its public opinion, said Hermann Borchardt in 1943, has decayed or been subjugated. In the era of its great emperors, Chinese public opinion held the maxim: "Honor the dead, and ply your trade well." The public opinion of the Persians in their own period of greatness said: "Tell the truth and shoot your arrows straight." The Greeks said: "Honor man, the image of the gods." And Roman opinion declared: "Thou shalt till the soil and respect the law." But the last public opinion of this type in the West existed in Europe, having force until about 1490, and it said: "Fear God and keep His commandments." After that time public opinion gradually perished through the eternal recurrence: the rich and sophisticated began to despise it, and the people fell away. Finally the artificial makers of opinion arrived, as they have in other cultures, and they have brought with them our modern enlightenment which tells the people there is no God, there is beauty in railroad building, and there is a more glorious future before them.*

These observations of Borchardt represent what is probably the most conservative position a modern student may take; it is an ultimate assertion of the traditional and non-controversial nature of public opinion. This position holds that controversy is not the birth of opinion, but that it is rather the death of all force in public opinion. Because the public, according to Borchardt, arises from social consensus, the loss of agreement means the slow death of coherence, and of the public (in this case, general) character of opinion. The more moderate position is that taken by George Creel in 1918 when he said, in discussing the work of the Committee on Public Information: "A great many people think that public opinion is a state of mind, formed and changed by the events of the day or the events of

---

tude" suggests permanent, customary, habitual, or traditional character. An attitude must be more lasting than a reaction to a passing controversy. Doob, however, distinguished enduring and momentary public opinion, and accepts public opinion as a part of culture. See L. W. Doob, *Public Opinion and Propaganda* (1948), 27, 35, 50, 60.

* Hermann Borchardt, *The Conspiracy of the Carpenters* (1943), 278-279.

the hour; that is, sort of a combination kaleidoscope and weathercock. I disagree with this theory entirely. I do not believe that public opinion has its rise in the emotions, or that it is tipped from one extreme to the other by every passing rumor, or by every gust of passion, or by every storm of anger. I feel that public opinion has its source in the minds of people, that it has its base in reason, and that it expresses slow-formed convictions rather than any temporary excitement or passing passion of the moment." *

II

The fact is that in modern democracies thought has been constantly disturbed by the uncertainties of controversy, by the unpredictable force of emotion in public attitude, and by the slowness with which opinion has moved to new or permanent points of crystallization. A phase of the principle of permanent and traditional opinion has been the belief in an evolution of public opinion toward a more profound conception of the common good and an abiding support of principles which work in the long run for national well-being. "Public opinion is a different thing from mere public feeling, whether taking the form of overwrought emotion or of easy going sentimentality," declared *The Independent* on June 14, 1906. "Public opinion is compounded of knowledge, discrimination and judgment. It is a product of intellectual activity. It is created by investigation, discussion and a critical review of a situation. It is a net result of a collective 'getting at the facts' and a collective thinking about them in a calm-tempered

* See George Creel, "Public Opinion in War Time," *The Annals of the American Academy of Political and Social Science,* 78 (1918), 185-194. Elizabeth B. White, *American Opinion of France from Lafayette to Poincare* (1927), 310, suggests that through our history when French thought marched with ours we have been inclined to be friendly. Thus, both French and American public opinion have been governed by long-run but intangible currents of community thought and ideals. Leon Blum has said that the great mass of French opinion has remained unchanged, "immobile as the deep mass of the ocean beneath the storm." See *The Political Quarterly,* IV (1933), 58-67.

way." The writer concluded by hoping that one day the metropolitan newspapers might become real organs of public opinion.

Public opinion is the mature judgment of the average man, thought United States Attorney General Charles J. Bonaparte in 1908. It is not sentiment, prejudice or factitious clamor. Opinion implies an evolution toward reason.* Most of that which passes for opinion is mere emotion and cannot rightly be called opinion, asserted *The New Republic* on September 18, 1915. Genuine opinion is neither cold, logical judgment nor irrational feeling; it is scientific hypothesis and it is not spasmodic, though it changes in the light of information and the development of reason in popular judgment.†

Those who believe in the educative force of modern democracy as the producer of rational opinion do not, of course, defend traditional opinion in the ordinary sense of the word, for they frequently would include emotional and irrational judgments under the heading of "tradition." Tradition implies judgments of value and a kind of deposit of truth. Yet those who believe in the evolution of public opinion toward the achievement of rational judgment would not object to the permanent maintenance of such a standard of public judgment, or, indeed, of a democratic tradition which insists on mature rationality in public attitudes. We might say, in this case, that public opinion is evolving toward a new kind of permanence, though the persistence or permanence of the irrational is clearly recognized in the discussions of public opinion which we have here observed.‡

* Charles J. Bonaparte, "Government by Public Opinion," *The Forum*, 40 (1908), 384-390.

† See C. L. King, "Public Opinion as Viewed by Eminent Political Theorists," *University Lectures, 1915-1916* (University of Pennsylvania, 1916), Vol. III, where real or rational opinion is distinguished from less reliable and more emotional points of view. It is, of course, important for a person to know what is rational and what is not, but such knowledge may not be essential in defining the concept of opinion itself.

‡ *All the Year Round*, 40 (1878), 77, observed: "It comes to this then —public opinion is the mingled outcome of education and feeling, of intelligence and emotion, of reason and prejudice, of tradition, sentiment and

Faith in the ineluctable movement toward a more rational and differentially permanent opinion has been rudely shaken in recent years by the emphasis on propaganda—that is, the psychological approach to the average and group mind. No doubt also the work of Walter Lippmann who, in *Public Opinion,* described opinions as stereotypes,* as pictures in our minds, has stimulated for Americans a doubt that the dream of a march toward rationality has serious foundations. Public opinion, in the Lippmann view, is the total of such pictures or stereotypes in a large enough group to constitute a public. But if the distortion is due to the character of mental processes and to the nature and complexity of the world, a permanent irrationality of opinion is postulated that undergirds the whole opinion process in modern society. Any such view must in effect deny the fluidity of opinion which it is necessary to acknowledge if we say that public opinion is concerned solely with immediate and controversial issues. For the permanent context of opinion, whether it moves toward the use of reason or remains with its emotional and irrational character, underlies all controversy and, indeed, governs the settlement of many public policies.†

Actually in modern times, some opinion is permanent and some is not; some opinion is the affirmation of knowledge and some is the assertion of prejudice and irrationality; some opinion is based on a concept of the common good and some is merely the satanic projection to others of the evil within the individual. The issue is whether we must define public opinion as the im-

---

interest." See A. T. Hadley, *The Education of the American Citizen* (1901), 17 ff; Woodrow Wilson, *An Old Master and Other Political Essays* (1893), 99 ff.

* Lasswell has argued that Thurman Arnold's term "polar words" is a richer expression than Lippmann's "stereotypes." *The Public Opinion Quarterly,* II (1938), 689, in a review of Arnold, *The Folklore of Capitalism* (1937), 147.

† For the influence of Lippmann, cf. D. D. McKean, "Public Speaking and Public Opinion," *Quarterly Journal of Speech,* XVII (1931), 510-511. See also the review of Lippmann's *Public Opinion* in the London *Nation,* 31 (1922), 734-745.

mediate focus of attention as in controversies, or whether the enduring background of any symbolism must also be called opinion in a public sense.*

It is possible for exponents of democracy to regard public opinion as the hypothetical result of an imaginary but continuous plebiscite. They may think of an ideal public opinion emerging from an ideal election, or from a system in which participation is ideal. According to this view, public opinion has not emerged from an organic entity called the state, but from the individual, and is constantly approaching rational principles, which will be perfectly expressed through the political process. Yet the fact is that the development of studies of social process as it actually operates has documented the imperfection of participation, and recognition of this imperfection has led—as we have seen—to minimizing the whole conception of the public as it arises from the actuality of imperfect participation. Nevertheless, granting the imperfection of democracy, and, therefore, the remoteness of "ideal public opinion," does not mean that there is no public opinion with which to deal. Those who have believed in the general will have depended on the rationality of man, while those who have studied the social process inevitably have come up against the irrational qualities of public opinion and the complex imperfections of participation in public decision. Yet it must not be assumed that the notion of political participation depends for its validity on the current rationality of opinion. The historian, for example, has in his search for the uniqueness of events assumed that public opinion is the summation of what a given collection of persons have thought on a given subject at a particular time. He has not felt impelled to say that such opinions are true or false, but he has been compelled to observe

* See the discussion of the Round Table on Political Statistics at the Second National Conference on the Science of Politics in 1924 in *The American Political Science Review,* XIX (1925), 123 ff. This group deplored the use of the term "public opinion," preferring instead the use of the term "attitude." "Attitude," for example, carries no implication of the degree of rationality in it. See Stuart A. Rice, *Quantitative Methods in Politics* (1928), 51 ff.

the effect of such opinion on the decisions made by particular governments.*

III

Is public opinion a new social factor, or is it as old as organized society? Bauer, for example, regards public opinion as based on tradition operating under continually changing techniques of publicity or communication. Tönnies, Allport, Albig and others view it as a new product of the new means of mass communication. Thus, public opinion becomes the controversial appreciations of urban and industrial civilization. In the extreme, it might be said that rural people, living outside the range of these issues, have no public opinion. We might call this the "great public" theory of opinion, for it associates the origin of public opinion with the middle class and urban development. Again, is public opinion in its nature permanent or is it fluctuating? The issue is whether or not public opinion includes traditional and basic values which form the context of decisions and the maintenance of social order. American students of opinion who are

* Robert C. Binkley, "The Concept of Public Opinion in the Social Sciences," *Social Forces*, VI (1927), 396: "Public opinion in connection with the will of the State is a *quantity of will;* in connection with the problem of the social process it is a *consensus;* in connection with the problem of history it is *summary*." Cf. Virginia R. Stedman, "Some Interpretations of Public Opinion," *Social Forces*, X (1932), 339 ff, who discusses the conflict between those who, like Lippmann, define opinion in terms of actual emotional behavior and those who define it in ideal terms like John Dewey in *The Public and Its Problems* (1927).

Among the modern evaluations of public opinion, one may mention E. M. Sait, *Political Institutions* (1938), 507-508. Sait was critical of the demand democracy makes on all citizens to have an opinion whether or not they know anything about public issues. Sait cited various writers—such as George Cornewall Lewis, Walter Bagehot, Frank Exline, James Bryce, Ernest Barker and William McDougall—who have believed that the popular will originates with the few. Cf. R. W. Kauffman, "The Great God Opinion," *The Cosmopolitan Magazine*, 49 (1910), 664-665: "We must get rid of the belief in the infallibility of public opinion." Also, W. B. Munro, "Is the Slacker Vote a Menace?" *National Municipal Review*, 17 (1928), 80-86; "The Worst Fundamentalism," *The Atlantic Monthly*, 138 (1926), 451-459.

connected with the polling institutes seem to assume that public opinion is largely controversial and fluctuating. The permanent elements in social attitude are often excluded from their views of public opinion.*

One issue of great importance is quite factual. Does the system of communication within social groups in modern times differ from that of the ancient world to such an extent that a significant qualitative difference is to be found? Is mass or general communication purely modern, or is it also ancient? The modern sociological view in the study of public opinion tends to minimize the effectiveness of communication in the ancient world. But other writers—as, for example, Bauer and Lin Yutang—have built their cases around the continued effectiveness of communication, while stressing its evolving techniques.

Is there ever such a thing as an organic and unified public opinion? Or must public opinion be always the divergent and conflicting pressures in the controversies between groups? These questions are but another facet of the issue between the alternatives of regarding public opinion as both permanent and fluctuating, or of considering it as merely a fluctuating force in group life. If the great changes in the history of opinion are to be found in the evolution of the techniques of publicity, then public opinion may be found in the much slower evolution of the permanent streams of social attitude. But if public opinion itself arises from the social conditions of communication in urban and contractual society, then the vast reservoir of social attitudes remains outside of what is technically called public opinion. A revolution may demonstrate fundamental splits in mass attitude on current issues, but likewise the duration of a social order may illustrate long-standing public agreement on fundamentals. But the long-standing agreement may be divided—as Tönnies be-

* See Paul F. Lazarsfeld, "The Obligation of the 1950 Pollster to the 1984 Historian," *The Public Opinion Quarterly*, XIV (1950), 617, where the idea is expressed that the polls are collecting data that future historians can use. The results of polls are source materials of tomorrow. Julian L. Woodward, "Public Opinion Research 1951-1970: A Not-Too-Reverent History," *The Public Opinion Quarterly*, XV (1951), 405 ff.

lieved—between unorganized, divergent opinion and organized, basic or fixed opinion. Even the modern polling techniques assume—as did Lowell—that except in revolution or civil war, all will accept the prevailing or majority opinion. Such acceptance implies, clearly, restraint or limitation on the part of the majority. Granting such restraint, the acceptance of majority opinion does not necessarily mean agreement on fundamentals throughout a society, for it can just as well be argued that the self-restraint of the majority permits disagreement on fundamentals.

IV

The modern sociological tradition in the discussion of public opinion shows an impressive diversity. But one of the most incisive of the differences is the conflict between those who consider process and believe in scientific study alone, and those who would see in the opinion process some advancement toward the attainment of humanitarian and rational goals. It has been recognized, however, that the concept building, the theorizing of a hundred years before the end of World War I, has been used in the newer and quantitative studies of public opinion. In other words, there has been a tendency in behavioral science to continue under empirical application many of the ideas of another age. The empirical approach, quite naturally, proclaims its intention of not considering the normative aspects of the opinion process, but such a result has hardly been achieved, since the empirical method is based quite often on the sheer avoidance of moral, ethical, and other evaluative issues.

Among the traditional students of the opinion process, let us consider Lester F. Ward, whose writings were notably influential around the turn of the century. The goal of our effort, Ward argued, is to attain correct opinions, and to use the scientific method in getting at social truth as the basis of progress. Many modern social scientists may agree with Ward that description comes first, and that beyond this there must be some technique of evaluating opinion. Indeed, the great effort of the social sciences has been to reach a science of society; and thus the truth or untruth of opinion must have a scientific foundation, as many modern social scientists assert. Progress consists largely in the movement toward mass opinions based on scientifically tested ideas. But the strong trend in the twentieth century toward humanitarianism in sociology, for example, and the insistence on reform and the belief that progress is essentially irreversible, suggest conflict with the demands of scientific method in dealing with attitudes.

Ward * represents powerfully the nineteenth-century social science tradition in this respect. Social order, he thought, rests on ethical actions, but progress depends on dynamic action. While the value of human action itself depends on the correctness of opinion and the importance of the subject matter of opinion, the great social aim is correctness of opinion. Ward believed that incorrect opinions tend to be corrected by the consequences which flow from them, and thus there is continually a trend toward greater social rationality. Though doubt is better than settled opinions which are not true, division of opinion brings no benefit if the opinions under attack are true. Controversy is not always a means of progress. However, dispute is not eternal, since we may reach agreement on certain things. Citing Euclid as an example, Ward argued that dispute in all things may not continue without end. Astronomy and the sciences in general demonstrated for him this proposition. Nor has the settlement of scientific questions induced intellectual stagnation or social degeneracy. Indeed, most actual differences of opinion are unnecessary, since it is the fault of social organization that incorrect opinions are held. It is, therefore, the duty of society to see that all questions which can be settled are settled, and that they are removed from the arena of controversy.

One barrier to the establishment of correct opinion is the preponderance of subjective influence; truth can be grasped, said

* See Lester F. Ward, *Dynamic Sociology, or Applied Social Science* (2 vols., 1897). First published in 1883.

Ward, only by the intellect, for it is not determined by the feelings. Opinions based on desires are as likely to be false as true, and universality of belief is no evidence of the truth. Ward regarded this confusion of belief with truth as the great fallacy of all known periods of history. What we need today is an extension of the scientific method to every department of human thought and opinion. Education, therefore, must be directed at the oldest and most universal, yet the worst customs, the most pernicious institutions and the most false maxims. The critic might suggest that on his past performance man shows little promise for the future, but the sharpest denunciation of the past has, in the history of social thought, been coupled with the greatest optimism for the future.

It was custom and religion that Ward believed to be the chief forces distorting our conceptions of duty. Citing Comte, he argued that the failure of human effort was due to the lack of correspondence between thought and reality. Success can come only from the right kind of opinions, for most of our thinking is worthless to progress and order. The only valuable opinions are those that, being freed from superstition and convention, are guided by positive utility. Sound ideas are dynamic ideas. Ward is well known for his support of positive action by government for progress; thus he favored "meliorism" (George Eliot's word), that is, humanitarianism without sentiment. Much of our present charity, he thought, is bad because it preserves the unfit.

Ward's contemporary, Arthur F. Bentley, is credited with stimulating much of the contemporary interest in the group process, and his interpretation of the public begins and ends with the analysis of the social group in its interaction with other groups.* Leadership and public opinion are closely related, but they are interlinked with the group process in government. There is no public opinion except that represented by the activity of a group

* Arthur F. Bentley, *The Process of Government; A Study of Social Pressures* (1908). Bentley was a prolific writer, but this volume is accepted as the classic statement of his position.

or a set of groups, and there is no unanimous opinion. Public sentiment or "public will" expresses better what the term "public opinion" crudely describes, but since the term "public opinion" is well established, Bentley conceded that it should be used. Public opinion has leadership and it is leadership, but all forms of leadership must be stated in group terms. And a political group is by its nature a case of leadership. Groups can only express themselves through their leadership.

Bentley regarded public opinion, however, as having the value only of the group which gives it expression. It is directed to or against other groups, and ordinarily it is highly differentiated, or specialized, in what it condemns or denounces. It varies in generality and intensity, because it reflects the group struggle permeating the social process. Nevertheless, public opinion is only manifested opinion, and there is no sharp line between opinion and action. Opinion groups are merely one variety of interest group. "No interest group," said Bentley, "exists which cannot be reflected by an opinion group." According to Bentley there is, therefore, no value in the distinction between interest and opinion, because all social process turns on the observable facts of activity. The problem of public opinion is in large part to determine what really are the social factors which try to express themselves in terms of ideas.

From the cold analysis of group activity manifested in public opinion, one may turn, as in the nineteen-twenties did Charles Horton Cooley, to the force of the environment and the march of group activity toward higher levels of rationality—that is, toward the attainment of democracy in a normative sense. Though Cooley was a strong environmentalist in his theory of the development of the social self or the personality, he had little patience with the psychological interpretations of opinion, such as the ideas of Gabriel Tarde. He believed that the psychology and pragmatism of William James was the best foundation on which to analyze the process of group-to-group communication as it had appeared in American thought. Social consciousness may be viewed either as it occurs in a particular mind or as it is observed in the co-operative activity of many minds. The social ideas of individuals are closely associated with those of other people, and there is action and reaction in forming the whole of social thinking. From this arises "public consciousness, or to use a more familiar term, public opinion, in the broad sense of a group state of mind which is more or less distinctly aware of itself." *

However, Cooley felt that there is also an enlargement of consciousness through social evolution, which has been greatly facilitated by modern transportation and communication. The public phase of this larger consciousness is democracy, which is in turn the organized sway of public opinion. Cooley was certain that the tendency of the world was toward democracy, and with Lord Bryce he had confidence in the public opinion which governed the United States. Public opinion in our time had become more rational and self-determining, and it was applying the fundamental principles in human nature to a larger social life. Thus, democracy means organization, and the co-operative product of communication and interacting influence; it is not simply a form of government in which heads are counted. Public opinion, as a product of the social process, is more than just a collection of individual opinions, as men like Bryce and Allport had regarded it. Cooley had confidence that public opinion, especially in democracies, was showing a development toward maturity and reliability. He had great faith in the common man, particularly in the use he would make of the new means of mass communication. Out of modern developments there was bound to come an expanded consciousness of the larger social whole. Cooley believed that likewise human nature is ready for a higher type of social organization than had hitherto been attained, but it is under democracy that the new stage will be reached. Had Cooley understood the force of propaganda, Lippmann's "art of creating consent," and the application of Freudian ideas to advertising, he would not, perhaps, have had such confidence in the rationality of public opinion.

* Cooley, Social Organization (1929), 10. See E. C. Jandy, *Charles Horton Cooley, His Life and His Social Theory* (1942).

A central issue in the observation of group activity and social interaction, is of course the structure of social control. Public opinion, to the sociologist, is one of the means by which social behavior is directed. But it makes a great difference whether we regard public opinion as the immediate and the controversial, or whether we consider—as E. A. Ross said—that it is "the primitive nucleus out of which the various agencies of social control have developed." Public opinion controls through the short-sightedness and impulsiveness of the mass, while other forms of control, such as the law, may restrain actions which are not generally or actively condemned by popular opinion.* Ross believed the religious and legal codes were far more intelligent than public opinion. Religion seeks to preserve the fundamentals which do not immediately appeal to the public, such as the family and property. The law is not sentimental, and it anticipates problems before the masses of the people are excited about them. More quickly than either public opinion or religion, the law can be used to suit the purposes of a dominant ruling class. Public opinion as the deep-seated and deeply felt social code of the masses exercises one form of control, but opinion as controversial must be less of an agency of social discipline, for it is as short-lived as the issues that give it meaning. On the other hand, propaganda seeks to shape opinion on both controversial and traditional issues, to focus it on some area of social conflict; and it must assume that public opinion so formed will be an important agency of social control. Propaganda which seeks to show that a particular policy is in accordance with the tightly held traditions of the larger social groups must surely be the more effective instrument of social direction.†

* E. A. Ross, *Principles of Sociology* (1920), 429-430.

† *Ibid.*, 283: "Nor does system-building exhaust mental co-operation. Common opinion—class, group, or public opinion—is usually the resultant of many individual contributions, the residue left after the offerings of each have been winnowed in the minds of the rest."

The close connection between tradition and controversy in propaganda is illustrated by the fact that a very considerable amount of propaganda is an effort to *interpret* a tradition in favor of one side or other in an immediate political controversy.

American sociology is committed to a dynamic approach to the study of public opinion. Public opinion is a means of expression of the processes of society, and it is related to the techniques by which social control is effected. It is a phase of conflict and co-operation in the modern community. The view of public opinion as a phase of social control has, likewise, led the sociologist to the study of propaganda.*

The cultural sociologist, however, insists that the basic culture traits, the culture pattern, must be understood if public opinion is to be understood. Thus, even though opinion may be subject to change, its changes are to be related to the context of permanent judgment. The mores, characterized by definite convictions, form the background for an active movement of opinion. Bogardus, for example, attempted in the study of race relations on the Pacific Coast to show the stages through which opinion moves from the mores to active judgments on current problems. The coming of the alien Japanese awoke and irritated the area's traditional mores, groups were formed and reactions to the new situation could be observed. Counter-groups then established themselves, and the two sets of social organization came into conflict, until one carried the field. But public opinion is a social process which in turn arises from the cultural foundation of conviction. Public opinion, Bogardus argued, arises out of a disturbance or proposed change in the mores. This public opinion is composed of lesser public opinions, or sub-publics; the larger public includes those who give any attention at all to the issue.†

* See William Albig, *Public Opinion* (1939), 1 ff, and *Modern Public Opinion* (1956); F. E. Lumley, *Means of Social Control* (1925); also Lumley, *The Propaganda Menace* (1933); Leonard W. Doob, *Propaganda, Its Psychology and Technique* (1935); E. J. Carr, "Public Opinion as a Dynamic Concept," *Sociology and Social Research*, XIII (1928), 89-129; G. A. Lundberg, "Public Opinion from a Behavioristic View," *The American Journal of Sociology*, XXXVI (1930), 387-405; Harvey Glickman, "Viewing Public Opinion in Politics: A Common Sense Appeal," *Public Opinion Quarterly*, 23 (Winter, 1959-60), 494-504.

† Emory S. Bogardus, "Public Opinion as a Social Force: Race Relations," *Social Forces*, VIII (1929), 102-105; Bogardus, "Analyzing Changes in Public Opinion," *Journal of Applied Sociology*, IX (1925), 372-381.

To know the immediate culture pattern is not enough, for in the end an understanding of the cultural undergirding of opinion must reach into an understanding of civilization itself. Not only this, but the understanding of different civilizations or broad cultural backgrounds is necessary. From this, we arrive at the whole issue of cultural pattern as the functional matrix of public opinion, for not only the given culture but the pattern of cultural evolution will determine what the content of public opinion is. On this basis, assuming the reliability of pattern, we can explain the existence of opinion and in some degree predict what opinion may be or will be. Here the different factors in a cultural situation must be stated; and, as MacIver argues, they indicate the different tempos of change. Cultural values, for example, are clearly slower to change than technology, though it must be equally clear that mere rapidity of change tends to provide a normative justification of it.*

The study of social pattern, however, has seriously divided social scientists, for some are unwilling to admit to the ranks such controversial figures as Vilfredo Pareto and P. A. Sorokin. Pareto and Sorokin have been concerned with describing what they consider to be the longer movements in cultural change, and to discover, if possible, the form of this pattern, or the elements of permanence which may be found in it. In such studies of the basic cultural matrix—in the work, for example, of such men as Oswald Spengler, Karl Wittfogel, Arnold Toynbee, and Eric Voegelin, who have sought to discover patterns in history, we reach what might be called cultural objectivity as to public opinion. For a given stage of cultural or historical development offers the governing conditions of opinion, and in a measure it specifies the content which opinion must have at a given time. This view does not depend on what the pattern is, for the pattern,

* R. M. MacIver, "The Historical Pattern of Social Change," in *Authority and the Individual* (1937), 126 ff. MacIver is noted for his discussion of community, in which the community, as a smaller group organization, is distinguished from society and the state. It is by the free expression of opinion that the state is held responsible to the community in modern democracies. See *The Web of Government* (1947), 192 ff.

whatever it is, predetermines, in this theory, the nature of the cycle of repetition.*

V

German theories of public opinion, and, indeed, most continental theories in this field, have not stressed the means by which the opinions of the people can be made an effective control over the actions of government. They have emphasized, rather, the traditional, religious, and cultural conditions under which opinion is shaped, and the means by which it has been or can be expressed. Though the folk spirit may be the foundation of the German nation and of its institutions such as law and monarchy, consent and its correlative participation were not accepted in Germany until the end of World War I as the foundation of either the state or of institutions. Thus, consent and participation were relegated to the background, while the statesman, the intellectual, and the public official took to themselves the task of expressing the larger cultural meanings of the folk spirit and the national tradition. The idea of public opinion lived under the shadow of Hegel's impressive and brilliant generalizations until the modern German trauma of the two world wars. In turn, much of the history of the idea of public opinion was to be found in its explosive and revolutionary struggles against ruling orders, such as the French Revolution and the German rebirth after Napoleon.

In the German definitions of *die öffentliche Meinung,* the "openness" of the public has been stressed. The public is the open and the general, and, in close analogy to the English use of the word "public," the term in Germany became a kind of

* In Sorokin's theory one should, no doubt, distinguish between the force of ideas or values in different culture mentalities. Values are obviously stronger in ideational and idealistic cultures, but mass opinion as a social force is characteristic of eras whose peoples tend to rely upon the sensate and visual modes of perception. Sorokin argues that determinism tends to run parallel with sensate culture. Mass opinion and the rise of public opinion would thus be associated with deterministic thought. See P. A. Sorokin, *Social and Cultural Dynamics* (3 vols., 1937), I, 66 ff, 404; II, 250, 347 ff. See Sorokin, *Contemporary Sociological Theory* (1928), 709.

descriptive phrase for the general community and for special communities or publics in which classes, intellectual interests, and group competence—such as that of the jurists and business groups—were to be found. In this connection, German social scientists might agree that public opinion is what a man will say out loud as a member of a special-competence group. With Bluntschli, they might say that until the power of religion was destroyed there could be no public opinion, for no previous types of society in which religion was powerful could survive in a time of the general communication of ideas. German liberal theory thus looked to urban and middle class society as the true home of public opinion, or at least considered that in the ancient world public opinion existed only under urban conditions with limited means of communication within special group interests. German conservative thought, however—as in Hegel—could see public opinion in older regimes, though the Reformation was, again, regarded as the beginning of the modern conditions under which public opinion could be studied as a separate social factor. But German Catholic thought, quite naturally, rejected the liberal idolization of urban, middle class, and commercial life; and in its own view of public opinion retained a sense of historical continuity. To German Catholic thinkers, the public was still the open and the general, but the history of public opinion became a history of the modes of communication and *Publizistik*, observable in poetry, speeches, drama, controversial writings, and the publication of news or matters of interest to most of the community, or to special groups, such as business and finance.*

If the term "public opinion" as we know it today is a product of the late eighteenth century, it also has clear historical antecedents, since—as Wilhelm Bauer observed—the problem of public opinion has been recognized throughout Western history.

* See Lorenz Stoltenberg, "Die Öffentliche Meinung," *Schmollers Jahrbuch*, XLVIII-2 (1924), 963 (211)-967 (215), for an analysis of Tönnies' ideas. Lother Bucher, "Über Politische Kunstausdrucke," *Deutsche Revue*, XII-2 (1887), 67-80, I, is an important article in the introduction of the idea of public opinion to the German learned world, though of course it was not the first by any means.

Bauer illustrates by citing the fact that the Greeks spoke of *óssa, phḗmē* or *nómos,* while the Romans spoke of *fama, fama popularis, rumores,* and in the closing days of the empire of *vox populi.* Medieval writers used the term *consensus,* which was modeled on the stoic *consensus communis,* and it signified traditional opinion. Machiavelli gave attention to the *pubblica voce e fama,* while Shakespeare repeatedly recognized the idea of the force of opinion in his drama. Bauer believed that it was in seventeenth-century England that one may first find the idea of public opinion clarified, and he emphasized William Temple's *An Essay on the Original and Nature of Government,* in 1672, which assumed that the source of authority is the prevailing opinion. But it was Locke, says Bauer, who "first" sought to supply a juristic and ethical orientation for the phenomena of public opinion. Bauer showed the spread of the concept from England to France in the eighteenth century, where Montesquieu is found speaking of *l'esprit générale,* and Rousseau expanding the idea already common in France of the *volonté générale.* In German usage, *Volksgeist* was a rough approximation of the term "public opinion." However, on the eve of the French Revolution *l'opinion publique* gained currency in the circle of Louis XVI's minister, Necker, and from there it moved into the speech of the Western nations. By its broadened use, however, the term has lost, Bauer believed, its incisiveness and its historical connotations.*

Bauer distinguished, first of all, public opinion from opinions merely voiced in public, for public opinion is a deeply organic force; it is both rational and irrational and it is both fleeting and permanent. But it represents unified group pressures and attitudes, and all of the essential social forces are involved in making it. There is both static and dynamic public opinion, the former being the opinion of tradition and usage, such as might be found in agrarian and barter economies. Dynamic opinion

* See Wilhelm Bauer, "Public Opinion," in *Encyclopaedia of the Social Sciences,* XII, pp. 669-674. Bauer's two main works are *Die Öffentliche Meinung in der Weltgeschichte* (1929), and *Die Öffentliche Meinung und Ihre Geschichtlichen Grundlagen* (1914).

strives consciously to be rational. It uses systematic publicity, propaganda, and agitation; and it is a product of urban culture, but it is, moreover, a product of the urban culture of all ages. It is to be found under Pericles, in the time of Cicero and Caesar, in the Renaissance cities and in modern urban and industrial situations. And through all ages one should study the techniques by which opinion was organized in a dynamic sense, through which appeals were made to the masses of the people.

The prophets in the ancient Jewish state used the market place and the temple to appeal to popular attitudes, and at a late stage even written documents. Greek society shows the constant effort to organize public opinion as a wealthy and aggressive urban civilization came into being. Pan-Hellenic festivals and conspiracies against the nobility show alike the process of organization. In Pericles, who developed political publicity to a high degree, the techniques of appeal to the Greek masses are clear, and the Greeks are forerunners of modern experts in publicity. In public deliberations it was, of course, oratory, developed to a fine and formal art, that was used to manipulate the opinions of the citizens. Next to oratory, the theater was a powerful force in shaping and appealing to static opinions in a dynamic context.

One of the contributions of Greek culture to Roman society was the importation of Greek methods of publicity. Oratory, the theater, and a pamphlet literature which attained sizeable proportions by the time of Caesar, were given wider scope in Rome than in Greece. The development of rapid communication through the road system and the recognition of the value of news, particularly under the empire, provided new means of directing public opinion. Bauer observed that by the time of Cicero news suppliers were a specialized profession. In 59 B.C. Caesar directed that *Acta Diurna*, reporting the activities of the Senate and Assembly, should be made available to the public, and news distribution became a powerful force in directing and molding the attitudes of the masses on public policy. The disintegration of the empire, of course, restricted these techniques of publicity, and, with the decline in efficiency in communication, tradition and custom had again time to become predominant in shaping local attitudes.

However, the conflicts of the Middle Ages were a constant stimulus to greater efficiency in communication. Both the medieval Holy Roman Empire and the medieval Papacy revived to some degree the ancient practices of communicating with a scattered population; and both sought, through their pamphleteers, to reach the masses with their appeals. The growth of medieval cities stimulated still further the latent revival of publicity, and with the invention of the printing press we find the beginning of the modern mode of mass appeal. Because of printing, the audiences or those affected by appeals during the conflicts of the Reformation and Counter-Reformation were larger than ever before. Commercial newsletters were developed by the merchants, and after the Reformation there were traveling booksellers. The collection and dissemination of information came again into the hands of specialized groups. Such news bulletins began in the commercial and trading centers early in the seventeenth century. The first English newspaper appeared in 1622, and in 1631 the *Gazette* appeared in France under Richelieu. In addition, during the seventeenth and eighteenth centuries, scientific and literary periodicals made their appearance. Bauer argued that these journals shaped the tastes of a growing middle class, or urban, reading public.

Great importance must be given to English and American experience in the development of the constitutional position of public opinion. In the English struggles over religion which resulted in the civil war, public opinion was shaped toward its parliamentary expression. Bauer regarded the Leveller spokesman John Lilburne as having played an important part in discovering the use of propaganda and in the development of periodicals devoted to stirring up opinion. With the expiration of the Licensing Act in 1695, the way was opened for the establishment of a free press. American techniques during the American Revolution reached the masses of the people, particularly through the anti-British pamphleteering of Thomas Paine, one of the most successful of all agitators and political propagandists. Likewise, the French Revolution shows a continuation of the use of the techniques of publicity in order to reach the masses; in that revolution public opinion came to be regarded with almost idolatrous reverence, and it became a powerful agency in the institution of organized democratic politics.

No small part of Napoleon's power was his exploitation of the emotional response of the masses, and the Napoleonic legend hardly yet has ceased to be a force in French public opinion. But the very techniques of mass manipulation which emerged with the French Revolution and the Napoleonic era were carried to the people against whom the French made war, and the broad appeal to the masses became, as a consequence, part of the public life of Europe. Metternich and his fellow-statesmen were unable to abolish the newly learned techniques of publicity. The post-Napoleonic ministers of the great powers could not eradicate the emotional power of the new slogans and symbols of the bourgeois revolution, and they could not undo the effect upon the people of the teachings of the revolutionary period, which had proclaimed that the masses should play an important role in the determination of public policy. Thus in the nineteenth century conservatives themselves were led to accept and use this new principle. Under its pressure they adopted nationalism, deserting a previous cosmopolitan and internationalist attitude.*

Probably the most dramatic recognition of all, however, of the force of the techniques of publicity and the belief of the masses that they should have a share in the state is the fact that twentieth-century totalitarian regimes have been unable to ignore political participation, and in consequence they have

* There is a considerable literature on French propaganda developments during the nineteenth century. One may note Lynn M. Case, *French Opinion on War and Diplomacy during the Second Empire* (1954); David L. Dowd, "Art as National Propaganda in the French Revolution," *The Public Opinion Quarterly*, XV (Fall, 1951), 532 ff. See also Peter Viereck, *Conservatism Revisited* (1949), for a perceptive study of opinion movement in the last century.

utilized an extraordinary development of the techniques of propaganda and censorship. Public opinion is a force in the whole Western world, because firmly imbedded in Western thought is the idea that democratic public opinion can be the ultimate and rational standard in directing politics. And with the growth of education and the means of mass communication, the principles and practices associated with this idea have only become more deeply fixed in contemporary minds.*

VI

Ferdinand Tönnies has received a more effective hearing than Bauer, but this is largely because of his reputation as a sociologist and only secondarily because of his studies of public opinion. The newness of public opinion and the idea of the peculiar problems of the present have been forcefully delineated in Tönnies' work. As a result, if the student of society wishes to examine communication and publicity, his attention can, under these assumptions, be concentrated on the modern period. He is not bound to make a comparative study of ancient techniques, since these are both qualitatively and quantitatively insignificant for the modern study of public opinion. It is probably another case of the struggle between the mind which sees the historical continuity of society and the mind which sees the reality of modern society in its differences from earlier and dimly remembered periods.

The anchor of Tönnies' system is the distinction between *Gemeinschaft* and *Gesellschaft. Gemeinschaft*, or community, is the

* See Wilhelm Bauer, "Das Schlagwort als Sozialpsychische und Geistegeschichtliche Erscheinung," *Historische Zeitschrift*, 122 (1920), 189-240. Here Bauer emphasizes the historical and changing background of words, showing how significance is changed through historical development. On p. 215 n, he replies specifically to Tönnies, denying that public opinion is essentially new. The specific issue of the modernity of public opinion is thus raised. Among the *Schlagworten* he studied in the context of their general social history are *Pax* from Roman history, public opinion, nationalism, imperialism, and capitalism—in each case showing the changing meaning of these terms.

historic, traditional, and inarticulate form of society. It is based on concord, custom, and religion. In contrast, *Gesellschaft* or society is the modern middle class, urban, industrial, and commercial form of social organization. It strives to be consciously rational, and it is based upon convention, legislation, and public opinion. The course of evolution is from the *Kultur* of community to the civilization of society.* Public opinion is distinguished by Tönnies from Public Opinion, the latter being a unified and active social force, distinct from its organs, such as the press, which assist in giving it expression. Three stages in the emergence of public opinion are suggested by Tönnies, *die feste, die flüssige,* and *die luftartige,* which Professor Palmer suggested should be the solid, the fluid, and the gaseous. The last, for example, would be the mere opinion of the day, as found in the daily press, while the other two are related to the more substantial types of expression used by the enlightened and the rational leaders of society, as in periodical publications and in books. While community and society are fundamentally different in nature, and the latter especially is characteristic of modern times, Tönnies shows that they may overlap. Public opinion is, indeed, sovereign in the modern state when society and community do overlap, as in practice is to some extent the case in nearly all societies today.

Tönnies is particularly concerned with a criticism of modern opinion. The great political leaders of the nineteenth century—Napoleon, Bismarck, and the English political leaders, for example—saw the importance not only of long-run opinion but also of day-to-day opinion. Yet each modern state must be studied for its specific characteristics in public opinion. In his study of the United States, Tönnies relied on Bryce and Ostrogorski, and he argued that America, like other countries, is led by its men

* Ferdinand Tönnies' great work on public opinion is *Kritik der Öffentlichen Meinung* (1922). Paul A. Palmer has summarized his theory in "Ferdinand Tönnies Theory of Public Opinion," *The Public Opinion Quarterly,* II (1938), 584-595. Tönnies' *Fundamental Concepts of Sociology,* trans. by C. P. Loomis (1940), may be consulted with profit on the idea of public opinion.

of wealth and education. With perhaps the thought of American acceptance of anti-German propaganda in World War I in his mind, Tönnies held that American opinion is colonial and gullible, and that it digests all that the British offer it to swallow. However, he also thought that permanent American opinion holds strongly to the values of our republican constitution and that Americans believed in democracy as the best form of government. It is gaseous opinion which is easily manipulated, while solid and permanent opinion resist the efforts of the propagandist. Tönnies felt that in contrast with the United States, British public opinion has more basic convictions than that of any other country. It claims to be rational, and its strength is in its solidity. French public opinion, however, is gaseous and emotional, though it claims to be rational.

Public opinion in any nation, therefore, according to Tönnies, is a social judgment to be sharply distinguished from the popular beliefs (*Volksstimmung* or *Volksgefühle*) which are found in the community or *Gemeinschaft*. It is on a basis such as this that the modernity of public opinion is to be argued. Not only does the development of public opinion in society control the state and through the state the background community, but it strives also to go beyond national boundaries. It seeks to establish an informed public wherever its common concerns are touched. Public opinion in this view, then, is the creation of a *Gelehrtenrepublik*, a kind of elite characteristically international in its scope of action. Its centers, however, are in cities, particularly the great cities of modern times and in institutions of learning.* But the public, as Tönnies sees it, is an assemblage of men and women, especially under urban conditions, where a common focus of interest or anticipated events draw them together. Its direction or its formal manipulation is another matter, just as the standards of formal correctness or utility in its behavior are drawn up by those who in a certain sense are part of it but not of it in an organic manner. "*Das Publikum ist eine Menge*

* Tönnies, *Kritik*, 77.

von Menschen—Männern und Frauen—, zunächst von solchen, die sich räumlich vereinen, z.B. im Theater; von Menschen sehr verschiedener Art, die aber miteinander gemein haben, dass die Gelegenheit, das Erwartete, das Interesse, sie zusammenführt oder zusammenhält." *

The principle that public opinion is a new force in the world depends in Tönnies—as well as in many other writers—on the close association between public opinion and the city. Public opinion is a middle class factor, and the middle class is peculiar to the growth of cities, the means of communication, the emergence of specialized elites, and the desertion of the traditional values which have given coherence to Western life. The city is the enemy of tradition and the worshiper of efficiency, and in its nature it must war upon community, just as community must struggle to preserve itself and to found again, after the process of urban destruction has run its course, the principles of a common and enduring civilization. The elites which lead the public—*i.e.*, the urban *Menge*—have assumed, of course, that the city is the place of intelligence, reason, and progress, and are the places where the sound modern foundations of social life may be found. But *das grosse Publikum* never actually gets together in any physical sense, though it makes itself felt as a totality. It is brought together by other means than place, for the press and the communication of ideas, either general or specialized, gives the scattered components of *das grosse Publikum* their common ground. Thus the sharing of opinion in society is a far different process than in community. Publicity (*Öffentlichkeit*) in its general characteristic is bound up with every developed (*i.e.*, urban) political life. Thus the market place, in the broad sense of that term, may, according to Tönnies, be its most continuous symbol.†
Moreover, interweaving through all the forms of publicity found in society are the various forms of social conflict—the opposition between rich and poor, capital and labor, city and country, the learned and the ignorant mass.

* *Ibid.*, 82-83.
† *Ibid.*, 100.

In spite of his theory that public opinion is a force especially characteristic of modern times, Tönnies recognized that the force of public opinion is related to its solidity, to a connection in fact with community, or to the overlapping of community and society. Decision, thus, may arise from the lasting or the permanent elements in opinion, and decision itself rather than controversy may be the most effective expression of public opinion. Controversy may or may not be part of the process by which the public seeks to make and enforce its decisions.*

* See Ferdinand Tönnies-Curtin, "Zur Theorie der Öffentlichen Meinung," *Schmollers Jahrbuch für Gesetzgebung, Verwaltung und Volkswirtschaft im Deutschen Reich,* 40 (1916), 2001-2030, for comment on Bauer, *Die Öffentliche Meinung und Ihre Geschichtlichen Grundlagen.* The general tenor of the criticism is that Bauer has failed to emphasize the writers and thinkers of modern times who made public opinion the new force that Tönnies holds it to be. Modern liberal parties which have demanded the support of public opinion are in part responsible for its force, but Bauer should have emphasized Jacques Necker, who above others in his time saw the power of public opinion, and Georg Forster, who was in Paris during the French Revolution and was the first to put the term "public opinion" into German. Forster saw, for example, the large city (*i.e.,* Paris) as the source of public opinion, and recognized that in Germany there was then (1794) no comparable phenomenon. Bauer also neglects Christian Garve, who saw in the Reformation the power of public opinion; Garve drew the term "public opinion" from the French use of the term. But there was no public opinion, according to Garve, if it came from custom or compulsion. Tönnies cites J. K. Bluntschli, in his article on public opinion in his *Staatswörterbuch,* VII, 345 ff, showing that the power of public opinion had grown enormously during the last hundred years, and that public opinion is primarily the opinion of the middle class; as the middle classes rise in power, so does the power of public opinion. Heinrich von Treitschke, Tönnies notes, adopted the same thesis. Ranke held that public opinion had been powerful in the new Europe (*Werke,* XXXVII, 87). Dahlmann and F. von Hellwald are noted to the same effect. The latter observed that public opinion began at the end of the sixteenth century. James Bryce's observation that public opinion is a new power in the world, especially since the rise of popular government, is brought into the lists against Bauer. See *The American Commonwealth,* Ch. LXXVII, Part IV.

Bauer's answer, of course, would be that only by careful historical study can we determine which elements in modern public opinion are new and which elements are continuous in human experience. A new surge of the power of opinion in modern times does not show that there have been no other periods in which a high degree of organization, communication, and effectiveness in popular thinking was attained.

CHAPTER 6

The Quality of Opinion

I

Behind the psychological problems presented by public opinion operating in a complicated world, there is an important history of psychological interpretations of human nature and politics. Thomas Hobbes is credited by C. H. Driver with beginning in his *Leviathan,* in 1651, psychological political speculation in England. He presented a doctrine of the association of ideas to explain both the content of the individual mind and the selfish motives animating political behavior. It was a doctrine of struggle, an evolutionary conception, a kind of natural selection of ideas of an unsocial nature. To suppose that the social contract arose as a catalytic agent which precipitated social impulses from antisocial behavior was indeed a weak hypothesis. How did man really become social if he is in origin a creature in a perpetual war of all against all, as Hobbes pictures him?

Nevertheless, associationist psychology remained a primary thesis. It became the foundation of diverse creeds, all of which held that to change the environment is to change the man. It was, as Driver argued, a doctrine of golden promise, and it filled the nineteenth century with its enthusiasm. It is found in the anarchism of William Godwin, the collectivism of Robert Owen, and the philosophic radicalism of the earlier part of the century. French thinkers like Condillac and Helvetius expanded the doctrine to an extreme degree. It was a doctrine more useful to reformers, to those confident of the final victory of rationality in man, than to those who held to the centuries-old conservative belief in a composite character of human nature.

The attempt to resolve the primary emotions, such as fear, love, and anger, into sensations was unconvincing, while the emphasis on habit introduced by Hume and reinforced by Bagehot in the nineteenth century has been more enduring in democratic thinking about public opinion. Habit can explain much, and it can serve no doubt as a bridge between an older associationism and the more modern experimental, mechanistic, behavioristic, and other similar views. Thus, one might say of thought in the nineteenth century that it tended to regard all opinions as secondary passions, derived from the laws of association. To the men of that period, opinions were not to be changed suddenly, for they were believed to be firmly rooted in instinct; re-education, or the reformation of intellectual habit, was regarded as the only way to bring about a change in the political climate.*

At the end of the last century, the psychological attempt to understand politics broadened into the present emphasis, in which psychology has become to many the most important key to understanding the problems of public opinion, democracy, and, indeed, the modern state.† Today, as in the past, the psychological approach to political theory is a tool of interpretation which cuts two ways. For it reinforces the principles both of those who seek an ultimately rational public opinion and of those who stress the

* See T. R. Edmonds, *Practical, Moral, and Political Economy* (1828), cited in C. H. Driver, "The Development of a Psychological Approach to Politics in English Speculation before 1869," in *The Social and Political Ideas of Some Representative Thinkers of the Victorian Age*, ed. by F. J. C. Hearnshaw (1933), Appendix, 251 ff.

† According to Berelson: "At about the turn of the century public opinion ceased to be a topic of general speculation and became the object of specific and detailed monographs. Among the earliest of these were a number of essays by Tarde, the French psychologist." It is noted that Tarde considered outside influences, such as newspapers, and especially conversation. B. R. Berelson, P. F. Lazarsfeld, W. N. McPhee, *Voting; A Study of Opinion Formation in a Presidential Campaign* (1954), 299-300.

pervading irrationality of political action. Psychological interpretations are the refuge of observers who claim to be "realistic," but also of those who concentrate on the description and analysis of the course of politics. In the new society the reformer and the dreamer have seen in psychology a fresh means of interpreting human nature, a way of discovering the needs of the mature personality; and psychology has been the foundation of much of twentieth-century social science. Psychology becomes, thus, one of the primary scientific foundations of a new social ethics. It provides a new methodology for the investigation of the world of politics and a renewed optimism for the future of democracy. Yet the practical use of psychology actually points in quite another direction. While the technical psychologist may be disinclined to draw large political conclusions, those who have been engrossed in the struggle for power have shown no such modesty. And the results of propaganda technique have confirmed the reliance of the men of power on the deliberate manufacture of public opinion.*

While the prophets of social science may look to psychology to assist in remaking man a little nearer to the heart's desire, the realists and political leaders have used the new mysteries to manipulate men as they are. The political problem, psychologically speaking, became therefore a question of the nature of men in the mass. What is the nature of group behavior? What is the quality of group opinion, as contrasted with the opinion of the individual? Is group opinion any different from the summation or addition of individual opinions? What is the crowd or the mob? Does the crowd do something to the reactions of the individual mind that nothing else can do? Is not politics simply the

* Driver lists the following writers as decisive in starting the new psychological age: Lloyd Morgan, *Comparative Psychology* (1893); *Instinct and Habit* (1896); L. T. Hobhouse, *Mind in Evolution* (1901); Wm. McDougall, *Introduction to Social Psychology* (1908); *The Group Mind* (1919); Graham Wallas, *Human Nature in Politics* (1908); *The Great Society* (1914); *Our Social Heritage* (1920); Curtis D. MacDougall, *Understanding Public Opinion* (1952), gives useful summaries of contemporary psychological theory on human nature.

problem of the nature of the masses? Whatever one may think of the issue of the individual versus the crowd, none can deny that psychological investigations of group behavior have profoundly shaken the confidence of modern thinkers in the rationality of politics. If men are irrational, they can be controlled by irrational techniques, and ultimately both force and deception are justified in governing. Both the fabrication of consent and the swift cut of the sword explain the coherence of modern populations. And the modern state is founded, thus, on the irrational juggling of symbols and the fear of the police. The rationalist has habitually begun his study of politics with the individual, while the psychological techniques of leadership begin habitually with the concept of the masses. But the individual in the masses is being looked at as a total psychological *Gestalt.* Instead of the personality being considered as a series of conflicting impulses, it is now held, it seems, that man strives for a unified, meaningful structure of his beliefs, perceptions, and attitudes. The use of psychological research in relation to public opinion is being governed more and more by the concept of unified mental structure. Attitudes thus tend to be regarded as a series of dispositions to react favorably or unfavorably to a class of objects.*

II

Wilhelm Bauer thought we should begin our study of public opinion with the masses,† and he observed that it was Scipio Sighele and Gustave Le Bon who first in modern times investigated the nature of the mass or the crowd. The psychological problem of politics is, thus, the means whereby ideas are transferred and shared among a great number of people. Critics of democracy

* An issue of the *Public Opinion Quarterly*, 24 (Summer, 1960), was devoted to the study of attitudes. See Charles Mackay, *Extraordinary Popular Delusions and the Madness of Crowds*, foreword by Bernard M. Baruch (1932), for discussions of John Law, the Mississippi and South Sea bubbles, the tulip craze, and the Florida boom.

† *Die Öffentliche Meinung in der Weltgeschichte* (1929), 8.

often assume that only irrational and emotional opinions and symbols are shared in this way. One might admit that irrational ideas are shared on a mass basis without admitting that only such ideas can be shared. But to say that rational ideas may be shared is to restore such a sharing to a central position in democratic philosophy.

In 1901 Sighele professed himself happy that Gabriel Tarde, Gustave Le Bon * and Victor Cherbuliez had used his ideas, for he wanted to spread the views of the Italian school of criminal anthropology, which based its tenets largely upon the study of collective psychology. But Sighele recognized that more than the crimes of crowds needed to be studied, no matter how important it was for judges to have recognized the different nature and the peculiar qualities of collective crime.† On the basis of the then current organic theory of society, Sighele proposed the inferiority of group decisions. Sighele held that in criminal law, group crimes should have a different and lighter punishment than those committed by a single individual. A crowd is by its very nature more disposed to evil actions than the individual, and by the process of imitation and collective suggestion irrational behavior easily spreads. As an example Sighele cites the fact that after an English Lord jumped into Vesuvius, many Englishmen did likewise.

Sighele regarded a crowd as a compact organism, but public opinion as a diffuse organism. He felt that public opinion cannot

* In 1923, Le Bon, citing his *Les Opinions et les Croyances*, based the power of propaganda on prestige, affirmation, repetition, and contagion. See Gustave Le Bon, "Genèse et Propagation des Idées," *Les Annales Politiques et Litteraires*, 81 (1923), 62-63. Amerigo Namias, "L'Opinione Pubblica," *Nuova Antologia*, CCXXI (1922), 148-154, argued that public opinion is part of the collective mind, from which not even the most intelligent can escape. Public opinion includes both powerful traditional judgments and fluctuating new opinion.

† See Scipio Sighele, *La Foule Criminelle* (2nd ed., 1901), preface. The first edition of this work was published in 1892. See also Sighele's *Le Crime à Deux* (2nd ed., 1910), where the prestige of certain personalities in the leadership of crime is stressed, that is, the hero as pictured by Thomas Carlyle. Sighele seemed greatly influenced by both Herbert Spencer and Carlyle. Sighele's works were published first in Italian.

be defined exactly, and he doubted that it could be identified with the most elevated intelligence of a given country. Indeed, to the extent that the superior intelligences are subjected to crowd influence, they are alike subject to political error. To seek public opinion, Sighele first sought the public and he found it in psychological terms. To Sighele, the public is a phase of collective psychology; it rises from the crowd. It can draw its characteristic unity out of groups of diverse kinds—from a mere audience in a theater to a serious association of persons separated physically but united in idea. However, the public can be reduced to a crowd when the fact of physical contact is predominant, as in the case of a crowd in a stadium. Sighele and his followers were unwilling to admit or emphasize that people may be united by a common political function—that is, the common life of citizenship and by participation in the affairs of the government. In modern times, however, physical separation has become the rule rather than the exception, for through the art of printing the *foule* has been superseded by the public. The public involves a moral contact, while the crowd or *foule* is by nature physical and emotional. The crowd is barbarous, while the public is essentially civilized. Yet in the second half of the eighteenth century when the true public emerged, it began to acquire some of the traditional qualities of the crowd. For with the press, the railroad, and the telegraph, the public attained a sense of immediateness and simultaneity, qualities a *foule* always has. But the crowd and the public move side by side, and Sighele argued that now we live in an age of both crowds and publics. Though Tarde insisted that we have reached an age of publics, Le Bon and Sighele, more impressed than he with mass irrationality, insisted that publics often descend to the level of crowds.

Thus, one must separate the psychological study of publics and crowds. There are all kinds of publics; they may be limited and specialized, but as they become more general they become more powerful. Publics in the nineteenth century were less defined and more fluctuating than in former periods. To this, the power of journalism had contributed, and Sighele believed that all articles in newspapers should be signed. Political parties, moreover, no longer stand for anything very clearly. By the second edition of his work, Sighele had followed this line of argument far enough to recognize the anti-liberal implication of his theories of crowd behavior. He felt impelled, therefore, to make some distinctions and to point out that the crowd was not always the enemy of progress, for in the liberal revolutions the enemies of the crowd were aristocrats and exponents of despotism, especially in the Latin countries. Here, Sighele turns against his own Italian background for he contended that the North European crowds were superior to those in Latin Europe, and he thought that this development had resulted from the fact that Latin education was retarded, and the youth were directed toward the bureaucracy, rather than toward industry and the professions. Sighele, like many continental liberals, was impressed by the progress of the Anglo-Saxons, and tended to contrast it with the corruption of Greece, Italy, Spain, and France.*

III

Among the men who have directed modern thinking toward the use of psychology in the study of large aggregates of individuals, Sighele's contemporary, Gabriel Tarde, occupies a place of peculiar importance, for he was one of the first significant investigators of public opinion to base his work upon the application of social psychology. Tarde held that imitation and invention are the elementary social acts, and progress is possible be-

* It seems clear that during the nineteenth century English writers were willing to grant a greater reliability to public opinion than in most parts of the continent. Looking back from the vantage point of the nineteen-twenties, Martin observed that Jefferson and Bentham had a profound faith in newspapers, and welcomed the transference of political power to millions of ill-informed persons. But English writers in the end followed the others in questioning the possibility of intelligent crowd or mass opinion. Martin accepted Lippmann's theory of the distorted picture of the unseen environment. See Kingley Martin, *The Triumph of Lord Palmerston; A Study of Public Opinion in England before the Crimean War* (1924), 15 ff.

cause of imitation, for it results in the substitution and accumulation of inventions. According to Tarde, democratic periods are those in which the distance between classes has been sufficiently reduced to allow the external imitation of the highest by the lowest. In modern times the old classes and distinctions have given way to new types—such as the publicists, financiers, artists, and politicians. Tarde remarks that all the new types are found in the great urban capitals, where, as Alexis de Tocqueville said, the sway of journalism must extend as men grow more and more equal. Where the great city dominates, majorities as well as political capitals attain prestige; the disposition to believe in the masses increases as public opinion increasingly dominates and guides society. Tarde observes that the lack of faith in single individuals inspires an unlimited confidence in the judgment of the public; and where all are thought to have the same light, by means of the communication of ideas, the truth is believed to be on the side of the greatest number.

Tarde points out, however, that in the modern world, in which custom is shattered, fashion predominates in the processes of imitation. Pride of birth, dogmatic belief, and political tradition give way to the progressive assimilation of the people's thinking into the irresponsible power of public opinion. The morality of an age of fashion resembles its politics, for leaders take care of interests in shortsighted ways. Still, the moment will arrive when civilization, at a point of culmination, will turn back to a higher level of morality.*

Tarde turned in 1904 to a specific discussion of public opinion. Social psychology, as distinguished from psychology, has no need for any mysterious collective being, for the public is a scattered crowd where mutual interaction and influence operates at greater and greater distances. Public opinion is the consequence of contacts or actions at a distance, since the public must be distinguished from the crowd. The principal meaning of "public," said

* See Gabriel Tarde, *The Laws of Imitation,* trans. from 2nd French ed. by E. C. Parsons (1903). The first edition of this work was published in 1890, the second in 1895.

Tarde, has arisen from the new or modern way of life. With the invention of printing especially, the new public came into being, for a collectivity purely mental in nature was produced, though each individual might be physically separated from the others. In this situation the currents of opinion in more developed societies must be studied, for it is the kind of communication between individuals which has generated the public. The formation of a public, *i.e.*, by suggestion at a distance, supposes a mental evolution much more advanced than is necessary in the formation of a crowd. For a public exists without physical contact, and its collective nature arises from accepting mental suggestions.

Tarde is one of the earlier writers to speak of "publics." The need for a distinction between publics arose, no doubt, from his attempt to offer a psychological explanation of mental unity on some point or other. No ancient writer, says Tarde, speaks of *his* public, and in the Middle Ages there were only crowds. Thought, Tarde argued, is the greatest social force, and the invention of printing was needed before there could be a public. In this connection Tarde's principle is like that of his contemporary Alfred Fouillée who stressed the influences of idea-forces in society.* About the time of Louis XIV—according to Tarde—the public began clearly to emerge, yet there were still torrential crowds. While the public was still a small elite, it developed rapidly during the eighteenth century, for only then such a large number of men undertook the same studies that it was impossible to know each other personally. In the latter part of that century, however, a growing political public tended to absorb the other publics—scientific, literary, and philosophic. True journalism, Tarde argued, dates from the French Revolution, the time of formation for a feverishly growing public. The crowds of the revolution were like others in past centuries, but the political public oriented around the new journalism constituted a primary difference from other periods. Thus the public is the social group of the future, as the means of communication continue to develop, such as print-

* See F. G. Wilson, "Concepts of Public Opinion," *The American Political Science Review*, XXVII (1933), 371-391.

ing, the railroads, the telegraph, the telephone, and other means not anticipated by Tarde.

It is easy to recognize in Tarde the prophet of the present-day study of public opinion; for in social study today, as in Tarde's own work, the emphasis falls on examination of the phenomena of mass communication and the publics it generates. We might also agree that Tarde bridges the differences between a sociological and a purely psychological approach. However, if the existence of the public is based on the communication of ideas and their power of distant suggestion, we might also urge that it is superficial to exaggerate the swiftness and penetration of modern communication, and at the same time minimize the effectiveness of social and political communication in periods before the invention of printing. Why should not Tarde have considered further the pamphleteering in England during the seventeenth century, and why not in earlier times the power of spoken communication? For if one man, say a preacher of the crusades, preaches to many audiences in different places, does he not attain, at a slower rate, the same results as does the modern journalist? And what of oratory and widely distributed writings of the ancient world? Or the influence of Greek and Christian teachers whose words were carried by students and by manuscripts to many people living at one time, and to succeeding generations? It is superficial to base the nature of the public on a technique of communication, rather than the fact of communication.

In any case, Tarde resisted the late nineteenth century trend to debase communicated thought and collective action to the level of the mob, as social psychologists such as Le Bon attempted. Tarde reserved for the public a higher place in the temple of rationality than was reserved for the crowd. Tarde's day was the era of the public or of publics, and publics rarely degenerate into crowds. All groups show a tendency to form publics by establishing journals, for general communication is necessary between associates in a group. However, the press, as distinguished from journals, provides an unstable basis of public action. While older political parties are more durable and less ardent, the fluidity of parties is hardly compatible with the tradition of stable parliamentary government. Yet the press does drain away the potential danger of crowds. In general, Tarde insisted that "public" and "crowd" (*la foule*) are the two extreme terms of social evolution. Opinion alone is characteristic of publics.

Tarde uses, therefore, a qualitative distinction between opinion (which is real or rational) and sentiments or emotional responses found in crowds. But is it only the rationality of opinion that distinguishes in this theory? Does not the modern system of communication provide a basis for effectiveness of opinion so organized? In the end, we must choose between criteria, for on the one hand we may say that public opinion is rational or well-founded opinion; or, on the other, that public opinion arises from the techniques or mechanics of action, or from its effectiveness in dealing with the enveloping social world. Clearly, Tarde recognized that the modern public of communication at a distance is effective, especially in politics. To evaluate opinion in terms of its effectiveness, in terms of its organization, or by the techniques used for its expression, results finally in a sociology of political participation. Tarde seems to waver between a test of quality and a test of effectiveness, but to the extent that effectiveness of action by public opinion is admitted—*i.e.*, the kind of communication and organization on which it rests—he has pointed in fact toward the idea of effective participation in making public decisions the primary characteristic of public opinion.

Opinion which is light and passing is contrasted by Tarde with tradition. The power of opinion today, he said, is against tradition, but more seriously this power also constricts reason. Thus, the preservation of the rational element in opinion is of the highest importance. The rational process can be observed in the transformation of individual opinion into social opinion. This process through the ages essentially has been carried out by conversation or the spoken word, until the invention of the modern press. The press has enhanced the power of numbers, it has worked toward the limitation of intelligence and character through the wide extension of opinion, and at the same time it has limited the power of governments. Parliaments, for example, are quite different institutions today than they were before the invention of printing. Conversation, to Tarde, was still important, and he cites with approval a letter of Diderot to Necker in 1775, which stated that opinion in its origin is the product of a small number of people who think before they talk.*

IV

Graham Wallas' influence on English-speaking scholars has been powerful on at least one point—his insistence on a re-examination of the intellectualist theory of politics. Wallas demonstrated that "human nature" as a set of psychological facts had often more to do with a political decision than carefully reasoned argument. For Americans, therefore, Wallas' *Human Nature in Politics,* in 1908, was a great turning point in the study of public opinion, for never since then has the rationalist view of public opinion—*i.e.,* the optimistic assertion that public opinion grows more intelligent and rational with each new year of our national progress—been expressed with the same fervor as was frequent with Wallas' precursors such as Lecky. The shadow of irrational opinion has been over us ever since, as well as the recognition that "the empirical art of politics consists largely in the creation of opinion by the deliberate exploitation of subconscious non-rational preferences." † In later years Wallas was disturbed by the enthusiastic acceptance of his ideas, and he was obliged to urge his readers to recognize that there was, after all, a rational element in the public mind which could be and often was embodied in public decisions.

If, in 1908, a protest was needed against the intellectualist assumptions of liberalism, by 1920 Wallas saw that, with the dis-

* Tarde said, "L'Opinion, dirons-nous, est un groupe momentané et, plus ou moins, logique de jugements qui, répondant à des problemes actuellement posés, se trouvent reproduits en nombreux exemplaires dans des personnes du même pays, du même temps, de la même societé." See Gabriel Tarde, *L'Opinion et la Foule* (2nd ed., 1904), p. 68.

† See Graham Wallas, *Human Nature in Politics* (3rd ed., 1921), 118 ff.

illusionments of war and industrial society, the danger was that people might be too tired to make the effort to see social ends and calculate the rational means by which they might be realized. Yet who can deny that the whole impact of psychology on the man who believes in democracy has been to make him a little more fatigued than he would have admitted himself to be in a period when faith in "reason" was stronger?

Wallas' original thesis was not, however, anti-democratic. His own feeling was that it should result in more realistic democratic politics. An examination of human nature in politics, he said, must begin with an attempt to overcome the "intellectualism" which results from the traditions of political science and from the mental habits of ordinary men. One must be aware of the attachment of citizens to symbols which take the place of complex sensations and memories. But when we have become conscious of the psychological process in politics, we are put on our guard against the exploitation of these processes by others. Moral purpose must not be lost in concern solely with psychological exploitation, and education must be a counterweight against "the advancing art of political exploitation." Yet there must be a re-examination of traditional ideas, especially of the principles of representative democracy. Prophetically, Wallas argued that the consciousness of psychology in politics will cause some to return to Plato's idea of a despotic government carried on by a trained class or elite. However, good government does require consent, and consent cannot be treated solely in terms of intellectualist principles of politics.

Can we recognize the weakness of men, in terms of psychological process, and still retain a high moral flavor in government? Wallas was not frightened of the recognition by political leaders of the emotional nature of the public, of its passions and desires, and its erratic behavior. Great political leaders always have had such recognition of the facts of mass behavior. Bolingbroke referred to "that staring timid creature man." * Yet, in his

* Cited from *Letters on the Spirit of Patriotism* (ed. of 1785), 70.

assessment of man as an animal, Bolingbroke resembled Plato, Swift, and Darwin. And Disraeli, the greatest of Bolingbroke's disciples, affirmed that we are not indebted to reason for the great achievements of man, for man is truly great only when he acts from the passions which appeal to the imagination. Wallas hoped that instead of Bismarckian and Mazzinian national homogeneity, we might create a political emotion based on realistic recognition of the justified unlikenesses of human beings. Darwin, he thought, might have provided such an idea, if he had not also proposed the struggle for life as a moral duty.

Wallas concentrated his attention on the individual, but his conclusions are not wide of the propositions held by those whose interest is the crowd or the mass. In both instances, students of politics have held that intellectualist liberalism and conservatism must be revised to fit the facts of life. And, in both instances, the central problem of the modern state, its corruption and its reform, is a psychological issue, to be solved in such terms.

Arthur Christensen, the Danish student of political psychology, has argued that political morality is at a low level under all forms of government, because politics is founded on crowds, and the ethical development of crowds proceeds more slowly than that of individuals. The rational investigation of crowds is, therefore, one of the first issues of politics, and Christensen trod the paths opened by Le Bon and Tarde at the end of the nineteenth century.*

While suggestion to Christensen is the basis on which individuals are made into crowds, a political outlook is determined in part by the temperamental differences which divide individuals into conservatives and progressives. Christensen held that, although social suggestion is founded on tradition and public opinion, and on contributions of the dead and the living, the crowd soul is only the sum of the single souls who compose it. While the mental life of crowds is very primitive, it is connected directly with parliamentarism, the most powerful of the social suggestions of our time. Liberalism has proposed both liberty and

* Arthur Christensen, *Politics and Crowd Morality*, trans. from the Danish by A. C. Curtis (1915).

equality, essentially contradictory ideas, but it is equality that has been the most powerful stimulus leading to democratic and parliamentary government. Still, our political history is dull, since it is primarily the history of the number of votes cast in given elections.

Christensen believed that the allegiance of the parliament to the crowd is demonstrated by the parliamentary tendency to ask, not what is the correct policy, but what is the will of the crowd. The politician under modern conditions is the leader of the crowd. Thus political forms which originated in democratic idealism are moving on to other forms, since there is a continual loss of idealism, and a continuous rise of the techniques of propaganda. According to Christensen, even whole states are crowds, enormous and heterogeneous crowds, governed by primitive feelings. There can be no development of a common authority superior to states, and Christensen felt, even in his own time prior to World War I, that psychologically the state seemed to have reached its ethical limits. Because individual morality had outstripped crowd morality by many centuries, politics and ethics were mutually exclusive. Crowds have no feeling of responsibility. Thus the recognized state morality is the generally recognized crowd morality.

Yet while the individual in his development inevitably outstrips the crowd, the crowd is capable of development. Public opinion—that is, with Christensen, the opinion of the crowd—absorbs new elements from individual morality. Public opinion is the bond of union between the individual and the crowd. But because of its interaction with the individual's opinion, public opinion may change faster than the accepted or practiced morality of the state. Public opinion, built on suggestion, affects the state strongly if it is united; but when it is divided, state action in democracies tends to take the more conservative opinion. In Christensen's view, the individual is the most advanced element in society, the crowd is less advanced, though it draws from individual morality through public opinion, and the state in its actual practices may be even more retarded and primitive than the crowd. Public opinion is the battering-ram that can force the crowd toward ethical development, and public opinion can be regarded as a kind of unofficial crowd morality, that is, state morality.

In contrast to these ideas, the American psychologist William McDougall insisted on the superior quality of group opinion. From Aristotle on, thinkers have been divided on this issue, for while Aristotle believed that a collective judgment may be superior to an individual one, the impact of social psychology has been in general to deny the higher intellectual value of collective judgments. While McDougall rejected German idealism, he affirmed the social nature of morality, and he cited Francis Bradley, the English philosopher, with approval on this point. Public opinion exists only in the minds of individuals, said McDougall, but it is the product of a collective mental life. In a healthy nation the standards of public opinion are higher than those of the individual in regard to right, justice, and tolerance. And this opinion with its high standards is more than the algebraic sum of individual opinions. In particular matters the judgments of public opinion may be higher than those of the average individual, even the best or most superior individuals. "There exists in every great nation the vague influence we call public opinion, which is the great upholder of right and justice, which rewards virtue and condemns vice and selfishness." *

But the true explanation of the superiority of public opinion is "the basal fact that the moral sentiments are essentially altruistic, while the immoral and non-moral sentiments are in the main self-regarding." Public opinion in a well-organized nation is largely the work of leading personalities, and it conforms with the best more often than the average. Great abilities, McDougall argued, are seldom aimed at the degradation of public opinion. However, public opinion is the informal organization of national deliberative life, while the formal organization of national deliberation, as in democratic government, may either fail or be successful in bringing the best minds to high influence in society.

* William McDougall, *The Group Mind* (1920), 264, *passim.*

Both the formal and the informal organization of public opinion tend to raise the collective mental process above the average. At best, the organization of collective mental life may embody the national tradition in political, religious, and scientific culture.

McDougall believed it was clear that emphasis on collective mental life means the rejection of the individualistic theory of public opinion. Public opinion to McDougall cannot be the mere summation of individual opinions. The political leader must be more than a delegate of so many individuals, for he must seek to raise national deliberation to a plane higher than a mere crowd. Public opinion is not a mere sum of individual opinions upon any particular question; it is rather the expression of the attitude of mind which prevails throughout the nation "and owes its quality far more to the influence of the dead than the living, being the expression of the moral sentiments firmly and traditionally established in a more refined form in the minds of the leaders of public opinion than in the average citizen." * Thus public opinion lives in the realm of moral judgments, and in fact may have little to do with the details of specific legislation. Controversy is, therefore, excluded as the primary representation of public opinion, and McDougall's portrayal of public opinion is much like Bauer's depiction of organic opinion. For McDougall, public opinion is essentially collective, it is the fruit and the labor of the group mind, and its evaluations emerge slowly and change slowly. Every enduring group has its own public opinion, though it is still a part of national opinion.†

* *Ibid.,* 271-272.

† McDougall argues that most highly organized groups display such a collective mental life that one may properly call it a group mind. The group becomes, therefore, more than the sum of the individuals composing it. The unorganized crowd is simple, emotional and fickle; but on the higher levels of organization these qualities are superseded by the higher qualities McDougall associates with public opinion. A high level of public opinion suggests the problem of how to prevent the emergence of crowd reactions. Cf. William Orton, "News and Opinion," *American Journal of Sociology,* XXXIII (1927), 80-93.

V

No one may properly consider the modern problem of public opinion without taking into account the Freudian analysis. To some, one of the great demonic forces in modern life is analytic psychology, since it can be used to explain away any pretense of rationality in human behavior. But the fact may be that as argument, Freudian analysis proves in effect more than it intends, and those who wish to exploit psychological power for the consolidation of political power have no need to pay attention to the therapeutic aspirations Freudians profess. Since Freud's ideas have entered generally into the thinking of political leaders, advertising men, motivation researchers, and public opinion surveyors, one extremely significant—and unexpected—result is that issues of public opinion have begun to be regarded as more individual than collective in nature. For the concept of an irrational crowd which submerged the potentially rational individual has given place to the idea of the individual with subconscious motivations. The source of irrationality in politics has become the single person, and the irrationality of the crowd is a reflection of what is true of each single individual. If mass action is irrational, it is because the individual is irrational.*

Psychoanalysis is clearly one of the most revolutionary of the forces at work in modern society. It is a force or a technique for organizing thought which may be used for practically every political or social purpose. It may be used in art to generate modesty and understanding of individual tragedy, and it may sharpen our perception of the inmost life of the individual. But it may also be used to restrict the idea that man has a free will or a moral nature, or that his reason is a creative force in understanding and making the world. It may be used to sustain those in power who have the interest and happiness of men at heart, but it may also be used by those who cynically seek power. The believer in

* See Ferdinand Tönnies-Curtin, "Die Grosse Menge und das Volk," *Schmollers Jahrbuch*, 44 (1920), 317-345.

democracy may use it, but the tyrant is much more likely to. It may be employed both by the revolutionary and by the conservative.*

None can deny that the Freudian theory of mind has an impressive range of applications to politics and to the examination of the nature of political opinions, judgments, or evaluations. It is not the logical structure of an opinion with which the Freudian concerns himself, nor its validity, but the inner and subconscious motivations which give rise to it and so provide the duration, extension, and intensity that the opinion may have. Since the Freudian does not ask about the validity of an idea, but only about its origin and function in the individual, the proponent of democracy who is concerned with the moral order of a society must insist that the validity of an idea is just as important as any other quality it may have. But inquiry concerning the truth of an idea restores the whole principle of rational judgment and moral or philosophical value. To ask whether an idea is true, restricts and limits immediately the psychological approach, whether or not that approach is Freudian. Psychology may bypass reason, but it cannot demonstrate by its own method alone that rational principles are impossible to reach or that they do not exist. Only when psychology is used in connection with value theory does it support the democratic approach to social life.†

* See Thomas Mann, "Freud and the Future," *The Saturday Review of Literature* (July 25, 1936), 3 ff. See also *Factors Determining Human Behavior* (1937), for C. G. Jung, "Psychological Factors Determining Human Behavior;" and Bronislaw Malinowski, "Culture as a Determinant of Behavior." Neither of these writers is impressed by free will or man's tendency to believe in the omnipotence of thought. Jules Rassak, *Psychologie de l'Opinion et de la Propaganda Politique* (1927), presents Freudianism from the left-wing point of view. He argues that the socialist is too rational; subconscious values must be used in attacking the privileged classes. A successful revolution requires that in the long-run, ideas supporting the revolution must enter into the subconscious, particularly those that lead men to accept collective rather than individual values. After force in a revolution, the work of the psychiatrist begins, for political opinions depend primarily on the subconscious and unconscious sentiments.

† See Harold D. Lasswell, *Psychopathology and Politics* (1930); *Politics,*

Freudian analysis is profoundly different from the logical approach. Unlike the principle of logical thinking, the Freudian method utilizes a technique of free fantasy, whereby the analyst may penetrate the motivation of individual opinion and behavior. Thus we see irrational technique being used, in theory at least, to attain a sense of the rational, as in the use of dreams to discover the traumatic incident hidden in the subconscious mind. Analytic psychology has assumed that the cure for irrationality of personality is not the logical penetration of behavior, but a round-about method of causing the hidden factors in the subconscious to reveal themselves. Moreover, the significance of political opinions cannot be grasped apart from the private motives they symbolize. The psychological view therefore must see politics as an arena of the irrational; politics is the process by which the irrational bases of society are brought out into the open, or a process by which such bases are used for the attainment of power.

Particularly important in the psychological analysis of politics is the study of symbols, because opinions become symbolic of individual motivation and they find expression in extremely diverse forms of behavior. Symbols are used in the displacement and rationalization of individual motives because of their ambiguity in relation to individual experience, and because of their general circulation. According to this view, the state may be described as a universal father substitute, image or surrogate; * the authority of the father may be transferred, thus, to the state, and various obscure or unseen motivations may be important in

Who Gets What, When, How (1936). During World War II his work in ideological intelligence suggested that psychological technique was being used in support of values, *i.e.*, American war aims, that were first of all rationally justified. Still, the question of how any value is to be so justified is not faced, since the principle of psychological technique is, or seems to be, his exclusive concern.

* Or a mother surrogate. See Sebastian de Grazia, "A Note on the Psychological Position of the Chief Executive," *Psychiatry*, VIII (1945), 267 ff. See also de Grazia, *The Political Community; A Study of Anomie* (1948).

shaping individual opinions of conservatism or radicalism. Such a conception regards political ideas as often almost wordless—that is, the drives of the subconscious mind are not formulated clearly in verbal symbols. Spengler also once urged that real ideas are wordless, and his statement is in close agreement with the psychoanalytical principle of the wordless drives of the subconscious mind.*

Among our own contemporaries, Lasswell has defined the public as composed of all those who follow affairs and expect to determine policy by discussion and by other means short of coercion. Lasswell considers that the public by nature has a common focus of attention, and there is consensus on democratic or constitutional principles, as well as a zone of tolerance for certain types of conflicts.† But in the modern world, politics is not the only avenue to power and status, and perhaps for many types of personality it is not even the chief one. The diversity of roads to power and status establishes differences in the types of personality in government and stimulates different types of organization for effective opinion. There has arisen a type of agitator who has an exaggerated belief in the efficacy of formulas and gestures in getting results, and his emotional transference or displacement is abstract in its nature. Civil servants are likely to show other personality traits. But to many the right to vote gives vent to personal antagonism toward rulers or toward authority they regard as disagreeable. The political man, the member of the public—as seen by Lasswell—begins with his private motives, and often these motives arise from maladjustments to the environment; these motives are then displaced to some public objects more ambiguous and universal than private motives; and

* Oswald Spengler, *The Hour of Decision,* trans. from the German (1934), 36.

† Lasswell, *Psychopathology,* 192; Herbert Goldhamer, "Public Opinion and Personality," *The American Journal of Sociology,* LV (1950), 346 ff, notes that while public opinion requires attention to public objects, personality characteristics profoundly affect the amount of attention that is given.

these displacements are rationalized in terms of the public interest for purposes of political action.*

Psychological study can be either a support or a substitute for logical and rational inquiry. In its description of behavior, psychological study may undermine the traditional arguments for a democratic society; but, on the other hand, the empirical and quantitative student of public opinion may seek to modify more abstract conceptions of public opinion by uniting fact and value in a common synthesis. Value may emerge from facts scientifically gathered—a process very different from any procedure possible to those philosophical views which require complete separation of fact and value. One of the more impressive of the efforts in our time to unite quantitative study with the theory of public opinion has been made by Bernard Berelson. While it is easy to overstate what speculative minds have insisted is essential in democratic theory and practice, it is also possible to create a moderate synthesis, using the latest psychological data. The issue is to bridge the gap between scientific procedures and values held by those who defend a free public opinion. Though the gap may seem to be widening today, it is possible that in the field of public opinion study some reconciliation may take place, provided the quantitative methods of study are not extrapolated to a denial of value inquiry.

The contemporary inquiry into the "personality" of the interviewee is, no doubt, grounded in an approach related to Freudianism, or at least to the view that an individual may not be conscious of the ideas he really holds or their relations within his personal system of thought. Berelson first insists that in a democracy all personalities are not suited for democratic life. The "authoritarian" personality does not fit, though traditional democratic speculation has assumed, more or less, that almost anyone may be trained to the practice of rational judgment. But there

* See Lasswell, "The Measurement of Public Opinion," *The American Political Science Review*, XXV (1931), 311-326; *Democracy Through Public Opinion* (1941).

can be no rational judgment for the personality distorted by prejudiced or fascist ideas. Thus a psychiatric issue is organic with the training of the mind to be logical in its conclusions.* Second, Berelson comments on the theory of participation, noting that in practice, voting, or other forms of political participation, have not been as extensive as the democratic theory of the last century assumed they would become. Less than one third of the electorate is really interested in politics. Still, non-voters, for whatever reason, may constitute a cushion for the intensity of interest shown by others. Third, Berelson points out that information and knowledge are needed by the democratic citizen, while the polls and surveys show that in fact twenty percent of the electorate is almost totally uninformed. By taking these situations into account, and by essaying improvement where possible, the "model" of democracy, and the theory of democratic communication can be restated. But Berelson believes that it will be an organic restatement, in that combination is necessary between the values demonstrated by logic and philosophy, and the information offered by empirical investigation.†

* T. W. Adorno and others, *The Authoritarian Personality* (1950), one of the "Studies in Prejudice" sponsored by the American Jewish Committee. Its methods have been subjected to intensive scrutiny and sharp defense. See, for example, E. T. Prothro and Levon Melikian, "The California Public Opinion Scale in an Authoritarian Culture," *The Public Opinion Quarterly*, XVII (Fall, 1953), 353 ff; Morris Janowitz and Dwaine Marvick, "Authoritarianism and Political Behavior," *ibid.*, XVII (Summer, 1953), 185 ff; Richard Christie and Marie Jahoda (editors), *Studies in the Scope and Method of "The Authoritarian Personality"* (1954); Charles D. Farris, " 'Authoritarianism' as a Political Behavior Variable," *The Journal of Politics*, 18 (February, 1956), 61 ff.

† Bernard Berelson, "Democratic Theory and Public Opinion," *The Public Opinion Quarterly*, XVI (Fall, 1952), 313 ff. Also, Morris Janowitz and Dwaine Marvick, "Competition Pressure and Democratic Consent," *The Public Opinion Quarterly*, XIX (Winter, 1955-1956), 381 ff; Elihu Katz and others, *Personal Influence; the Part Played by the People in the Flow of Mass Communication* (1955) (the Decatur Study).

One of the problems of creating an informed public opinion is the very complicated issue of the right of access to public documents. There is, for example, very little right to documents on federal matters, and no right of access whatever to federal administrative documents. Public welfare considerations are prominent in access to information on juvenile delinquency

There are many psychological approaches to opinion other than the Freudian, but the Freudian approach in its many variations has been a profoundly revolutionary interpretation. One is tempted to feel that the advertising and public relations firms, whose services command startlingly large sums of money, go back in their foundation to the insistence that men have motivations below the conscious level. The modern psychological revolution seems to be in essence a "manipulative approach" to the content of a mind or minds, but the manipulative approach goes against the ancient rationalist proposition held by generations of philosophers who believed that force or coercion cannot work on the mind, and that the convictions of the individual and his rational perception of the world are inviolable. We are not ready, it would seem, to surrender the principle of Plato and Aristotle, Aquinas, Spinoza, and Locke that there is a rational core in man which inevitably resists the forceful or insidious outside formation of conviction or judgment. It is natural and rational for men to attribute their actions to love of self, but it is also natural to recognize that love of others and the existence of a common good are also effective forces. The manipulation of the mind is dangerous, but it would seem that on opinions grounded in depth the techniques of manipulation are not as effective as some have thought might be the case.

It is easy for the critic to see the danger signals. People are over-organized and pressed on all sides by the demands of the complicated operations necessary in modern civilization; propaganda is a menace to rational political judgment, and dictatorships have explored to the limit the power of propaganda. In the marketing of goods there is a growing use of psychiatry and the techniques of behavioral science to encourage the sale of merchandise, and special use is made of a depth approach which exploits the desire for status. The professional persuaders grow bolder each day in their invasion of the privacy of our minds.

---

and rape cases. The states have passed many statutes dealing with public knowledge in matters of public record. See Harold L. Cross, *The People's Right to Know: Legal Access to Public Records and Proceedings* (1953).

Those engaged in motivation research, whether in academic life, in research organizations, or in industry, sit down together to explore the state of their science. Communists and totalitarians have used a complicated system of "brainwashing," and are able to induce false confessions by provoking nervous breakdowns and distortions of individual perception or suspension of the normal concern for reality. Beyond this, there is a flood of drugs which affect the nervous system, and in turn the understanding of the world, together with the content and intensity of belief. People are taught in their sleep, images are engineered, and the theory of subliminal perception plays a role in the strange modern assault on the quality of opinion. Education for conformity moves on apace. Those who disagree may be charged with being victims of mental illness and in need of treatment for mental health by those engaged in "social engineering." The untoward ideological or political position is often taken as a sign that a person may be well along on the road toward mental illness.*

Psychology serves both for the preservation of rational opinion and for the stimulation of irrational behavior. The therapeutic value of psychology cannot be denied; it is certainly acceptable to help the marginal man make some sort of adjustment to his society. What we have been commenting on, however, is the revo-

* There will be no effort to cite literature in detail, but if one wishes to keep up with new research adventures of our time, the following are exceptionally valuable: *Prod* (Political Research: Organization and Design); *The Public Opinion Quarterly*, in which nearly all relevant material is listed, including the summaries of the proceedings of the American Association for Public Opinion Research; *Items*, published by the Social Science Research Council, is a high-level report on developments in research method. The most widely read books in recent times which deal with the manipulation of opinion are Vance Packard, *The Hidden Persuaders* (1957); *The Status Seekers* (1959); also, Nicholas Samstag, *Persuasion for Profit* (1957). Stanley Kelley, Jr., *Professional Public Relations and Political Power* (1956), has stressed the influence of public relations experts in political campaigns. Perhaps one should recall William H. Whyte, *The Organization Man* (1956), and the literature it has provoked, as well as William Lynch, *The Image Industries* (1959). There is a large body of important literature on advertising, but see particularly O. A. Pease, *The Responsibilities of American Advertising; Private Control and Public Influence, 1920-1940* (1958).

lutionary use of techniques of persuasion on what might otherwise be called normal people. The "social engineers" seem to accept certain ideological positions, and to consider the critic or the deviant simply a case for therapy. Still, democracy and constitutionalism, the rights of man, and the principle of the consent of the governed are rooted in the belief that man has a moral nature and a rational capacity which can be expressed politically for the common good. It is one thing to recognize that rational ideals have not been attained, or that high moral standards in civilized life are yet but goals or ideals. It is quite another to place the irrational aspects of behavior at the center of politics and to behave as if the truth or falsity of principles is irrelevant.

CHAPTER 7

Systematic Techniques

I

If we assume that man has a reasonable, moral nature which is expressed in politics, there are appropriate techniques to be used in reaching this goal. If we assume, on the other hand, that because of the psychological nature of men, the quality of opinion is inherently irrational, there are appropriate techniques to implement this conviction. The history of modern democracy and constitutional government is in measure the development of techniques which rely upon the rational capability of citizens. In contrast, the attack upon democracy uses an opposite body of techniques which assume the irrational nature of at least a very considerable portion of the people. In support of democracy, political technicians have assumed it is possible to bring the qualitatively satisfactory aspect of opinion closer to governmental decision. In the opposite case, political technique has been used to corrupt democratic procedures on the theory that it is the duty of those in power to mold the individual citizen to the decisions of the few. On the one hand, democracy assumes majority decision to be ultimately a reflection of assumptions which are rationally justifiable; and, on the other hand, the opposing technicians regard majority decision as manufactured by the engineering of social approval. When propaganda or the manipulation of symbols important to ideological intelligence fails, censorship or the elimination of ideological opposition is effected. If closing the ordinary means of communication does not succeed, then suppression and coercion may be resorted to, and, within the effective limits of these techniques, political ends may be sustained with mass support.*

II

The essential question for those who believe in democracy is whether something may be done that will assist the reasonableness of citizens to emerge in concrete political situations. Broadly, the democrat has proposed that education will elevate the functioning of democracy. It is for this reason that mass education has been one of the tenets of the democrat, and it is for this reason that popular or mass education has been almost universally supported from the middle of the last century down to the present time. It has been believed by progressives since the eighteenth century that education will enable the people to accept the findings of science and to understand social problems.

Education has generally been associated with the principle that an informed citizenry is necessary to rational participation in politics. From a common school education which sought to stamp out illiteracy, we have moved in more modern times to the idea of education in social questions, that is, to a broad knowledge of the world around us. But when educational techniques have sought to inspire a particular kind of political behavior, *i.e.*, the approval of specific policies or ideas, the basic conflicts of modern society have separated education from the general democratic consensus. Thus education reaches a point where it is charged with the overtones of propaganda.† But no

* See H. D. Lasswell, *Democracy Through Public Opinion* (1941). On censorship, see Lasswell, "The Relation of Ideological Intelligence to Public Policy," *Ethics*, LIII (1942), 25 ff; James R. Mock, *Censorship, 1917* (1941); James R. Mock and others, "The Limits of Censorship: A Symposium," *The Public Opinion Quarterly*, VI (1942), 3 ff; Edmond Taylor, *The Strategy of Terror* (rev. ed., 1942).

† According to Ernst Kris and Nathan Leites, education deals with non-

believer in the possibility of rational decisions by the masses has been willing to deny the pre-eminent importance of citizenship education. For education is still the background technique of democracy and popular government; a free citizen is one who knows something of the world around him, and he is ideally one whose mind is not distorted by the forces either of propaganda or censorship.

The democratic aspiration toward education has expressed itself on two levels. On the one hand, there is the general type of education which instills the principles of Western civilization and enables the personality to function in variable capacities. On the other hand, there is the specific type of education which enables the individual to do better a certain kind of work. As of old, we have both the *artes liberales* and the *artes serviles.** Professional and technical training permeates our whole society, and there is practically no important profession today which does not require a long process of training for its neophytes. One can say, indeed, that a high level of training is part of the work of civilization, but it is not always clear that technical and vocational education is democratic, because the admission to a career in "management" in a modern corporation tends to be limited to those who have a college diploma. Technical education, such as training on the job, often merely hardens class lines.

Freedom of thought and discussion, associated with freedom in political participation, must be the basis of democratic public opinion. In education, this has meant that individuals may seek the kind of philosophical and religious education they want. It has meant that freedom is freedom to choose one's metaphysics, and it has meant the right to make for oneself the decisions important in one's life. Freedom has meant in education the right

---

controversial issues, while propaganda attempts to influence the attitudes of large numbers of people on controversial issues of relevance to a group. See their "Trends in Twentieth Century Propaganda," included in *The Process and Effects of Mass Communication*, ed. by Wilbur Schramm (1954), 488.

* For an invigorating discussion of classical liberal arts education, see Albert Jay Nock, *Memoirs of a Superfluous Man* (1943), 96.

to choose a system of values from the riches of the liberal arts. But it has also meant that freedom to establish schools is essential in the freedom of the mind.

The technical and vocational training offered in higher education indicates the specialization and the group pressures which characterize a highly developed society. As new groups attain professional status they turn to the universities to train and select their personnel, whether as civil servants, the employees of business, or simply those admitted to the practice of a given profession. At the same time, the humanities and the social sciences are regarded as educators of the soul, as providing the breadth of personal perception necessary to the well-rounded individual. Moreover, the educational process, as democracy views it, does not stop with the professional certificate; for adult education, both in a general and in a professional sense, continues far into life.

The democratic manner of life is committed to education, and its philosophy of progress remains closely tied to educational progress. Rational citizenship now, as in earlier times, is held to depend on the educational development of the personality. Democratic governments will, therefore, continue to spend huge sums of money to provide education for those who are willing to make the effort. Education is central in the techniques of freedom.

III

Even the most ardent defender of popular government, or of government by public opinion, must recognize there are proper techniques for the handling of mass hysteria, the phenomena of the crowd, and there are times, such as in war, when a democracy must resort to the iron curtains of propaganda and censorship. His acceptance of this situation does not mean that the believer in democracy has abandoned his belief and become a totalitarian, for devices designed to control irrationalism in politics are subordinated to the larger rational procedures of organized civil life. The focus is still on the idea of rational progress.

We are faced with the fact that conditions may arise which require even the most eager democracies to control the mass of their citizens. Psychological techniques may be used to enlist the emotions on the side of educational effort, but they may, likewise, be used to control the aberrations of individuals and groups. They may become debased techniques for the manufacture of a distorted and vicious consensus. One may say that most of the techniques used by totalitarian regimes are also sometimes necessary for the preservation of democracy, but one must also say that the standard for their use is a definition of the goals of democratic life. A mob is sometimes a fact of existence, but it is a matter of the deepest principle whether a whole citizenry is consciously made into a mob, or whether mob phenomena are limited in their influence on public policy. Hearnshaw reports that the word "mob" came into use at the time of the conflict surrounding the Test Act in 1678 in the reign of Charles II. Shaftesbury was regarded as the leader of the London mob, a word which came from the Latin *mobile vulgus,* the fickle crowd.* Mobs or crowds were then, however, no new thing, nor can one say that the techniques of dealing with political mobs or crowds are particularly new. However, in a physical sense, the "mob" has all but ceased to exist in modern times. In the democracies, there are other ways for the people to express their resentments than by taking to the streets; while in the totalitarian states, modes of repression are such that spontaneous mobs do not form.

Bauer has emphasized the continuity of public opinion and the change in techniques of publicity, or one might say the evolution of techniques for dealing with man in the mass. Many of these techniques have remained as steady throughout the centuries as has the very existence of generally shared opinions.

* F. J. C. Hearnshaw, *Conservatism in England* (1933), 98. Cf. Christopher Hibbert, *King Mob, The Story of Lord George Gordon and the London Riots of 1780* (1958).

The conservative, it is said, likes to read Plutarch and Thucydides because a sense of historical repetition arises from the description of the great movements of the masses, and the techniques that have been used either for the mass movement or against it. In this view, then, the improvement of the means of communication is incidental to the hard psychological substratum which constantly emerges and even dominates or directs new techniques of publicity, communication, and mass control.

Mass phenomena, therefore, evoke the systematic techniques appropriate to their control or direction, and all regimes must use such devices as the occasion may arise. Democracies as well as autocracies must understand the problem of the mass or crowd. Group hysteria is a rare but objective fact of politics. It is a duty of the statesman to understand and to overcome hatred and illusion through his knowledge of the mass soul—as Baschwitz pointed out.* The statesman's task is at its height in war and revolution, for it is here that the techniques of propaganda, censorship, and coercion can be most useful or most detrimental. It is those who oppose a particular war, or who favor a particular revolution, who also have the strongest feelings about the psychological qualities of mass action. It is they who study most carefully the systematic techniques which emerge into full bloom in these times.

When a war is opposed, it is charged that support for war or foreign policy is manufactured through a conscious exploitation of the psychological weakness of men in the mass. Those who support such policies may agree that support is highly emotional rather than rational, but in such cases emotional behavior is defended because it is regarded as a support for the rational propositions leadership has laid down for the guidance of public decision. In either case, the existence of mass emotional action is correlated with the use of systematic techniques in relation to public opinion. In 1917 James Harvey Robinson spoke of "the still small voice of the herd." Quoting Bertrand Russell, who

* Kurt Baschwitz, *Der Massenwahn, Seine Wirkung und Seine Beherrschung* (1923).

opposed World War I, he observed that "men fear thought as they fear nothing else on earth. . . ." He approved Trotter's contemporary argument that the only psychology is social psychology, for beliefs are the products of society and man always listens to the voice of the herd. Trotter emphasized human gregariousness and suggestibility as explanations for a large part of the furniture of the mind. If we think we are harkening to the voice of God, we may be sure that we are listening to the voice of the herd. The more confident we are, the less reason there probably is for our opinion. Robinson himself contended that obedience to the herd is more dangerous in modern times than it ever has been, for it means the acceptance of preposterous anachronisms and a refusal to consider the lessons of experience. Mental instability is unsuited to the modern scientific era.*

Yet the revolutionist cannot condemn mass action or mob hysteria, if such action supports the revolution which he believes will bring the better tomorrow. A revolutionist, if he accepts a Marxian analysis of society, for example, must look on the right kind of mob as a highly progressive force.† For then it is the task of the revolutionary elite to lead the mob in the direction of predetermined goals. Crowd psychologists, like Sighele and Le Bon, are in this view highly superficial, for they exclude any defense of the revolutionary mass aroused by particular historical junctures. According to this way of thinking, a scientific and sociological view of the masses must be provided from the study of historical and revolutionary situations. Revolutions come with the help at least of the masses, but Geiger observes that *die Masse erwächst aus der sozialen Dekadenzerscheinung der Mechanisierung und ist einer Faktoren der Überwindung dieser Mechanisierung*. Thus, a relation of social classes is the proper tech-

* See James Harvey Robinson, "The Still Small Voice of the Herd," *Political Science Quarterly*, XXXII (1917), 312-319, a review of Bertrand Russell, *Why Men Fight* (1917), and W. Trotter, *Instincts of the Herd in Peace and War* (1916).

† A. Rossi, *A Communist Party in Action*, trans. and ed. by Willmoore Kendall (1949).

nique for explaining the herd, and it likewise provides for the technical direction of the masses.* The historical value of the masses, to this school of thought, is simply the historic value of revolutions, and the social revolution may restore the relation between value and form in society. The mass evokes a spirit of protest from *Gemeinschaft* against *Gesellschaft*, against the mechanization of social relations, and the enslavement of men in society. The crowd psychologists are superficial because imitation, contagion, suggestion, and other factors assume the existence of groups and they do not in any case explain their prior origin. In no case, however, does this view hold that the historical function of the masses can be explained in purely intellectual terms; the non-intellectual is not always or necessarily retrogressive, if the historical situation demands mass revolution.

Not even a revolutionist, not even a scientific rationalist like Robinson, can protest, however, against the study of pattern or techniques of control in mass action. The leader must foresee the moment when mass discontent breaks away from democratic and constitutional procedures, the signs of the times must be known to him, and he must be ready to restore balance to group action, whatever his philosophy of history may be.†

IV

Between education and propaganda stands the systematic technique of publicity. Like education or propaganda, it is an attempt to reach the population through the media of mass communication. It arose along with the consciousness of propaganda, but in a more direct sense it is an outgrowth of modern advertising. After World War I, there were hundreds of articles in magazines and journals on the techniques of publicity. Each

* Theodor Geiger, *Die Masse und Ihre Aktion* (1926), 38.

† See Hadley Cantril, "Causes and Control of Riots and Panics," *The Public Opinion Quarterly*, VII (1943), 669-679. Here a code of behavior is proposed by the social psychologist for dealing with mobs, riots, and panics in Europe after World War II. Also, Saul K. Padover, "Patterns of Assassination in Occupied Territory," *loc. cit.*, pp. 680-683.

pressure group, interest, or functionally organized group, conducted self-examinations and clinics on its publicity techniques, and they studied how best they might put themselves in a favorable light before those outside the group. Educational circles tried to "sell" the public school to the citizens; public health interests tried to persuade everyone that public health measures should be supported; business, professions, corporations, universities—every conceivable group did its best to develop an effective system of publicity. As the techniques of publicity emerged, so did each organization's awareness of the value of public relations; and the new profession of the public relations counsel made its appearance in American life. In the discussion of public relations, the experts considered themselves propagandists—though they were at the same time propagandists who were doing a vital public service.

Publicity exists solely for the purpose of changing, directing, and coloring public opinion. The public is usually regarded as those who participate, or who could be induced to participate in some action. Opinion itself is regarded as the attitudes and states of mind of the public toward the given institution or institutions. Public opinion, in turn, is seen as a collection of individual opinions. The individual's opinion is a result of his history and his present situation. Publicity is, thus, effective when it can reorient the experiences of the individual in such a way that his actions will be different in future situations.

The first recognition of the effectiveness of publicity seems to have come following the exposure of the trusts during the administration of Theodore Roosevelt. Edward L. Bernays has noted that in 1908 T. N. Vail, president of American Telephone and Telegraph, used the term "public relations," and the new term began to displace the older use of "publicity." From 1919 to 1923 it became common to speak of the new profession as "counsel on public relations." * Big business, which hitherto had sometimes

* Bernays, *Public Relations* (1952), 70, 79. See also his "American Public Relations, A Short History," *Gazette* (International Journal of the Science of the Press), II (1956), 1 ff. In this article he states that the new

adhered to a policy of the "public be damned," was forced to find a means to soften the public indignation resulting from the scandals of the time, and it hit upon the idea of extensive publicity.

From that time on there was a gradual increase, especially in the United States, in the literature about publicity. Then, at the time of World War I, the great possibilities of publicity as a science were realized. There seems, also, to be a relation between attention paid to publicity and states of emergency or decline in business conditions, for fewer articles on publicity were published during the high prosperity periods of 1916-1919 and 1924-1928 than during depression periods. During the deep depression after 1929 there was a great increase in the listed articles, though it should be remembered that the indexing of periodical literature was also more extensive. However, there is some ground for concluding that a depression, with the resulting decrease in trade volume, creates an interest in reaching the public through publicity.

Yet the most significant change in our time is the recognition that public opinion is not simply to be obeyed or evaded, but that it may be molded and directed to suit given interests. The old term of "appeal to public opinion" was gradually replaced by the principle of "directing public opinion." It is to this end that publicity today is oriented with as much scientific accuracy as possible. Publicity men, public relations counselors, and the experts in advertising have liked to believe that the public may be made to think along any desired lines, and if their objectives could be attained in their entirety, public opinion would cease to be anything but a weapon or a force generated and controlled by the terrible few.*

---

profession of public relations arose between 1920 and 1929. The word appeared in *Webster's Dictionary* in 1920.

* According to H. L. Mencken, *The American Language, Supplement One* (1945), 578: "Public relations counsel was launched by Edward L. Bernays of New York, one of the most distinguished members of the fraternity. It had been preceded by *councillor in* (or *on*) *public relations*, occasionally used by Ivy L. Lee (1878-1934), another eminent publicist."

V

Propaganda is, of course, the major technique of control and direction of mass action on controversial issues in the modern world. After World War I, there was a sudden focus of attention on the techniques used in that war, and there was a powerful current of popular and intellectual disillusion.* The assumptions

---

See Ivy L. Lee, *Publicity* (1925). One of Lee's few publications is "The Court of Public Opinion," *Administration,* I (1921), 736-738, in which propaganda is classified as "underhand," while publicity is for the enlightenment of public opinion. Publicity is a "light-of-day proposition." But enlightenment requires skilled public relations counselors. L. W. Dodd, "Publicity," *The Saturday Review of Literature,* IV (1924), 113-114, said the earth had been made into "one stinking altar to publicity."

Among other works on this subject, see C. F. Higham, *Looking Forward; Mass Education Through Publicity* (1920); *Advertising; Its Use and Abuse* (1925). In Higham's mind, propaganda and publicity were about equivalent, but their main function was to spread information either about products or the values of civic life. Bernays has published, for example, *Crystallizing Public Opinion* (1923); *Propaganda* (1928); *Take Your Place at the Peace Table* (1945); *Public Relations* (1952); as editor, *The Engineering of Consent* (1955), and numerous articles. Bernays has used much of the psychological and social science material available on the nature of the public mind, assuming, indeed, the great power of emotional, instinctive, and irrational elements in individual judgment. In *Propaganda,* p. 37, he says: "The propagandist who specializes in interpreting enterprises and ideas to the public, and in interpreting the public to promulgators of new enterprises and ideas, has come to be known by the name of 'public relations counsel.'"

Government itself has got into the public relations business. It is assumed that the average man will not understand the problems of government, and that these problems must be presented in such a way that the public and special groups may understand and concur with the administration. Note F. E. Rourke, *Secrecy and Publicity; Dilemmas of Democracy* (1961).

* See Harold D. Lasswell, *Propaganda Techniques in the World War* (1927). On propaganda, consult in general James R. Mock and Cedric Larsen, *Words that Won the War, The Story of the Committee on Public Information, 1917-1919* (1939); Ellis Freeman, *Conquering the Man in the Street; a Psychological Analysis of Propaganda in War, Fascism, and Politics* (1940); F. E. Lumley, *The Propaganda Menace* (1933); Leonard W. Doob, *Propaganda, Its Psychology and Technique* (1935); F. C. Bart-

of propaganda as a technique rest largely on the belief that there is an irrational segment of political behavior. In any period of intense difference between people, the "opposition" will be charged with being hysterical, irrational, selfish, or other undesirable qualities will be attributed to it. Propaganda has been defined as a burning glass to focus the warmth of popular emotions on a specific issue, rather than being a *primum movens*. F. M. Cornford defined propaganda in 1922, in his subtle manner, as "that branch of the art of lying which consists in very nearly deceiving your friends without quite deceiving your enemies." *

Propaganda is a technique for the creation of opinion; it is the manipulation of symbols and not an appeal to reason, for it seeks to correlate symbol manipulation with emotional currents already present in the minds of the citizens. Propaganda assumes, indeed, that the intelligent man must work in a world that he recognizes to be non-intelligent.† Yet propaganda also assumes the oligarchical manipulation of symbols. Propaganda is directed by the few toward or at the many; it applies the iron law of oligarchy to the systematic techniques of public opinion. Thus, the arrival of propaganda and those who manipulate it has divided the citizen body into groups of different psychological capacity, for society is composed, then, of those who rationally

---

lett, *Political Propaganda* (1940); J. W. Albig, *Public Opinion* (1939), and *Modern Public Opinion* (1956); William Hummel and Keith Huntress, *The Analysis of Propaganda* (1949); D. L. Harter and John Sullivan, *Propaganda Handbook* (1953); Frank I. Cobb, "Public Opinion," in Senate Document No. 175, 66th Cong., 2nd sess. (1920); I. C. Willis, *England's Holy War* (1928); J. W. Meaney, "Propaganda as Psychical Coercion," *The Review of Politics*, XIII (1951), 64 ff.

* See Cornford's *Microcosmographia Academica, Being a Guide for the Young Academic Politician*, foreword by W. K. Guthrie (5th ed., 1953), foreword. See Lindley Fraser, *Propaganda* (1958), and Wilson Smith, *Professors and Public Ethics; Studies of Northern Moral Philosophers before the Civil War* (1956).

† See Lasswell, *Democracy Through Public Opinion* (1941); Wyndham Lewis, *The Art of Being Ruled* (1926); F. G. Wilson, *The Elements of Modern Politics* (1936), 266 ff.

use the irrationality of others in order to get power, and those who are the objects of such manipulative attention. If once there was a difference in the legal capacity of citizens, as in Roman law, the techniques of propaganda assume that the psychological capacity of men separates the oligarchical rulers from the masses who are ruled. Propaganda becomes a demonic force, a system of satanic techniques, that all men of political capacity are driven to use. Even the democratic rationalist must use propaganda as a counter-offensive weapon against anti-intellectual and anti-democratic forces.*

Propaganda is a body of systematic psychological techniques for acquiring control over opinions and the actions of its objects. It is, on the positive side, a system of appeals to the emotional responses which will favor a supported policy, and it assumes in this case that what is proposed is in degree emotionally harmonious with what already exists in a segment of the popular mind. On the negative side, propaganda is a system of appeals to emotional clusters of symbols to show that a given policy contradicts what is already in the minds of the citizens. In other words, propaganda seeks action or seeks to restrain action by using appeals to emotional slants. The technique of appeal may vary from situation to situation. At times pertinent information may be withheld, at times facts may be distorted or wilfully misrepresented, at times the purpose of propaganda may be veiled and the group supporting it may try to hide its identity; and the manner of presentation may be sweetly rational or burning with emotional fervor. For some propaganda, one means of communication may be more effective than another; and a judgment of effective communication is part of the task of those who would crystallize public opinion in their favor. Nor does the systematic technique of propaganda always imply that it is rationally or logically in-

* Lasswell, *Politics* (1936), distinguished between elites and masses. On pp. 217-218, he said: "The broad masses are seldom sufficiently active, or sufficiently radicalized, to bind themselves firmly to special means of expression." The most distinguished exponent of the "iron law of oligarchy" is Robert Michels, *Political Parties*, trans. from the Italian (1915).

valid, for it is the technique of appeal that characterizes propaganda.*

Education may be distinguished from propaganda in that in theory its objectives are general in nature, and specific action or public decision is not usually supported by it. It seeks, in the social sciences, to instill a knowledge of a body of literature, a method of procedure, as well as specific solutions. Nor is the primary appeal of education directed at symbolic congruence between action and emotion. Properly, education strives for the rational and the scientific, though one could hardly argue that educational effort precludes an emotional appeal for the support of reason and science. In the ideal, educational effort could not distort or withhold facts. And in the long sweep of its effort, it seeks to provide the individual with skills, techniques, and information which will, in theory at least, enable him to live up to his intellectual and social capacity. Decisions do not flow from education directly, though they may and do from effective propaganda. Likewise, the correlative technique of censorship and the extreme technique of coercion are excluded by definition from the proper procedures of education.

Whatever view one takes of the contemporary problem of public opinion, the issue of the systematic techniques of propaganda is always central. It is central with any political leader, any reformer, or any civil servant who is interested either in getting action and support or in preventing action or the rise of an opposition. Yet the wide popular knowledge of propaganda tech-

* Daniel Lerner, *Sykewar; Psychological Warfare Against Germany, D-Day to V-E Day* (1949), 5, says the propaganda function is "the emission of a unilateral flow of symbols selected to persuade a given audience toward a given end." The issue is simple: Is it effective? See also P. M. A. Linebarger, *Psychological Warfare* (1948). W. H. Mallock, "Scientific Methods of Propaganda," *Fortnightly Review,* CXI n.s. (1922), 300-308, urged the organization of anti-revolutionary and conservative propaganda. In speaking of World War I propaganda, Victor Morgens, a Norwegian writer, in "Politik, Propaganda, Presse, Publikum," *Deutsche Rundschau,* 213 (1927), 171-178, said the English technique was to "tell a lie and stick to it." Cf. Murray Dyer, *The Weapon on the Wall; Rethinking Psychological Warfare* (1959).

niques, especially through advertising and through competing political discussion, protects much of the public from the full force of propaganda. Propaganda's full power emerges only when it is supported by other means of control—in particular by censorship and suppression. Under a regime of free communication, propaganda is often dangerous and powerful, but under a totalitarian regime it becomes fatal to the spiritual dignity of man. In a democracy it is still assumed that men have a capacity to reason and to discriminate between the false and the true; under tyranny it is assumed that man is only a system of wants and manipulable emotions.*

Modern propaganda is different from that of previous eras in at least two respects. There is, first, a conscious attempt to use the findings of psychology in approaching the individual and the social group; and, second, a close association of the procedural aspects of propaganda with the new means of mass communication. Science has, no doubt, intensified the power of propaganda, but it has likewise strengthened the capacity of the objects of propaganda to resist by counter-offensive techniques. Propaganda is not, therefore, different in quality from previous periods—or even from the ancient world—but it is psychologically and technically intensified, and it is vast in quantity.

VI

The principle that opinion may be "made" carries with it, logically, the idea that the effectiveness of manipulation may be measured. And beyond this lies the general proposition that psychological and mathematical techniques may be used to measure both attitudes and opinions. The development of these techniques of measurement, culminating in the wide use of the public opinion poll, is clearly one of the significant advances in the application

* See E. D. Adrian, "The Nervous System," in *Factors Determining Human Behavior* (1937), 11, who argued that physiology offers only one certain method by which human behavior can be improved, and that is by breeding men with larger brains.

of psychological ideas to public opinion. The technique itself is a combination of psychological principles and statistical devices which give useful results. That is, public opinion, if it exists on any given question, may be measured; and it may be measured either as long-run or permanent, or as fluctuating on matters of a controversial and immediate nature. Propagandists may watch public opinion to test the effectiveness of their work; political leaders may study polls to decide whether public policy is being accepted; advertisers may discover by these techniques whether their money is being effectively spent; in war, governments may test whether their efforts to shape ideological intelligence are being crowned with popular support, and the individual citizen may judge whether he is following along with his fellow citizens, or whether his own opinions are becoming more and more unlike those of the general population. The citizen who enjoys the feeling that he is on the noisy band-wagon of the majority can act accordingly, while those who hold minority sentiments may be roused to more feverish activity. Moreover, all groups in the public want to know the effects of today's opinion on tomorrow's decisions.

Psychological emphasis on instincts gave way after World War I to the study of attitudes. Attitudes flower into opinions, and both may be measured by the new techniques. At least instinct as a concept was narrowed and separated from attitudes and patterns of behavior which clearly involved social influences. As a result of behavioristic studies, the political importance of instinct—so heavily stressed by earlier psychologists—rapidly diminished. William James had encouraged this trend by his emphasis on habit, and social psychologists, such as W. I. Thomas and C. H. Cooley, insisted that the important concepts for their work were attention, habit, sympathy, suggestion, attitudes, and emotions. The Freudian "wish" likewise entered the picture, but the upshot was that a social psychology based on habit and attitude provided materials which are observable and statistically measurable. John Dewey's work on the theory of human nature was a powerful stimulus to this type of study and technical application.*

Polling techniques measure, primarily, opinion on current and controversial issues, yet to secure accurate results the small percentage of the population selected for answering the pollsters' questions must be classified in accordance with prevailing attitudes and probabilities of response. Atypical groups must be ignored, and only those who contribute to the prevailing stream of mass response must be consulted and their views tabulated. In so far as polls are concerned with controversial questions, they are akin to the problem of judging the effectiveness of propaganda; but it is difficult to separate polling from the underlying thesis of social psychology which holds that attitudes provide one of the foundations of opinion.

Emphasis on attitudes, of course, implies a theory of permanent or long-run opinion, rather than a definition of public opinion purely in terms of controversial issues. Attitude has been customarily defined as the sum total of a person's inclinations and feelings, prejudice or bias, preconceived notions, ideas, fears, and convictions about any specific topic; it may, indeed, be imperfectly or hardly verbalized at all. An opinion, in contrast, is a verbal formulation of an attitude, or it is a verbal symbol of an attitude. Attitudes, in turn, are to be measured in terms of the acceptance or rejection of an opinion, though it cannot be assumed that one will always act in accordance with the opinions verbalized for one specific situation. But there is both controversy and variety in the definition of attitudes and opinions. Attitudes may mean inferred states of readiness to act in an evaluative way, in support of or against a given stimulus situation. An opinion or a belief is a view, then, upon which we are willing to act. In 1935 Gordon W. Allport suggested that an attitude is a "mental and neural state of readiness, organized through experience, exerting a directive or dynamic influence upon the individual's response to all objects and situations with which it is related." Nor is opin-

* See *Encyclopaedia of the Social Sciences*, I, p. 206; John Dewey, *Human Nature and Conduct* (1920).

ion here considered merely the "verbalization of an attitude," for opinion is a more rational, expressible construct, dealing with some problem, issue, or uncertainty in discussion. Some analysts therefore believe that opinions are not the direct expressions, exhibitions, or descriptions of attitudes.* Albig has been impressed with the variety of meanings in the use of the word "attitude," particularly in modern sociology and social psychology. Today's uses range from the temporary set of the organism on to the relatively permanent and complex tendencies to act. W. I. Thomas, said Albig, was the first to emphasize the concept of attitude as basic in social psychology.†

Attitudes and opinions are quite obviously qualitative, intangible, evaluative, or normative; and in the ordinary sense they cannot be counted, weighted, or scaled. Yet one of the most remarkable of the developments in the last few years has been the use of empirical and quantitative scales for the measurement of attitudes and opinions. Mathematics has come to the aid of the remarkable imaginations of those who have devoted themselves to experimenting with this type of method, and who have profited

* Cited in *The Process and Effects of Mass Communication,* ed. by Wilbur Schramm (1954), 209, 218, 222.

† William Albig, *Modern Public Opinion* (1956), 152 ff. Miller has said that during the last few years "interaction" has tended to replace the study of attitudes as the defining character of social psychology. G. A. Miller, "Language and Communication," *The Public Opinion Quarterly,* XVIII (1951), 111. Some also have questioned the propriety of separating opinions and attitudes in quantitative studies. Some students of public opinion using quantitative techniques have employed attitude and opinion interchangeably, G. D. Weibe, "Some Implications of Separating Opinions from Attitudes," *The Public Opinion Quarterly,* XVII (Fall, 1953), 328 ff.

There is, of course, a voluminous literature on attitudes and attitude measurement. The best of the pioneer works was, it seems, L. L. Thurstone and E. J. Chave, *The Measurement of Attitude* (1929). See D. D. Droba, "Methods of Measuring Public Opinion," *The American Journal of Sociology,* XXXVII (1931), 410-423. It is said that the questionnaire method dates from its use by Fechner and Galton about 1885. See Mildred Parten, *Surveys, Polls, and Samples: Practical Procedures* (1950); F. F. Stephan and P. J. McCarthy, *Sampling Opinion; An Analysis of Survey Procedure* (1958); W. S. Torgerson, *Theory and Methods of Scaling* (1958). One of the most recent treatments of the quantitative studies of opinion is V. O. Key, *Public Opinion and American Democracy* (1961).

by many mistakes in order to improve the methods available for the survey of what human beings may be thinking. Not only have new methods been devised, but the quantifiers have attempted to indicate just how theoretical conceptions can be related to the empirical data collected by the surveyors and the pollsters, and those who have sought to scale the trends in the personality. From predicting elections—as in the less than happy efforts of 1936 and 1948—the technique has moved on to an inquiry into the qualities of the personality, as in the collection entitled *The Authoritarian Personality* by Adorno and others, which appeared in 1950. Here an attempt is made to evaluate the personality without the individual being aware of it, through "projective questions" (projective techniques extend, of course, to non-verbal devices) designed to reveal the unconscious personality or undiscussed convictions.

The quantitative study of the human mind or personality has, indeed, become one of the most ambitious of the research programs in the social sciences. Such studies are also generously supported by the foundations, because they cross disciplines and experiment with new methods, and because the projects are therefore generally co-operative, involving a number of social scientists. In detail there are two important issues: the statement and selection of values behind a study, and the complicated and ingenious techniques which quantitative work may employ. The quantitative study of the qualitative tends in nearly all instances to become formal, and to lose the shading of "life in the situation." Leiserson, for example, has criticized the Lasswell-inspired type of study because the hierarchy of authority is considered in too formal a manner. Rather, he insisted there should be study of the relatively autonomous units of political influence in each of which the instrumental conception of opinion may be said to apply.* The critics of the quantitative techniques insist that they

* Avery Leiserson, "Notes on the Theory of Political Opinion Formation," *The American Political Science Review,* XLVII (March, 1953), 171 ff. See also Daniel Lerner and Harold D. Lasswell and others, *The Policy Sciences; Recent Developments in Scope and Method* (1951), which is

are not truly objective, while those who use them are concerned to show that internal devices are available to validate the accuracy of any given survey of attitudes or opinions. One critic has insisted that though the precision of polls has increased, "value judgments still permeate the entire field . . . the personal judgment of the researcher continues, and undoubtedly will continue, to play a paramount role." *

From the relatively simple methods of trying to predict how an election will turn out, modern research ranges far beyond mere studies of public opinion. Critics have stressed that the individual may be approached at any time by an interviewer, asking for his most intimate thoughts and judgments on the world about him. If a person declines to take the authoritarian personality test, it may be declared that his refusal itself proves that he is an authoritarian. If he refuses to accede to "depth interviews," someone else will be interviewed and the system of correlations will, by mathematical techniques, place him where he belongs anyway. Through "correlations" the mind of the nation is being transferred to IBM cards. Even the individual who claims his natural right to privacy is nevertheless denied it by the mathematical results derived from sampling methods and extrapolated from the proper cards.

Stouffer has observed that interviewing as a method of inquiry is universal in the social sciences. But he notes as well the new inventions for social research, new inventions which make the interview an engine whose power has not been subject to calculation. There is the card, the recording of opinions, and the

---

composed of studies on the possible roles of the social scientist in making policy decisions; M. B. Smith, J. S. Bruner, and R. W. White, *Opinions and Personality* (1956).

* Robert Ferber, "Value Judgments and the Public Opinion Polls," *Current Economic Comment*, 18 (August, 1953), 23. While the literature on this subject is astonishingly large, one recent effort may be cited: E. A. Suchman, and Louis Guttman, "A Solution of the Problem of Question 'Bias,'" *The Public Opinion Quarterly*, XI (1947), 445-455, cited in *Public Opinion and Propaganda*, Daniel Katz and others (1954). It is suggested here that "intensity" questions can be used to objectify the questions forming the scale.

application of mathematical principles to samples.* These methods have spread from the United States to many parts of the world. In France and Mexico, for example, pollsters are at work on the discovery of the thought of the individual about public affairs, and in West Germany the exemption from the channels of communication grows less with the establishment of the "Institut für Demoskopie" and "Emnid." In 1955 there was an international meeting of pollsters at Constance, and among the 300 international guests was George Gallup, the "father of all public opinion polls." There may be soon, indeed, "world" polls of public opinion, world public opinion research centers, and polls of parliamentary opinion. These developments will constitute the great "breakthrough" in public opinion research.†

The range of investigation covered by the quantitative technique is difficult to state. Governmental agencies of every sort, as they reduce their problems to statistics, derive much of their information from interviewing the individuals who may be concerned. Party organizations, congressmen watching their districts, businesses seeking wider markets, all use interviewing and advanced quantitative techniques. Comparative ideology, the

* See preface to *Interviewing in Social Research,* H. H. Hyman and others (1954). Albig, *op. cit.,* 156 ff, 164 ff, discusses the measurement of attitudes and opinions. However, the literature can only be suggested; for instance, the many articles in *The Public Opinion Quarterly* may be consulted and the other references cited. Such a bibliography is only for the expert or the polling technician; however, see especially Louis Guttman, one of the most inventive minds in the field, "An Outline of Some New Methodology for Social Research," *The Public Opinion Quarterly,* XVIII (Winter, 1954-1955), 395, and the literature by Guttman cited on pp. 403-404. Also, pp. 443-445.

† Among relevant literature, see Wilhelm Hennis, *Meinungsforschung und Repräsentative Demokratie* (1957), who stresses the importance of the difference between choosing and thinking, and between public opinion and popular sentiment. Public opinion research (Demoskopie) has been influential on the political parties in West Germany in the formulation of their programs. Note also Pierpaolo Fergiz, *Il Volto Sconosciuto dell'Italia: Dieci Anni de Sondaggi DOXA* (1956); *The Public Opinion Quarterly,* XXII (Summer, 1958), 181, "Thirteenth Conference on Public Opinion Research;" *Sondages,* the French publication on polling, with a European bibliography on the subject.

status of the middle class, and a multitude of other matters have been studied in this way. From the close alliance between election polling and market research, one moves on to the deeper issues of public philosophy. In each field models are established which enable the investigator to select and organize his material. Deutsch, for example, has used cybernetics and the theory of communication to construct usable models for the study of nationalism.* The point at issue is perhaps this: the study of communication must be made scientific; and to be scientific it must apply the theories based on quantitative analysis in close relation to models which are suited to the quantitative data available for study. Attempts have thus been made to test the receptivity of people to various kinds of materials and appeals, with the same material at times being attributed to sources differing from high to low credibility. College students have been common and readily available guinea pigs, and they seem not to mind being deceived occasionally in the cause of scientific method.† Studies of ideological affiliation have recently been stimulated by quantitative inquiries into the deeper, latent attitudes on communism. Stouffer studied attitudes toward the nonconformity of atheists, socialists, communists, and former communists or those suspected of being so. It would not be surprising that those with strong religious or Christian convictions should be more concerned about communism than others, yet the inquiry did not raise forcefully the issue of whether communism was a revolutionary movement engaged in subversion and espionage.‡

In more specific relation to the study of public opinion, certain observations may be made. As it stands today, the quantitative

* Karl W. Deutsch, *Nationalism and Social Communication* (1953); see also his "On Communication Models in the Social Sciences," *The Public Opinion Quarterly*, XVI (Fall, 1952), 356 ff.

† C. I. Hovland, I. L. Janis, and H. H. Kelley, *Communication and Mass Persuasion; Psychological Studies of Opinion Change* (1953).

‡ Samuel A. Stouffer, *Communism, Conformity and Civil Liberties; A Cross-Section of the Nation Speaks its Mind* (1955).

study of public opinion and society has been a slow development, with periods of high and low intensity of effort. However, it must be said that the sampling process used in order to predict the outcome of elections was the first and main stimulant for this vast effort of our generation. Few would question the mathematical ingenuity or brilliance of many of the efforts to quantify public opinion, the attitudes of social classes or elites, and the possibilities of marketing products of one kind or another. But it is also clear that it is dangerous to assume that the pollster is merely an objective inquirer into public opinion. Nor can one assume that the people, who in a democracy are supposed to be sovereign, have no interest in what the political views of the social scientists may be. The pollster has an ideology just as does the person who is interviewed and correlated.

Every technique for dealing with public opinion, therefore, is shadowed with postulates about the nature of proper public decisions.* A technique, it may be argued, is in itself neutral, and its import is always within the particular situation in which it is used. But some students of opinion surveys have believed that the polling techniques may be regarded as a potential substitute for ordinary political procedures, such as the formation of an electorate, the conduct of elections, and the submission of some public questions to voters. Polling would acquire under these conditions a constitutional position equal to the present techniques

* The criticism of the polling techniques has been vigorous. See Edward L. Bernays, "Attitude Polls—Servants or Masters?" *The Public Opinion Quarterly*, IX (1945), 264-268b; Lindsay Rogers, *The Pollsters* (1949). Rogers' argument centers finally on the proposition that the polls cannot measure a public opinion that does not exist, which is often the case with issues presented to the pollees. But Rogers also presents the powerful argument that the pollsters have not thought much about their premises, such as: Do we want representative government or a town-meeting society?

The failure of the polls to indicate the outcome of the presidential elections of 1936 and 1948 stimulated an extensive literature on what is wrong. See *The Polls and Public Opinion*, ed. by N. C. Meier and H. W. Saunders (1949); Frederick Mosteller and others, *The Pre-Election Polls of 1948* (1949). See especially Joseph Alsop, "The Wayward Press: Dissection of a Poll," *The New Yorker*, September 24, 1960.

by which opinion is correlated with public decision.* But then the public would have no initiative of its own, and there might be some question whether there is any public at all. It has been sarcastically suggested that all we need in modern government is a competent body of civil servants and a United States Polling Authority. If the civil servant wished to follow public opinion, he could discover it by statistical computations; but if he did not wish to follow it, the Polling Authority could be used to determine the estimated amount of governmental propaganda needed to produce the desired public opinion. However, public opinion polls have no constitutional standing. Public decisions are not made in this way in a democracy, for even if the representative or the political leader studies the polls, it is he who makes the public decision within the range of his power.

VII

Public policy in the field of public opinion may move in either of two directions. Techniques may be employed which tend to strengthen the force of opinion on government, or techniques may be employed that tend to increase the force of government on mass opinion. The new psychological techniques we have been discussing are dangerous when they are not controlled by democratic philosophy, but on additional grounds they are dangerous because confidence has faded in specific democratic reforms. To give the eighteen-year-olds the right to vote is merely a gesture, for one can hardly think that this reform will alter significantly the course of political decision. The Jacksonian reform movement faded out, as did the nineteenth-century continental movements for direct government. Likewise, the second era of

* Cf. Harold F. Gosnell, "The Polls and Other Mechanisms of Democracy," *The Public Opinion Quarterly*, IV (1940), 224-228. G. M. Connally and H. H. Field, "The Non-Voter—Who He Is, What He Thinks," *The Public Opinion Quarterly*, VIII (1944), 175 ff, have proposed the use of polls to explore the mind of the non-voter. Cf. Julian L. Woodward, "Public Opinion Research, 1951-1970; A Not-Too-Reverent History," *Public Opinion Quarterly*, XV (Fall, 1951), 405.

democratic reform in the United States which came toward the close of that century and produced such devices as the direct primary, the initiative, referendum, and recall, has no counterpart at the present time. Instead, a leading principle of reform has been to strengthen the executive and administrative branches of the government.

As the power of government in shaping public opinion has increased with the growth of executive leadership and with the growth of complex and technical functions in government, another movement, the rise of pressure groups and the organization of functioning groups into a kind of guild system, has at the same time fragmented public opinion. With the government seeking to balance one pressure group against another, it has become increasingly difficult to perceive a general, overall public sentiment, or any form of actual general will.* Stuart Chase once spoke of Big Business, Big Labor, and Big Agriculture, but one might add to the list Big Government and the pressures on public policy which arise from the growth of administrative structures. The democratic ideal of the informed and participating citizen, however, implies the possibility of such a sharing of well-founded opinions that we can reach a kind of general will that bypasses the pressure groups.

Those who would increase the force of government on opinion have the history of the twentieth century before them, for every fascist, communist, or dictatorial regime has relied heavily on new developments in propaganda, censorship, and suppression. Those who would increase the force of opinion on government have before them the history of democratic aspiration, its failures and its successes. What techniques can be adopted by those who want a greater force of opinion on government? While mass education must include a philosophy of the state and its historical and moral obligations, while the citizen's thought must affirm the rational and the moral elements in men, the believer in democracy must take thought about the necessity of forming his own

* See Stuart Chase, *Democracy Under Pressure* (1945); David B. Truman, *The Governmental Process* (1951).

techniques. He must realize that a new era of democratic reform is vitally needed if the practice and force of free opinion is to be preserved.

What are the systematic techniques to which the democrat in our day may turn? The old ones to be sure, for democracy is hardly possible without the preservation of representative and constitutional government; that is, government which lives under the law and respects the limitations that the long-run popular will has embodied in the constitution. The democrat must fight also for the preservation of civil liberty—the liberty that assures to individuals a respected right to criticize the government, that assures to them, indeed, the moral worth and dignity involved in life, liberty, and property.*

Still, it must be recognized that democratic reforms have tended to reach a maximum effect and to fail to get their anticipated results. In the eighteenth century, annual elections were considered important, along with other devices such as the separation of powers. We know today that annual elections are hardly a sure guarantee of freedom, yet effective elections today are clearly of profound significance, especially in view of the corruption of the electoral process. We must renew our study of elections, and the new period of democratic reform must revise electoral procedures so that, if possible, they will be effective against authori-

* One of the issues in the field of civil liberty is, of course, the qualities of a free press. There is a vast literature, both criticizing and defending the modern newspaper, radio, and television. In general, the issue in a democracy is: What restrictions on the press, radio, and television are compatible with a democratic and free communication of ideas? Must communists and fascists be allowed to use the free communication of ideas in order to destroy civil liberty? Obviously, a democracy may protect itself, but there is not much agreement on how it should be done. See, for example, the following: Norman Angell, *The Press and the Organization of Society* (rev. ed., 1933); R. W. Desmond, *The Press and World Affairs* (1937); Edward C. Hayes, "The Formation of Public Opinion," *The Journal of Applied Sociology*, X (1925), 6-9; Wolfgang Stein, "Vorlesungen für die Presse," *Preussische Jahrbücher*, 204 (1926), 1-24; Lothar Bucher, *Der Parlamentarismus Wie Sie Ist* (3rd ed., 1884); H. A. Münster, *Geschichte der Deutschen Presse* (1941); C. A. Siepmann, *Radio, Television and Society* (1950); F. C. Irion, *Public Opinion and Propaganda* (1950).

tarian tendencies. Democracy must somehow learn to recover its stolen elections. In retrospect, both waves of democratic reform in the nineteenth century in the United States left their permanent deposit, and this deposit is still an assurance of freedom. But the study and further development of popular control in the modern Leviathan is urgently needed. Democratic thinking must consider how to control the new developments which restrict the force of opinion on government; proponents of democracy must study the control of propaganda; they must find a way to make sure that modern means of mass communication are used in favor of free discussion; they must keep a vigilant watch on the tendency of government to resort to censorship; and, above all, they must combat the practice of suppressing the communication of ideas. But each of these objectives requires constant experiment and the revision of policy.

However, there is another factor which the democrat must also take into account. In the complex society in which we live, there is much evidence which leads us to doubt the power of public opinion to control the trend of events. No doubt public opinion is, finally, only one of the forces which determine the structure and operation of a political system. If we admit the long-run trends in an economic order, admit the force of geographical conditioning of our life, admit that a level of technology casts its imperative over a whole society,* that institutional construction is slow, and that inertia is powerful—admit all this and more and we are conscious of the objective limitations on the power of public opinion. Perhaps we should admit, likewise, that on the psychological level human nature offers stubborn resistance to the allure of reason, morality, and science, and that this also is an objective limitation on the functioning of public opinion.

Beyond all these considerations the functional creativeness of public opinion remains. It is the task of the democrat and his leader who would strengthen the force of opinion on govern-

* See H. A. Innis, "Technology and Public Opinion in the United States," *The Canadian Journal of Economics and Political Science*, XVII (1951), 1-24.

ment to know the possible creative power of public opinion, and to provide, if possible, the conditions under which it can best control the course of society. For creative public opinion is not the only force in the world; it is only one among many—powerful though it is. Where opinion can function, it should be provided with free channels of communication, and where its action is unlikely to be effective, democratic education should try to make the reason plain. It is here that the systematic techniques which favor democracy should be most carefully organized.

Beyond systematic techniques, the philosophical problem remains. Beyond sociological objectivism and psychological analysis, the judgment of the content of public opinion is the task of science, reason, and moral purpose. For human purposes are also psychological facts, and the stuff of social life. Public opinion by itself cannot be the only standard of political action. There is always a theory of human behavior behind it, and in the end public opinion is itself a technique by which such a conception shares in the creation of public policy. But it is a technique that is conducive to freedom and to the realization of the norms of individual and social purpose. "If man is irrational," said Phyllis Doyle, "force alone will constrain him, and an orgy of intolerance is justified. If he is rational, then persuasion will win his ear and a sweet reasonableness will be suggested as the proper means whereby to assert the authority of the community over its erring members." * The poet or the mystic might say that finally all evaluations, all norms and purposes, are to be explained only by poetic insight or intuition that grasps a world seen only in part. Science as empiricism or as rationalism can be singularly unmoving, however important it may be. For Western man, one can see in the differences between Nietzsche's *Thus Spake Zarathustra,* Housman's *A Shropshire Lad,* or *The Little Flowers* of St. Francis, contrast and contradiction as fundamental as may be imagined. Evaluation is something that is added beyond a simple psychological analysis of man.

* Phyllis Doyle, *A History of Political Thought* (1932), 14.

PART III

GROUPS AND THE ORDERING OF OPINION

CHAPTER 8

Public Opinion and the Intellectuals *

I

A study of the relation of intellectuals to public opinion suggests the outlines of a sociology of the intellectuals as a functioning social group. The *libertas philosophandi* † has long been asserted by the educated elite, and in pre-democratic days its theoretical relation to public opinion was quite clear. Philosophers have had the civil liberty to criticize government, but the same right was not generously extended to the vulgar conscience, or the common men who composed the "open public." Actually, the rise of democracy has not fully clarified the issue, though the mass or Gnostic movements of modern times have asserted the right to judge the government, the intellectuals, and any other group that might stand in their way. The democratic intellectual can hardly say that the mass in revolt does not have the right to judge him, but he can and does say that public opinion must be reformed, purified, educated, or directed by the latest developments in scientific hypothesis. More especially, however, the modern self-conscious intellectuals have directed their fire against

* Republished from *The American Political Science Review,* XLVIII (June, 1954), 321 ff.

† Robert B. Sutton, "The Phrase *Libertas Philosophandi,*" *Journal of the History of Ideas,* 14 (April, 1953), 310-16.

other groups or elites who have a following and who in fact provide a pluralistic leadership of public opinion.*

Yet in this type of discussion, the intellectuals have seldom analyzed themselves as Julien Benda attempted in *La Trahison des Clercs.* In general, the intellectuals have raised the question of the conditions of culture, and whether or to what extent the intellectual may offer his loyalty to it. And because the *libertas philosophandi* has so often involved the assertion of revolutionary and highly negative judgments, the existing popular culture, so often permeated with Western religious ideas, has come in for harsh criticism. A moment of reflection will suggest that, on the contrary, the intellectuals should look in a scientific spirit at other groups whose traditional judgments do not agree with theirs. It is easy for the clerk to laugh satirically at the country bumpkin, who in a democracy may occupy the highest political post, but he might on occasion look at himself in all humility, without the arrogance that the possession of knowledge (not necessarily wisdom) so often induces. In any case, one of the issues of analysis in contemporary politics and culture is the examination of the intellectual; the creation, one might suggest, of an inwardly directed sociology of the intellectuals.†

The issue becomes finally one of philosophy. One must acquire a metaphysical focus before any such tension as that between public opinion and intellectuals can be fully understood. But in the discussion there is seldom a proper confrontation of issues, since less fundamental controversies and the praise and denunciation of personalities obscure what otherwise might be an enlightening area of discourse. In a basic sense, the issue is the

* See, for example, José Ortega y Gasset, *The Revolt of the Masses,* trans. from the Spanish (1932). Or, in contrast, Julien Benda, *The Treason of the Intellectuals* (*La Trahison des Clercs*), trans. by Richard Aldington (1928).

† Crane Brinton, "Something Went Wrong: Three Views of the Heritage of the Early Nineteenth Century," *Journal of the History of Ideas,* 14 (June, 1953), 457-62, deals with this issue by being sharply critical of Peter Viereck, who had offered criticism of the contemporary intellectuals. See my "The Social Scientist and His Values," in *Ethics and the Social Sciences,* ed. by Leo R. Ward (1959), 1-23.

liberal affirmation of various forms of empiricism against variations of theistic philosophy, or the struggle between the affirmations of scientific and religious interpretations of man.* It becomes the conflict between the interpretation of "secular democracy" and some modern form of a sacral or religiously influenced society. However, this is only the fundamental form of the question, since the number of secularized ideologies is large and the number of morally and religiously influenced systems of ideas is also considerable in the diverse modern political structure of the West.† For example, the contemporary struggle over the content of education surely involves the most fundamental of philosophical problems, but the battle is actually fought in a half-light, or with a spotlight illumination of personalities in a fog of personal recrimination and epithet.

II

We must keep in mind a distinction which is of profound significance. There is a difference between the intellectuals and intelligence. There is intelligence throughout society, and wherever it is it should be used in private lives and in the operation of government. Intellectuals in the European sense—that is, the intelligentsia—have a special kind of intelligence. They are functioning groups of society, like any of the professionals—lawyers, doctors, engineers, professors, journalists, and more recently the scientist of whatever kind he may be. Intellectuals as a group are characterized by their specialized study and function; they have gathered information, and by the logic of their professional status they use such information to make judgments about the world

* See J. Grimmond, "The Principles of Liberalism," *The Political Quarterly*, 14 (July-Sept., 1953), 236-42.

† Lord Acton in the nineteenth century was interested in counting the number of systems of thought which might be used to explain political movements in his time. Since Acton was attempting to reconcile British liberalism with his own religious ideas, he tended to blunt the conflict between liberalism as a secular system of thought and Christianity. See G. E. Fasnacht, *Acton's Political Philosophy* (1953), 140-41.

around them. For long centuries they have sat in judgment on the popular mind, and here we have an issue which was as important yesterday as it is today. The intellectual has often seemed to say: "You must forgive us if we seem a little proud, and if we feel that the power of organized society should be largely in our hands. You must forgive us if we disdain the ideas of the common man, because when the common man agrees with us we will like him. We want to remake him in our own image, if only to the extent that he is willing to accept our leadership when important questions of public policy are involved. We are not opposed to freedom, but we feel more capable than other men of defining freedom and justice."

Reflection on the rise of the modern Western intellectual class since the revival of the study of Roman law in the twelfth century, the reintroduction of Greek or Aristotelian philosophy into the great European universities and the rise of medicine and theology as disciplines may lead one to think there is more than a grain of truth in such a statement. Some intellectuals, like the theologians and the medical men, have generally had a large following among the "vulgar." Others, like the humanists with their knowledge of ancient tongues, and the philosophers who have rejected the religious beliefs of ordinary men, have been at war with society for nearly five hundred years. In our time, the spectacular achievements of the scientists in particular have separated them from ordinary people. In the scientist many have seemed to see fulfilled the idea of the "superman;" and for the first time in American history, the scientist as the aide of the military has been envisaged as the next possible destroyer of civilization, rather than its obedient servant.

The great symbolic intellectual figure, however, has been the philosopher, the lover of wisdom.* This symbol has been forceful ever since the beginning of Greek speculative thought. It found a powerful exponent in Plato, and perhaps Pythagoras as well. True knowledge was a mystery which only the initiated might savor.

* Cf. Eric Voegelin, *The New Science of Politics* (1952).

In Plato's allegory of the cave, the mass of ordinary men have their backs forever turned to the light of true reality, and see only its shadows passing before them. Some years ago Walter Lippmann * described public opinion as a set of stereotypes which partially informed men use to explain the world; and Lippmann's stereotype is in function much like the shadowy images reflected in Plato's cave: the stereotype does not include a proper range of information; it is distorted; it is merely a picture of the world and not its reality or truth. Thus, every man who becomes in his heart an intellectual—that is, a philosopher of some kind or other—must make a great decision; he must decide whether or not the ordinary man actually does sit in a cave with his back to the light. He must decide whether or not common opinion about the world is merely a set of stereotypes, or distorted images. He must decide whether to sit in judgment on the world and all poor mortals who inhabit it. It is a profound and disturbing issue, and if one is a proponent of democracy, the issue is all the more difficult. To the aristocrat, at heart there is no issue, because to the aristocrat knowledge is like all good things in being the privilege of the few.

And now we reach a striking paradox. The intellectuals, who are most passionately for the earthly salvation of mankind, and the reform of men and institutions, are those who least respect what may be called the traditional values of any long-standing or operating community. For, in truth, no existing society can be called a utopia, and men never do actually escape the frustrations of living or the failure of their characters to fulfill their own potentials. Nevertheless the modern intellectual Gnostic will say that in a democratic society man can be educated to greater awareness of what ought to be done to make society better; in other words, public opinion can by education be slowly recast, and loyalty for a new, transfigured society can be deliberately created. But when the tradition-bound mortal refuses the new light, the intellectual in a democracy logically can only accept

* Walter Lippmann, *Public Opinion* (1922).

defeat and start over. In a totalitarian society, however, those who refuse what the intellectual believes to be the light may be put in concentration camps or sentenced to slave-labor; others can be driven by fear into silence in order that they may survive in a world where the social dissenter is regarded as the enemy of mankind. Meanwhile, those who run the slave-labor camps would say that they greatly love the people, that their eyes are upon a golden future, and that the pain of today is justified by the promise of tomorrow.

Against intellectuals of this type, are those who might be called conservatives.* These are men whose thinking respects the tradition of a people; they are willing to believe with ordinary men in their religion, and in the common wisdom which ancestral experience has fed into the minds of those who are not intellectuals. Similarly, they believe that values—good and evil—may be demonstrated by methods of logic and reason. Science has its facts, and no one would wish to deny them, for they are part of truth; but justice and morality are also facts that live in the great current of truth which is carried by the intellectual traditions of religions and nations. Moreover, these conservative intellectuals tend to say that they do not believe a new society is immediately possible; they may say also that men are unfortunate or evil in their deeds—not because of a lack of knowledge, but because of a lack of character—because, in short, men are sinners. Perhaps there is more humility in such an intellectual, and there may be less of lust for human power, or, let us say, less *superbia* and *pleonexia*—although these qualities are yet there, even if only in their pride in the fact that men follow and love them. They tend to agree with St. Paul that the least of God's children may have as much moral wisdom as the philosopher; that the knowledge of the Christian, informed by his faith can fearlessly be measured against the secular and positivistic morality of an unfriendly world.

In the extreme, then, we have two great types of intellectuals

* See Russell Kirk, *The Conservative Mind* (1953); Peter Viereck, *Conservatism Revisited* (1949).

in relation to common sentiment, or the public opinion of any society. The philosopher in the Greek sense, the lover of wisdom, and the Christian thinker tend to agree that all men can share in the transcendental aims of the human soul. There is always a higher wisdom which ordinary men keep alive and share, and sometimes induce others to accept as the proper standard of their behavior, both private and public. The other type of intellectual —the modern Gnostic—Plato would call a Sophist: he teaches success in life; he has few standards; he is Machiavellian; * and though he may exploit tradition for purposes contingent to propaganda, he has a profound contempt for the traditional morality of the society in which he works.

Let us now try to state more clearly the practical and philosophical aspect of this issue as it concerns public opinion. How can the functioning citizen of a democracy get along with the intellectuals? On the other hand, how can the intellectuals get along with the members of a democratic society? What kind of intellectuals and what kind of citizens work best with each other? One thing is clear. Ever since the founding of the great Western universities, one of their functions has been the training of public servants—the teachers in the schools, and members of professions such as medicine, law, and theology. In the history of Western governments, the transitions of society can be marked by the changing character of the intellectuals who have served the government. One can almost say, indeed, that the intellectuals, of whatever kind, formulate the policies of government in any detailed or specific sense, regardless of the form of government. But the lawyer trained in the Roman law and the common law who became the adviser of modern absolute rulers was different from the clerk or the cleric who preceded him before the rise of these systems.† Moreover, the techniques of the trained servant of

* Cf. Max Lerner's introduction to the Modern Library edition of Machiavelli's *The Prince* and *The Discourses* (1940).

† Christopher Saint-German's *The Doctor and Student* in 1518 may be regarded as a statement of the older position of the supremacy of the higher law, but the Student in the dialogues expresses many of the ideas of absolutism.

government vary with different systems, but in the democracies of our time so much is secret that policies are often formulated and put into effect before there is any publicity. Immanuel Kant was facing this issue when he said that any policy of government might be accepted if it were compatible with publicity, and this was to him one of the most essential pillars of freedom. In general, in a democracy today the expert or the professional man is merely made to act somewhat more slowly and cautiously than if he had the backing of an absolutism. With the idea of career public service becoming increasingly accepted, even a change in political regimes may not alter greatly the advice on particular policies as it is received by a new President or Congress.

Thus, the relation between public opinion and the intellectuals is not primarily a matter of the form of government, though one could hardly deny the importance of different systems of making political decisions. One can range a gamut from the Greek devices of popular participation, through the emergence of nineteenth-century democracy, and on to the corruption of traditional democratic devices in modern totalitarian systems, and it will be seen that the important issue is what kind of philosophy the intellectuals hold and what kind of traditional values the people believe in. Sometimes the intellectuals and the common man agree on basic propositions and sometimes they do not, though it is generally true that whether there is agreement or disagreement there is a difference between the statement of traditional belief and the manner in which the intellectuals argue their propositions. What kind of truth is sought? What reality is desired? What is involved here is not just a question of economic motivation, for all men, however they may reason, must have the necessities of life; it is not just a matter of psychoanalysis or class status either, for men, whether intellectuals or not, have their frustrations and mental disturbances. In the end it becomes a question of values, or what kind of values should be reflected in the spirit and policy of government. It is a question of how values are determined and sustained, and it is a question of what these values are.

While the tension between intellectuals and ordinary people

is always present, this tension—sometimes growing and sometimes in abeyance—has been peculiarly characteristic of the modern world. It began at the end of the Middle Ages or in the early Renaissance in the universities of northern Italy; and throughout its advance, the secular theory of intelligence has increasingly dominated intellectual thought. It was not a new conflict, because it was present among the Greeks and the Romans, and indeed it may be found in any society that has left a literature for posterity. We sometimes call it humanism, sometimes liberalism, sometimes scientific thought; sometimes it is our modern historicism, and sometimes it is neo-Platonism as against the older medieval Aristotelianism. But it meant in essence that the human mind at its educated best is autonomous, that reason gives men their own law, that the quest of reason is more the creation of standards of justice, than finding a justice which already exists in some kind of moral order inherent in the universe.* From the time of the Renaissance, Greek philosophy was especially used as an alternative to Christian philosophy.

In this growth of the pagan revival with its accompanying secularism—which to some is the essence of modernity—there was an increasing separation between the intellectuals—that is, professors, philosophers, lawyers, and medical men—and the common man. The bridge between them had heretofore been their common Christian faith, but this was slowly eroded away. All through the centuries since the Renaissance one can find the intellectuals increasingly talking about the vulgar, the plebs, the unlettered; and there is in general a fear of what people in the mass can or will do. Many political philosophers, for example Jean Bodin, have considered the plebs violent and uncertain,† a force to be guarded against rather than obeyed. In the genial, Elizabethan *Religio Medici* of Sir Thomas Browne (1605-1682)

* See C. N. R. McCoy, "The Turning Point in Political Philosophy," *The American Political Science Review,* XLIV (September, 1950), 678-88.

† Jean Bodin, *Method for the Easy Comprehension of History,* trans. by Beatrice Reynolds (1945), *passim.*

we read that "Every man is not a proper Champion for Truth, nor fit to take up the Gauntlet in the cause of Verity." * To the intellectual, whether he was a Catholic, a Puritan, a Lutheran, or what not, the common people were an uncertain lot, unlearned and filled with superstition; and the storm was always latent behind the façades of peace. Whenever the lettered and the learned saw that the people disagreed with them, the people were in error: the intellectual aristocrat was always right; the common man was always wrong. This proposition has not changed through modern history, though the character of philosophy and the dominant types of intellectual effort have changed, and changed fairly frequently if one considers a broad enough sweep of event.

Intellectuals have always been divided, of course, for by their nature one intellectual must be critical of another, this being one of the aspects of the autonomous reason, the reason emancipated from all standards save those which are self-imposed. We are concerned here, however, with the dominant form of intellectual life which sought to serve the state, and to share in the training of its civil servants. First, we may observe a shifting away from Christian values and toward Greek philosophy, toward both Plato and Aristotle, and such of the learning of the ancient world as was available. It was literary and philosophical study independent of the Christian order that was at stake. The great values of the past, shared indeed with all men, were to be proved in a different way. But soon the values themselves came into question, and the revolutionary intellectual, who believed he might reshape the world around him, began to make his appearance. From the time of the development of science, the materialistic and empirical attitude of mind became stronger, and it began to be thought that if values could be proved, such proof could be only by a scientific method. Finally, in the nineteenth century the social scientists began to think of values as not being provable at all, or else provable merely in a utilitarian or quantitative fashion. But the intellectual was rapidly getting to the point where, in

* Modern Library edition (1943), 327.

social life, he could believe hardly anything. Values, the judgment of men and nations of the past, were regarded as simply a relative phase of culture. From Christian and humanistic learning we moved toward a scientific treatment of what most men thought. It seemed possible that we were approaching ethics and politics simply as a subdivision of a kind of descriptive anthropology.*

III

If one seeks the fundamental cleavage between different types of intellectuals, one has no easy quest. The nature of the quest has been described in various ways by many who have sought the fundamental issues of philosophy. But if one keeps in mind the relation of men to a human order, the issue may be stated like this: is there such a thing as a transcendent order, or is all reality—including social and private experience—immanent? Is reality only the here and now? Is this the only divinity men can know, and can it be discovered only by some application of what may be called positivism in social science? The predominant Greek philosophy which has survived as the core of many centuries of liberal education asserted the existence of a transcendent order, and so did Christian thought, whether based on Plato or Aristotle, or on a more direct examination of the implications of the Bible and Church tradition. The soul of man was open to something more than empirical data. Thus, Greek and Christian thought was looking for a spiritual reality transcendent to all men, whether they were among the learned or the vulgar. In more recent times, it is precisely the denial of such an order that has made up much of modern epistemology and metaphysics. Indeed, it has been the effort of many intellectuals to deny metaphysics by denying the existence of the spiritual and the transcendent. And it has been precisely this denial that has caused much of

* Contemporary American philosophy, especially pragmatism and positivism, may illustrate this point. There is much valuable material on the issue in H. W. Schneider's *A History of American Philosophy* (1946), Ch. 39.

the conflict between the intellectuals and the democratic citizen.

It is said that Plato's God was always busy with geometry; and that, according to some scholars,* is a peculiarly aristocratic and snobbish idea of science. It was a science beyond the comprehension of ordinary men; it was beyond the possibility of their participation in it. One may say, naturally, that Plato failed as a statesman or as adviser to kings and tyrants, but that in his *Laws* he seems to be trying to construct a society that would raise men to the highest level of which they are capable, and that in truth it was to a level very far from any modern idea of democracy. The dialectical wisdom which the rulers were to study in the *Republic* was only for a few, who in turn could direct the rest of society with wisdom. Here was a transcendental order clearly anti-democratic in implication. However, in Aristotle, both in the *Ethics* and in the *Politics,* the conservative mind comes closer to ordinary human habit, and there is a much more generous attitude toward what common people may think. They may still be directed by philosophers who have in mind a transcendent order, but the ordinary man participates in virtue. Moreover, the collective judgment of men is praised in Aristotle as a good standard for political behavior. One feels that the criticism of the city state in its time of decay was much milder in Aristotle than in Plato, even though Aristotle held that some men were slaves by their nature. On the other hand, Aristotle's praise of the common judgment was stated in the light of higher rational standards that were drawn from a knowledge of the purposes of nature. And some have gone so far as to assert that Aristotle had a profound influence even on the Stoic ideas of the natural equality of men. These points are emphasized because it seems that the path of reconciliation between the learned and the vulgar is the common acceptance of a transcendent order. This order may be known more intimately by those who are philosophers, but it is shared in and known to some extent by the education of all men in the habits of virtuous

* See Benjamin Farrington, *Science and Politics in the Ancient World* (1939); Alban D. Winspear, *The Genesis of Plato's Thought* (1940).

living. In this situation reason and faith have a common and supplemental function, and faith does not become the object of derision by those who have stressed the unlimited creativeness and autonomy of the educated reason. But it is also clear that there is a great dualism in human existence, for all men are existentially in both an immanent and a transcendent order, and the higher objectives of the transcendental are never to be realized in their fullness in that which is immanent and directly social.

It may seem paradoxical, but the intellectual who accepts a transcendental order which is above all men can be more easily reconciled to democracy and the forces of public opinion than one who does not. Such a view is critical of much of the current theory of democracy. For in the intellectually predominant view of the present, democracy is almost incompatible with any standards which philosophy and religion may propose.* It is asserted by some that only a philosophy of pragmatism is compatible with democracy. In other words, democracy must be based on something like William James' radical empiricism, or the instrumentalism of John Dewey. Or one might say that because no standard of human justice can be proved, the only standard is that which is approved by some majoritarian procedure.

If this proposition is accepted as describing the current philosophical situation, then its acceptance must arise from some qualities within the intellectual himself; it must be a kind of existential expression of the tensions of his life. In a direct sense, the reason for acceptance may be found in the attitude of the intellectual toward political power. Those who deny a transcendental realization must attain whatever objectives they have in mind in the organization of society, and the attainment must be brought about primarily through the force of the state. Thus, they are driven to seek power; or, if they fail, their sense of futility may lead them to deride it. On the other hand, those who, like Boethius, seek the consolation of philosophy, tend instead to speak

* See Karl Pribram, *Conflicting Patterns of Thought* (1949).

of the vanity of the world. To such as Boethius, the order of wisdom is both here and beyond, and knowledge can be its own reward and spiritual consolation. Such an intellectual's primary activities are teaching and writing, so that the *artes liberales* will become the proud possession of the coming generation. He is happiest when he is directing a school—the Lyceum or the Academy in Athens—or perhaps the cathedral schools which preceded the foundation of the Western universities. What he asks is freedom from the ruler, not freedom to direct the government.

One is driven, therefore, to the conclusion that the intellectual who rejects the higher order of human experience is existentially a seeker of power. The free commitment of his will may be to him a painful experience, but in the end he has tried to remake the world; that is, historically, he has sought to be the servant and the adviser of kings. His writings, like those of Pierre DuBois or Marsilius of Padua in the fourteenth century, become the manifestoes of the new and planned society. From the time of the rise of science and the troubles of the Reformation and Counter-Reformation, the idea of a utopia has been congenial to such intellectuals. From the eighteenth century to our time there has always been an intellectually led political revolution in the making. The Tudor humanist, for example, might stress obedience to the king,* but he also dreamed of the kind of society that autonomous human knowledge might make. Humanism was far more committed to the historic belief in a divine order than was the intellectualism of the eighteenth century, but the humanist was trying to be a philosopher and a bureaucrat. Consider, for example, the controversy over the objectives of Thomas More in his *Utopia*. Some have said that he was merely justifying English imperialism, but most students have said either that he was trying to reform society or that he was deriding the possibility of any reform. More was a great servant of the king, and he finally died as a martyr for his religious faith. But in the *Utopia* he seems to

* See Irving Ribner, "Sir Philip Sidney on Civil Insurrection," *Journal of the History of Ideas*, 13 (April, 1952), 257-65.

be struggling with the problem of personal power.* Should he seek power in order to reform the world, or should he say that the injustice of the world could not be cured, because of the corruption of men and government? Latterly, some have said that More was really arguing with himself as to whether he should be a lover of wisdom and the liberal arts, or seek to reshape society nearer to the heart's desire. There is no question here of what the people may want, for the philosopher working within his own philosophy may there say what justice is and what is proper for the people. But as a bureaucrat he would surely be at war with common opinion.

If we consider the seventeenth century, the picture is clearer. The ideal of science has dawned, and the literary humanism of a previous time is being pushed aside or into the darkened background where it has been ever since. Men seek now to wrest away the secrets of nature through mathematics, and through the new scientific methods. They would—like Francis Bacon, another servant of the throne and author of the first scientific utopia, the *New Atlantis*—develop a new technology and create a kingdom governed by scientists continually engaged in scientific experimentation. But it is the government of a society that is at stake; it is science and politics hand in hand, and there is no room for the traditions and values of ordinary men who might turn away from the chilly efficiency of the new technology. When you do not believe in the traditional religious and humanistic values, you may call yourself a modern and believe in science. And when you believe that the methods of natural and physical science can be applied to the social relations of people, you must turn to the state, for the state is the means whereby the new objectives can be attained. Likewise, one does not bother with ideas of natural rights and limitations on power when the state becomes the chief agency for the attainment of scientific results, whether those results are simple technology or the creation of a new social theory, as Robert Owen proposed.

* See Eric Voegelin, "More's Utopia," *Österreichische Zeitschrift für Öffentliches Recht*, Band III, Heft 4.

IV

At this point a digression into the history of political ideas is appropriate. With the beginning of the seventeenth century, certain major and traditional views in politics had emerged. There were the Calvinists, the Lutherans, the Anglicans, the Catholics, the minor and dissenting religious sects, and there were those who against all other traditions sustained the authority of the state and who were the proponents of various doctrines of sovereignty. It is clear, of course, that all of these views were internally divided, but each took a position on the central issue of time: the relation between religion and politics. One can generalize as follows: those who supported a religious tradition, especially when it was on the defensive, were likely to be exponents of the consent of the governed, tyrannicide, and the power of the traditional estates or parliaments of the realm. They were more inclined than the defenders of sovereignty to seek the support of the general population. On the other hand, it was a time of the emergence of the modern conception of the authority of the state, modeled not a little on the authority of the Roman Empire and the civil law, which had been used as a support for imperial power. Those who asserted the sovereignty of the monarch were not interested in what the people thought, but only in their obedience to the law. The doctrine of sovereignty was a kind of civil theology that was to take the place of the various Christian theologies which struggled against each other in Western Europe. Under the Tudors and the Stuarts, English official doctrine might be moving toward the assertion of the divine right of kings as the civil theology of Anglicanism, and Lutheranism had similar doctrines, though not so well stated. But the divine right of kings was simply a passing phase of the argument. It is not the argument upon which the power of the modern state was built.

The question involved here is the function of intellectuals in relation to what might be called the general currents of popular opinion. It is clear that the religious traditions appealed with success to the general body of citizens, otherwise the religious wars would not have been fought, kings would not have been assassinated, and widespread and violent repression of religious dissent would not have been possible. To be brief, the secular, empirical, and scientific intellectuals were on the side of political authority, and to them a strong monarchy became all too often a symbol of the denial of the power of the people. The intellectuals framed the new theory of power. Though the lawyers had long used the model of the Roman emperor in the analysis of kingly power, the secular mind used the new mathematical and scientific theories to justify the supremacy of the state over all dissent. In other words, much of the political theory of that time—political theory which now finds itself ensconced in the standard treatises—is a defense of political power. The lawyers, the humanists, the poets, the philosophers, and the writers of systematic works in political analysis were generally on the side of sovereignty. One should not underestimate the force of protest, the defense of popular consent, and the emergent theory of constitutional liberty. But down to the eve of the French Revolution the *philosophes* were often supporters of the monarchy and they were contemptuous of the ideas of the ordinary citizen. Ignorance, faction, and sedition comprised the treadmill of the common man. The idea of the centralized and powerful state was rationalized by the intellectuals; it is a lasting, but perhaps unhappy, contribution to the history of modern times.

In no small degree Machiavelli became the symbol of the organized power of the state, though he was denounced often by those who used him most. Sir Thomas Browne said of him: "I confess every county hath its Machiavel, every age its Lucian, whereof common Heads must not hear, nor more advanced Judgments too rashly venture on: it is the Rhetorik of Satan and may pervert a loose or prejudicate belief." * In contrast, Francis Bacon,

* Sir Thomas Browne, *Religio Medici,* Modern Library edition (1943), 344.

one of the great apostles of scientific method, and who was slightly senior to Browne, read avidly the Italian historians such as Paolo Sarpi, and he said: "We are much beholden to Machiavel and others that wrote what men do, and not what they ought to do." * Here is an essential credo of the new science of national power; here is the principle that description, and not values, forms the core of the effort of the student of politics. The people must be managed and prevented from organizing so that discontent can never be a force on government. Thomas Hobbes, on the other hand, had few reservations as to the action of a totalitarian state. Not only must the common people be told what to think; the preacher and the professor must be dealt with in the firmest way. But Hobbes tried his hand at theology, and he rather fancied himself as a theologian. He reduced obedience to God to obedience to whatever theology was incorporated into the civil statutes of the realm. Anyone who resisted the prince or the government was not only violating a civil law and worthy of condign punishment, but was also a rebel against his God. Moreover, the sovereign could command whatever he could get away with. Religion was thus reduced to a necessary annoyance; at best it was a department of government, as under the peculiar English system. Behind Hobbes' religious ideas, moreover, was a materialistic and utilitarian philosophy which in effect left no room for natural or divine law, for under Hobbes' covenant of death each individual had conceded all to the sovereign power of the state.

Fortunately for England, the long decades of disturbance and revolution ended, and a man like Locke could take many of the same philosophical ideas and create a moderate political philosophy which even led in the direction of religious toleration. And that great skeptic, Hume, like William James, insisted that we must believe, but always under a powerful government that did not allow for the religious assertiveness of other days.† In

* *The Essays of Francis Bacon,* ed. M. A. Scott (1908), LXXX.

† J. B. Shouse, "David Hume and William James: A Comparison," *Journal of the History of Ideas,* 13 (Oct., 1952), 514-27.

both Locke and Hume, the ideas of the common man get a hearing, and the stabilized custom, tradition, and public opinion of a nation may be considered in the calculations of public policy. But one of the great sources of modern liberty is the insistence on a genuine religious liberty, and though Locke moved far in that direction—farther than Milton—religious freedom was not a fact of political life. For example, Spinoza is cited for his defense of intellectual freedom, but it was the freedom of the philosopher that he defended. Spinoza's comments on religious liberty are often omitted from the books giving selections from his works. In his *Tratactus Theologico-Politicus* he argues in Chapter XIX that the right over matters spiritual lies wholly with the sovereign, and that the outward form of religion should be in accordance with public peace, if we would obey God aright. This is Hobbes all over again—the sharp Erastianism, or state supremacy over religion, that was characteristic of the critical and intellectual mind of the time. Some like Giambattista Vico in his *New Science*, might argue that in the custom of nations the right of the common man to share in society is an embodiment of the natural law, but Vico was a forgotten figure in his Neapolitan isolation until almost the beginning of the nineteenth century.

With these ideas in mind, some comment must be made on the modern age of revolutions which began with the French Revolution. The philosophers of France in the eighteenth century played a large role in bringing about the revolution, for the intellectual origins of the French Revolution are among the most important, as Daniel Mornet has argued in his study of the subject.* The intellectuals, such as Rousseau, provided the ideas that a Robespierre might use, even to the establishment of the worship of reason. Ever since the eighteenth century the battle over political ideology has centered on the philosophy of the French Revolution. A liberal must believe in it, and a conservative cannot. Burke and Wellington stand against Sieyès and Napoleon, and their suc-

* See Daniel Mornet, *Les Origines Intellectuelles de la Révolution Française* (Paris, 1933), *passim.*

cessors adopt similar intellectual and ideological postures. The revolutionist would destroy the things the people love in the name of the people; the conservative would preserve the things the people love in the name of duty. But the participants in ideological battle may be consoled by Alexis de Tocqueville, who believed that the French Revolution had already occurred before 1789, and that the institutions of France had long since undergone a deep-seated remodeling.

The philosophical battle over the French Revolution and its successor revolutions is different in at least one respect from the present struggle over the Russian Revolution. Both those who accepted the French Revolution and those who rejected it believed that values in social life could be demonstrated or proved. Values such as justice, liberty, natural rights, were accepted by both sides; Burke and Thomas Paine were trying to prove the same thing, although with widely variant theories of how to prove them. But since then values have tended to become myths, and power has tended to become technique in the atheistic humanism of the nineteenth century, as in the thought of Feuerbach, Comte, and Nietzsche. Against the relativist and pragmatic democratic intellectual, appears the Marxian, the supporter of the Russian regime and its expansion, who insists he has a scientific answer to everything. And in the cold light of the all-encompassing ideal of science, it is hard for the intellectual to say why the values of democracy can stand against dialectical materialism. To say, as some of the followers of John Dewey have done, that group experience, the dominance of the group, will give us answers, is surely futile, when the processes of group interaction produce the irreconcilable conflicts of modern times. C. Wright Mills in *White Collar* has suggested that to many intellectuals the revolution has become vulgar and the system of democratic society is accepted in a purely mechanical manner. To resist the new revolution, there must be an alternative faith. While we have many enthusiasts for revolution like Richard Price among us, there are on the other side few with the critical insight of an Edmund Burke.

V

But common men still believe in many things. They are largely opposed to the secular intellectual whenever they understand what the clamor of wordy battle is all about. If the common herd, as Browne said, follows the intellectual, you may have a revolution to remake society; but if the functioning citizen distrusts the intellectual leaders of important segments of society, the progress of society may be retarded, and retarded sharply in battle concerning values which are as old as the struggles between Plato and the Sophists. In a democratic society where there is a free communication of ideas and free elections, the people can at least make some sort of effective choice among the remedies offered them by those who edit the pharmacopoeia of the better world.

What then do the intellectuals promise? They promise a secular democracy, in which somehow spiritual values must take care of themselves. It is said that with psychology, the frustrations of the common man can be removed; with engineering and science, we can produce more worldly goods than he can consume; with economics, we can give assurance of a stable economy and high wages; with proper government policies, there can be liberty and security, and the lasting peace that poet and saint have so long prophesied. Art can be made popular and it can be appreciated; there will be plenty of novels to read, and entertainment will not be lacking. The great revolution, it is sometimes said, has already come and is behind us. The new frontiers of welfare beckon. But in all this there is another note: public opinion must be obedient; it must follow; and it must not be recalcitrant. Men must select the proper leaders and then not criticize them. It is surely uncertain whether the democratic citizen of our time is going to accept this prescription and such a leadership. It is not certain that he has accepted the secular democracy. Perhaps he wishes, as has the common man in other periods, to be creative.

CHAPTER 9

The Middle Class *

I

Two ancient symbols—public opinion and the middle class—have nearly always been associated in some degree. Public opinion has stood, first of all, for participation in the government of a society. Such participation has raised the issue of the quality of opinion or the quality of the participation in the government of *res populi.* From the time of the Greeks at least, the middle class has been regarded by certain conservatives, or let us say, Aristotelians, as having moderate, intelligent, and balanced opinion. Though public opinion and the idea of the middle class have been often associated, each has had different and divergent lines of emergence; different theoretical problems have been presented, and some of this development is to be outlined here. Yet at the tense moments of the eighteenth-century revolution, the French Revolution and its children, they were joined together in close doctrinal union at the height of a historical crisis.

The significance of this doctrinal union between public opinion and the middle class is to be found in other ideas associated with it. These ideas will be referred to as "the associated doctrines." These doctrines make the problematic of the two primary ideas clear, and they illustrate the theoretical force which brought

* Republished from *The Review of Politics,* XVII (October, 1955), 486 ff.

them together at a height of history. Such were the doctrines of progress, parliamentarism, the liberal or anti-Christian conceptions of ethics, and in times of crisis the principle of "dictatorship," which has seemed necessary since the days of the Roman Republic in order to meet the sterner contingencies of national survival. For the English, as Donoso Cortés insisted, dictatorship in crisis was always included within the power of Parliament. The Duke of Wellington understood this well in dealing with public disorders.

However, in the less mature parliamentarism of the continental liberals, it was necessary not only to have a theory of crisis and dictatorship, but also to make some provision in public law—*i.e.*, the state of siege—to enable institutions to surmount their critical moments. The defense of Napoleon III, by some who might well be called conservatives, is a recognition of the need for such provisions in public law. Walter Bagehot and Donoso Cortés were both in Paris to watch the progress of the Third Napoleon, and they both looked with considerable favor on the course of events. Said Bagehot, concluding his letters on the *coup d'état* of 1851:

> Mazzini sneers at the selfishness of shopkeepers—I am for shopkeepers against him. There are people who think because they are Republican there shall be no more 'cakes and ale.' Aye, verily, but there will though; or else stiffish ginger will be hot in the mouth. Legislative assemblies, leading articles, essay eloquence—such are good—very good—useful—very useful. Yet they can be done without. We can want them. Not so with all things. The selling of figs, the cobbling of shoes, the manufacture of nails—these are the essence of life. And let whoso frameth a Constitution for his country think on these things.*

Business men and scientists agree on one thing at least: too much interest in religion is bad for trade and for the bureaucratic position of the scientists. The associated doctrines held such a

* Walter Bagehot, *Literary Studies* (Everyman's Library, 1911), I, 331. See also Juan Donoso Cortés, *Obras Completas,* ed. by J. Juretschke (2 vols., Madrid, 1946), for Donoso's letters from Paris.

view. There was a vast optimism as to the intelligence of the middle class; as to its capacity to express the best of public opinion; and as to its willingness to stand for progress in industry, technology, empire, and the more balanced or sensible parties in parliamentary majorities. The proof of the intelligence of the middle class was to be found, it was thought, in the progress of the nineteenth century, and more especially in the commercial and industrial progress of Great Britain. However, the contemporary crisis is an era in which, for the first time since the rise of the idea of progress, there is a general questioning of its inevitability. The era of revolution and international war from August, 1914, to the present has produced a crisis of uncertainty, which suggests that both public opinion and the middle class have passed the zenith of their practical influence, and the doctrinal support they have received from the intellectuals of Western Europe.*

II

England was a model for the idea of public opinion in the nineteenth century. The continental writer on the subject inevitably had to use material drawn from British experience, simply because of the success of the British Parliament, the British Empire, the British armed forces, the stability of the Crown in the face of European revolutions, and the liberties accorded the subject in the expression of ideas. One might say that the success of the British came to be looked upon by some as the success of the middle class, or that the public opinion of Great Britain was regarded as being purely and simply the public opinion of the middle class. In any case, many Englishmen considered their country to be a kind of modern realization of the

* Charles A. Micaud has spoken of the sense of guilt of the French intellectuals: "The guilt of the intellectual . . . is first the product of the intellectual's belief that he is a bourgeois by origin and way of life. He must atone for this original sin. He has economic and cultural privileges for which he must be forgiven." See "French Intellectuals and Communism," *Social Research,* XXI (Autumn, 1954), 290.

Periclean ideal, the exemplar of progress, political stability, and prosperity, as well as of intellectual and cultural achievement. The British Constitution became the model for conservatives on the continent, just as English "parliamentarism" became the model for the critic and the liberal. But for the Englishman there was a particular philosophy—the utilitarian system—which justified the power of public opinion in the emergent parliamentary democracy of Great Britain.

When Jeremy Bentham began writing on politics and ethics he spoke of "the Legislator" very much as the ancients or Rousseau might have spoken of him; the standards of public ethics were not, apparently, to arise from the public opinion of British or any other society, but from Bentham himself. Philosophic radicalism * spoke of "the popular sanction." Bentham referred in the 1823 edition of *The Principles of Morals and Legislation* to both the wide use and the French origin of the term "public opinion," though he preferred to use "popular sanction." Even when Bentham and his group moved over to the support of political democracy, it was apparent that the public to be trusted was the English middle class, which in England was viewed as the most rational political class which had ever appeared in history. Consciousness of public opinion was, indeed, acute in England from the beginning of the nineteenth century; its organization, its manipulation, its use in politics, and the level of its perceptiveness, were all issues in the English consideration of the issue of political participation.†

* English writers contributed the word "radical" to the political vocabulary; "liberal" originated in Spain, it seems, around 1812, and spread rapidly to Western Europe. "Conservatism" was contributed by the French through Chateaubriand around 1818. "Socialism," "communism," as well as other words of this sort, are likewise French contributions. See G. Bastide, "Notes sur les Origines Anglaises de Notre Vocabulaire Politique," *Revue des Sciences Politiques*, 58 (1935), 524 ff; Arthur E. Bestor, "The Evolution of the Socialist Vocabulary," *Journal of the History of Ideas*, IX (1948), 259 ff.

† R. L. Hill, *Toryism and the People* (1929), 36, notes that between 1832-1846 the extra-parliamentary political association in England succeeded in mobilizing and regimenting public opinion. As public opinion thus be-

In the sustained self-examination conducted by British thinkers following the French Revolution, new interpretations of society were proposed. As elsewhere, the struggle between the emergent and conscious conservatism of the new age and the critical, radical, or liberal trend clarified the issue and made inevitable a wider appeal to public opinion by all who considered political questions. In effect, such discussion meant that man's power to shape his own society, his standards of morality, and his ability to create his future were increasingly asserted. In an atmosphere in which the moral world was becoming subject to formal plebiscite, deterministic philosophies had difficulty in retaining their hold. Malthus might propose against Godwin the objective factors which he believed determined the course of history, but neither Malthus nor climatic determinism could be warmly accepted in a day in which the middle class, especially, was being called upon to vote for one moral order against another. It was felt that whatever the forces might be which shape history and human character, they could be engineered. Such was the view of men like Robert Owen, but such also were in degree the views of those who lauded the public opinion of Englishmen.

Both the engineering concept of the environment and belief in the reason of men led to a deeper appreciation of Bentham's "popular sanction." But if the radicals and utopians moved steadily toward a sharper criticism of political institutions, they did not carry with them that new and powerful group of economists who, in many ways, symbolized for the world the achievements of Britain in industry and commerce. Broadly, the economists favored the mixed constitution—that is, the British system

---

came effective, the possibilities of the political campaign were realized. The reformers at the time of the Reform Bill in 1832 believed in universal suffrage, and to them middle class rule had become the rational ideal. Even James Mill, that great believer in the rationality of man, had contempt for popular movements. See Mill to Brougham, in Alexander Bain's *John Stuart Mill* (1882), 363-364. Robert Owen put some of his faith, as expressed in *The Crisis*, in the new public opinion that was arising in the world. On the influence of public opinion during the early nineteenth century, see Melvin M. Knight, "Liquidating Our War Illusions," *Journal of International Relations*, XII (1922), 485 ff.

which had gradually taken shape after the revolution of 1688. There was still at the time a strong tendency to regard the historical and chartered share of the people as the proper democratic ingredient in a political system. Political thinkers of the time therefore resisted the ever-widening demand for an extension of the right to vote. Hume, Adam Smith, Malthus, McCulloch and Senior were for a widely extended economic freedom, but they did not propose to grant the same right to the people in politics. For the people were, or could be dangerous, if they had a power in voting which went beyond the established liberties of the British system.* Yet, the democratic idea had been spreading in England since the time of the American Revolution through the labors of Price, Priestly, Cartwright, and others. The right to vote was increasingly argued to be the inalienable right of all, for it was held that personality and not property should be the basis of representation. More Englishmen than ever were asking for the right to vote, in addition to the assurance of such civil liberties as freedom of the press, of meetings, and of associations.†

* William D. Grampf, "On the Politics of the Classical Economists," *The Quarterly Journal of Economics*, LXII (1948), 714 ff.

† See Elie Halevy, *The Growth of Philosophic Radicalism*, trans. by Mary Morris (1928), 122 ff, who stresses John Cartwright's *Take Your Choice* (1776). One may, of course, cite the various reform movements of the time in this connection, such as Spence's agrarian communism, Howard's prison reform movement, Wilberforce's criticism of slavery, and Robert Owen's proposals for the reorganization of human nature and economic society. It was significant, then, that by 1817 Bentham espoused the cause of parliamentary democracy in his Plan for Parliamentary Reform. Bentham favored, with the Radicals in general, universal suffrage, annual parliaments, and election by ballot. Bentham wanted secrecy, universality, equality, and annuality of the suffrage.

It is fairly clear that Bentham turned to democracy after he had discovered the existing ruling class was unwilling to accept his proposals for reform. In his *Constitutional Code*, Bentham wanted an omnicompetent legislature, with no bill of rights, since, if we have the sovereignty of public opinion, nothing should be regarded as definitive. A bill of rights is conservative, and it is against the reforming spirit. He rejected, of course, the idea of a mixed state and the separation of powers.

On the other hand, the pages of Blackwood's Magazine from the period immediately after the fall of Napoleon to far into the nineteenth century

In the larger sense, however, Englishmen were becoming more enthusiastic about their public opinion, especially in contrast with other nations. William A. Mackinnon saw the test of civilization in the growth of the middle class, which exhibited particularly rational qualities. But, in turn, it was the British middle class which he took for his example.* The task he set for himself was to answer the question: what is public opinion? And his answer was that public opinion "is a sentiment that depends on the degree of information and wealth, which together may be styled civilization, and also with a proper religious feeling that exists in any community." But he held also that the rise of the middle class is the test of the growth of civilization. Because of commerce and manufacturing, England had the greatest middle class, and nowhere else is public opinion as powerful. Now the power of public opinion, argued Mackinnon, rises in proportion to its information, proper religious feelings, the facility of communication, and the capital existing among the individuals who compose the community. In turn a government becomes liberal in exact proportion to the increase in the power of public opinion. Moreover, the increased use of machinery brings an extension of capital, and thus augments the middle class and the power of opinion. Mackinnon was convinced that machinery changes the relative position of classes by increasing the power of the middle group. But the security of liberal government and liberty (ideas which Mackinnon did not clearly define) is the strength of what

---

demonstrate the conservative fear of the new power of public opinion. Rationality was not the primary quality of the masses, and yet the Tories were called on to pay more attention to the power of opinion in politics. Isaac Disraeli praised the ability of Elizabeth I in guiding public opinion. "This was the time of first beginning in the art of guiding public opinion. Ample volumes, like those of Fox, powerful organs of the feelings of the people were given them . . . In the revelations of the Verulamian philosophy, it was a favourite axiom with its founder, that we subdue Nature by yielding to her." See Isaac Disraeli, *Amenities of Literature*, new ed. by his son Benjamin Disraeli (1867), 376, 380.

* William A. Mackinnon, *On the Rise, Progress and Present State of Public Opinion in Great Britain and Other Parts of the World* (2nd ed., 1828), *passim.*

he chooses to call public opinion. By implication at least he seemed to think that only in Protestant England does one find a society as it ought to be. Catholic societies are simply lumped with all the other backward areas of the world. "Public opinion may be said to be that sentiment on any given subject which is entertained by the best informed, most intelligent, and most moral persons in the community, which is gradually spread and adopted by nearly all persons of any education or proper feeling in a civilized state." *

Negatively, Mackinnon ventured that popular clamor is not public opinion. Clamor is strong to the degree that the lower classes are ignorant and numerous in comparison with other strata in the community. And one might easily see that Mackinnon thought popular clamor had less power in England than in any country of Europe. He did not believe, considering the framework of his definition, there was any public in the ancient republics, and it was, therefore, unfruitful to discuss them. Thus to him English history is the greatest illustration of the growth of public opinion. With improved means of communication, the spread of education, a free press, and the development of transportation, public opinion emerges. Liberty and freedom increase and governments become more liberal and popular.† Prejudice and superstition vanish before proper religious sentiments, information, and civilization. Magna Carta attained little result because at that time there was no middle class; and the rise of the middle class in England explains the acceptance of the Reformation. Capitalism, commerce, and manufactures arose, likewise, because of the spread of the Reformed religions. Writing before the Reform Bill, Mackinnon insisted that the House of Commons as constituted at that time did represent the public opinion of the community more effectively than if it should be elected by universal suffrage and by ballot. The Commons represents the

* *Ibid.*, 15.

† The similarity of these ideas to those of Tönnies, who found public opinion in the commercial and contractual *Gesellschaft* may be readily noted.

property of the country—that is, the middle and upper classes. Universal suffrage would simply substitute the lower classes and popular clamor for public opinion. As the lower orders rise into the middle class, they will share in the existing representation of public opinion. In England, all persons share an equality of opportunity, and all classes are open to the talent and industry of each individual. Hence, any conflict between classes is impossible. Still, a larger upper class would provide added security for the British Constitution, the most perfect ever contrived by man.

Mackinnon felt that England had been fortunate while the Continent lagged far behind. With the rise of such a middle class as that of the British, a new public opinion will foster peace between nations. The rise and fall of nations may be traced in the rise and fall of the middle classes, for when the nourishment of the middle class fails, the power of a society declines. Despotism emerges from an expanding lower class. Moreover, if the French lower orders had been Protestant, the excesses of the Revolution would not have been so great, since there would have been more moral restraint. French public opinion was not sufficiently strong to withstand the lower class.

James Mill and John Stuart Mill can, however, be regarded as the great formulators of the radical and liberal view in England. It was a view that demanded, indeed, the freedom and education of public opinion. Perhaps the Philosophic Radicals believed as much as any other group ever has in the rationality of man, and in the ease with which rational political principles and practice may be attained. It is said that James Mill converted Bentham to political liberalism in about 1808, and then to Philosophic Radicalism. But the summation of James Mill's position may be found in his article on Government in 1820 for the *Encyclopaedia Britannica.* Man can be rational, and if he is let alone in the pursuit of his rational ends, a free society can be achieved. John Stuart Mill records that his father had such faith in reason that he considered all would be gained if the whole population were taught to read, if all kinds of opinions were addressed to it, and if it could through the suffrage nominate a legislature to give effect to the opinions it adopted. If a new legislature should abandon the representation of the customary class interests, it would reflect the general interests, honestly, and with sufficient wisdom.* James Mill was opposed to the power of the landowning families, and he favored the middle class. But John Stuart Mill was concerned with limiting the power of political groups. His *Representative Government* solved the problem by insisting on legislative control of the executive, and on the establishment of an identity of interest between the representatives and the country by short terms and by an enlarged suffrage. John Stuart Mill proposed the rationalization of the modern system of democracy and the power of public opinion which is, in general, accepted in our times. His essential proposition seemed to be, not that any particular expression of public opinion will be rational, but that the trend is in the direction of progress.

In John Stuart Mill's *A System of Logic, Ratiocinative and Inductive* one may find much of the credo of modern social science. But in it, too, one may find an argument for the long-run trend toward progress—a progress that can justify an immediate and broad faith in the right of all individuals to have a share in political decisions. Mill must not be accused, however, of having too much of an immediate confidence in men, nor in having any unlimited faith in the justice of the majority. And in *Liberty*, he said: "Despotism is a legitimate mode of government in dealing with barbarians. . . ." Circumstances must conspire with ideas to bring them into a rational and scientific system. Men are stupid and selfish as individuals and stodgy as a mass.† Moreover, in his idea of representative government, there should be ample safeguard against the tyranny of the majority, a principle he drew from Tocqueville's *Democracy in America*, as he recounts in his *Autobiography*. Still, the principle of a science of society prevails. The hope of the growth of rational-

* J. S. Mill, *Autobiography* (1873), Ch. IV.

† *On Liberty*, Ch. iii; *Dissertations and Discussions*, II, 269, "The Claims of Labor."

ism and the justification of the new system must rest finally on the progress of society through the stages of August Comte, from the religious period to the metaphysical, and from the metaphysical to the positive or the scientific.

Having rejected the concept of the historical cycle as found in Vico, Mill took instead the idea of a trajectory of progress. Progress is, in the long view, a linear march of men toward a rational perception of the interests and the laws of society. Properly understood, history does afford empirical laws for society. Progress, under this view, is a kind of rational necessity, though great men may determine the celerity of the progressive movement. It is, in the end, the intellectual element that is predominant in bringing about progress. "The intellectual changes are the most conspicuous agents in history . . ." History must be either cycle or progress, and Mill, like his utilitarian associates, took progress.

But A. D. Lindsay has raised this question: can a public opinion as intolerant as Mill describes it be induced to pass tolerant laws without itself being converted to tolerance? Such laws, in Mill's theory, might be the work of an enlightened minority; or, even if the public is intolerant, it may be convinced that intolerant laws will defeat its own ends. There are limits on the power of the state, especially when one realizes that coercion is often a useless and a dangerous instrument in affairs of the human spirit. So Lindsay concludes that the *Representative Government* combines Mill's enthusiasm for democratic government with the most pessimistic apprehensions as to what public opinion is likely to be.*

In *Utilitarianism* we are assured that the influences working for the improvement of the human mind are on the increase: these tendencies will generate greater feelings of unity and happiness with the rest of the community. But *On Liberty* tells us that "the majority have not yet learnt to feel the power of the

* See A. D. Lindsay's introduction to the Everyman edition of John Stuart Mill, *Utilitarianism, Liberty, and Representative Government,* xviii-xix.

government as their power, or its opinions their opinions. When they do so, individual liberty will probably be as much exposed to invasion from the government, as already it is from public opinion." The doctrine of liberty, Mill argued, applies only to human beings in the maturity of their faculties; the tendency of the modern world is "to stretch unduly the powers of society over the individual, both by the force of opinion and even by that of legislation." People tend to "like in crowds," the mind bows to the customary, and mediocrity is ascendant. Even in England where the public is primarily the middle class, public opinion is still the opinion of the mass, "that is to say, collective mediocrity."

Thus Mill's argument for liberty tends to become a searching criticism and a condemnation of much that has been prevalent in modern society. Liberty was in increasing danger; public opinion seemed to be all-powerful; and the public was "an overruling majority." By the Hare system of minority representation, Mill believed that "the very elite of the country" could be brought into Parliament in order that the basic tendencies of public opinion could be checked. Since mediocrity is implied in an extensive franchise, the system of proportional representation might reverse the trend of the times. "The modern regime of public opinion," said Mill in *Liberty*, "is, in an unorganized form, what the Chinese education and political systems are in an organized; and unless individuality shall be able successfully to assert itself against the yoke, Europe, notwithstanding its noble antecedents and its professed Christianity, will tend to become another China." Yet Mill's defense of representative government is strong; it educates the people; and his enthusiasm for a common and general participation in the affairs of government seems unstinted.

Among the significant treatments of public opinion during the last century, one must rank high the labors of James Bryce. Much that was said of public opinion by Englishmen—Coleridge, Carlyle, Bagehot, Acton, H. S. Maine, and others—might point to the immaturity of public opinion; they might urge caution, and show hope for the future emergence of popular intelligence;

but they did not write extended treatises on the nature of public opinion, such as one may find in the pages of Bryce's *American Commonwealth.**

For Bryce, a central theme was the sovereignty of public opinion in a democracy, especially in the United States. He viewed that sovereignty then with no fear; rather, he welcomed it and saw in it one of the foundations of American greatness. Yet in Bryce one can discover the distinction that in subsequent years has so troubled the students of public opinion, the distinction between opinion and "real" opinion. There is little individuality in American opinion, Bryce believed; because of the lack of substance in opinion, it is rather sentiment than thought that the masses can contribute. The upper classes know their interests better than the lower groups, where sentiment predominates. Though aristocrats furnish the people with ideas, nearly all the great political causes have made their way first among the middle or humbler classes. The trouble with mere sentiment, as Bryce saw, was its passive character, its inability to spring to the leadership of democratic movements. What leaders know of public opinion is, therefore, largely sentiment. And "the longer public opinion has ruled, the more absolute is the authority of the majority likely to become, the less likely are energetic majorities to arise, the more politicians are likely to occupy themselves, not in forming opinion, but in discovering and hastening to obey it." Thus, in the United States, where there is no formal ruling class, public opinion has as much power as it has ever had, even as much as the citizens had in the Assembly at Athens or Syracuse.

During the last century, those like Bryce who saw the middle class as the vehicle for the sovereignty of the "proper" public opinion, believed, likewise, that the fundamental issues of society had been resolved. There was to be no conflict on fundamentals in the future; indeed, it would be the age of internal peace and international security. Bryce was unimpressed with the forebodings of Tocqueville, and he could not accept the prophetic analysis

* See the author's article, "James Bryce on Public Opinion: Fifty Years Later," *The Public Opinion Quarterly*, III (1939), 420-435.

of Alexander Hamilton. Until late in his life, he seemed unaware of the portentous issue of propaganda, especially by governments. To Bryce, the newspapers were the chief organs of public opinion, and papers in the United States contained "more domestic political intelligence than any, except perhaps two or three of the chief English journals." The American press served the expression of public opinion and subserved the formation of opinion better than did the press of any part of the European continent. Our newspapers, he insisted, are above the level of the machine politicians. While in Europe the public meeting, discussion, and conversation are more important than in the United States, our general habit of reading papers make this less necessary. After World War I Bryce discovered propaganda. The press came to be viewed as an agency of propaganda, rather than as the true mirror of public opinion. And it was in international relations that he came most to fear the press.

The discovery of propaganda and the reality of class conflict, especially as a result of the Russian Revolution and the rise of socialism, came too late in his life for Bryce to examine its consequences for middle-class public opinion. To have understood the full force of these two political realities would have meant the desertion of much of his nineteenth-century optimism about the future of democratic government. Neither Tocqueville nor Mill nor Bryce could ever realize that the minority can be even more tyrannical than the majority, though Bryce felt that in America the majority was never the tyrant that Tocqueville believed it to be.

III

In the most optimistic of nineteenth-century thought the perfection of the British Constitution was associated with the perfection of middle-class opinion. The middle classes were aligned with the aristocracy, and both were allied against the lower orders of society, which were excluded from participation in the political system under the mixed constitution. In Greek theory, however, the middle class was a balance between extremes; and the mixed constitution was, in the work of Aristotle, a system which was possible of attainment. The political balance was between oligarchy and democracy, between the political energies of the rich and those of the poor. Nor should one confuse the philosophical perfection of the "mean state" in Aristotle's *Ethics* with the average city or the middle range in the possession of wealth. The whole political community might attain some greater ethical perfection, as indicated in a mean state of virtue, but it would not imply that the middle class had any monopoly on virtue. For virtue is something in which all might share, and the man of perfect virtue was outside of any class in an economic sense; he was the realization of philosophic perfection.

Following the French Revolution, however, there was for a time a passionate admiration and laudation of the middle class. None were quite sure just who the middle classes were, but somehow the English Constitution both before and after the Reform Bill of 1832 gave the world the model of balance, mixture, and the attainment of a middle-class society that was increasingly prosperous and enlightened. That time has passed—the day of middle-class perfection is gone—but its sincerity and its hope for progress were deeply real to the minds of another generation. The British Constitution stood to the European of the day as the model of mixture, stability, and the proper amount of popular participation to be allowed in government. In such an atmosphere, the attempt to restrict the suffrage to the middle class was also an attempt to preserve the mixture and balance of the Constitution. It was with Mackinnon the defense of the British system and the condemnation of any extension of the right of suffrage to the working class. It was a theory of alliance between the aristocracy and the middle class that he had in mind, for he regarded the government as a joint enterprise between them. It was a doctrine of moderation, of political perfection, and almost the perfection of the British middle class itself.

Perhaps it is the principle of moderation that is the element of historical continuity between the ancient world and the modern.

Social stability, moderation, the middle class (which implies a wide distribution of wealth), and the mixed or balanced constitution have marched through the pages of doctrine from ancient times to the present. Aristotle's polity was not a democracy in his view, because the people did not alone have an unrestricted supreme power. The modern American democracy is rather like the Aristotelian polity or balanced constitution of the city. Aristotle sought to base his moderation on the general distribution of wealth, and the restriction of the numbers of the very rich and the very poor. Yet moderation in politics requires more than a mere distribution of wealth; it is not merely a question of economics and politics. Ultimately, moderation for the ancient world, as for every generation, must be a question of virtue and reason, as Cicero saw when he summarized the philosophy of previous generations. The Ciceronic *res publica* was to be built on the mixture and balance of the Roman Constitution, but it was still to be a republic of reason and virtue; it was again a matter of philosophic moderation as the foundation for a political arrangement of offices.* Can we not see also the virtue of moderation as the principle of St. Thomas' mixture and justice in the constitution? Yet one can hardly find the middle class in St. Thomas; for virtue, reason, and law are broader and more fundamental than any class; they transcend all classes, and they deny the sovereignty of any class, since they affirm the sovereignty of law and of people who have certain qualities of intellect and will. Though one must show responsibility in the ordering of his wealth, still the mere distribution of wealth is not going to achieve justice in a state that lacks a Christian character. Without just individuals, there will be no moderation in the social personality. Moreover, virtue and reason, not mere class, would be the foundation for any commendable political opinions, and for the popular political participation which inevitably stands forth in the Thomistic conception of government.

* See Cicero, *De Officiis,* trans. by Walter Miller (1913), I, xi, 142 ff, for a discussion of "moderation." Moderation and temperance are frequently discussed by Cicero.

It was, let us say, frankly a Thomistic balance and a Christian system of moderation that Richard Hooker sought in England at the end of the sixteenth century. It was at this time he rejected the excesses of the Puritan movements, the mass and Gnostic movements of revolution which would first reform the church and then overturn the state. Hooker wanted to turn to the professional classes, not just the shopkeepers, many of whom happened to be Puritans. Instead of shopkeepers he would turn to the lawyers, to the universities, and to the well-trained clergy, for sanity in ideology and for the support of the Constitution. Moderation would come, here, from the classes of skill and virtue, the professional and functional classes, and not merely from those who ranked in wealth between the rich and the poor. And writers today have discovered Hooker to be the founder of British conservatism.* Surely, it is the defense of the mixed Constitution, the moderation of the educated, the rationality of the Anglican clergy, and the service of the professions, rather than of a mere middle class that gave him his claim to be a conservative. To Hooker, the Roman republican ideal would not be strange; he might with Cicero look to its restoration, but also to its reincarnation in the Constitution of the Tudor period, or the system of the Elizabethan Settlement.

In the end, this conclusion can be reached: the search for moderation, as shown in the literature of politics, is too broad for the middle class. The search for moderation includes all men, from the philosophers of the ancient world to those of the Renaissance, but not to the immoderate Jacobins of the age of liberalism. When one searches for moderation in politics, he may well defend the mixture and balance of the Constitution; he may well defend a census for the suffrage, but he cannot remain contented with the middle class, either in the liberal formulation of the ideal or with the middle class as it has been exemplified in history.

Indeed, the seeker for moderation in politics and in public opinion may well join with some of the socialists in their charac-

* Russell Kirk, *The Conservative Mind* (1953), 6, 18, 33.

teristic excesses when they rejected the middle classes both high and petty. Aristocrats and proletarians have denounced the middle class from the time of its modern emergence to social influence; the aristocrats, because the bourgeoisie lacked culture, a fine sense of responsibility, and moderation in politics; and the socialists, like Karl Kautsky, because the middle class men were the victims of all political or ideological absurdities. It is just as the communists say today: the middle-class people are fascists at heart. Christians often say the middle-class people are the epitome of greed, and they have, in the hardness of their hearts, no charity. The ancients let the middle class stand between those who are natural or normal participants in the class struggle. One can accept the historic theory of balance in the Constitution, as Polybius did, without being committed to the sovereignty of a class, middle or otherwise. Let us seek for moderation, for the constitutional ideal; let us recognize elements in a social structure that exhibit moderation and competence in opinion. The problem is to find such elements of a social structure, and to determine which of them comes closer to practicing the ideal one may have for public policy. But it should be remembered that the middle class, or any "class," can never be more than just a part of the state, while public opinion is by definition a universal idea.

The middle class in literature is, of course, far from the complexities of any actual situation. It is in its literary form a typical liberal concept of the aggregate or group, a statistical character, which takes no account of the existential. It knows no individuals, but it characterizes a great mass of them without individual differentiation. It is social rather than existential. The middle class in England that the utilitarians, the Bagehots, the Mackinnons and many others discovered was the middle class of the eighteenth century. It was a time of expanding empire and the rise of new social types, while the theory of balance and mixture in the Constitution was discovered to have existed for generations. De Lolme and Blackstone may be called to witness, as well as Hume and the classical economists. Students have listed them, the new types and the new middle class, which was universalized and idealized in the nineteenth century during its short reign—that is, down to the wars and disasters of the twentieth century. And the types were more than the "shopkeepers" who were used to symbolize lamely the England of the middle class.

A professional group is not a mere statistical conception, adopted for methodological purposes. Such a group is an observable fact in any society, and it is the kind of group on which a pluralistic theory of social organization can be built. Yet in the abstract, the discussion of the "middle class" suggests the statistical conception rather than the total and observable social fact. May not one say that a fatal weakness of the whole middle-class theory is that it has always been statistical, and that as a "class" it has not been the type of group one could properly use to construct a pluralistic theory of human society? Moreover, it is easy to confuse the useful or mechanic professions, and those based on the *artes liberales* with a class, or the statistical aggregate called a class, such as the middle class. It is obvious, also, that when the ancient writers distinguished the "useful" occupations from those based on knowledge, such as the labors of a gentleman, they were not then thinking of the middle class, which was essentially and merely a statistical notion of the distribution of wealth. Inevitably, criticism of the shopkeeper, the merchant, or the industrialist leads to a rejection of the middle conception of society.*

In the England of the eighteenth century there were adventurers, philosophers, economists, literary men, merchants or shopkeepers, industrial leaders or the members of management as we would now say, journalists and periodical writers, bureaucrats or civil servants, clubmen, the Methodists, and Freemasons. Some were

* Cicero, *De Officiis,* I, xlii, 150 ff; I, xlv, 155. T. R. Malthus may be cited as one who was both friendly and critical of the middle class. He was critical, for example, of merchants and industrialists. See Richard B. Simons, "T. R. Malthus on British Society," *Journal of the History of Ideas,* XVI (January, 1955), 64-65. To argue that the middle class should "rule" society is, no doubt, as fallacious as arguing that the working class should be sovereign. A conservative doctrine finds a place for both, and extends to both a share in political power.

approved here and others there, but hardly could the opinion of all of them agree or be approved by all others. The recognition of the function in social life of these groups led, quite naturally, to class collaboration rather than to an accentuation of class conflict. Collaboration meant in turn moderation in politics, and a rejection of the mass movements for the terrestrial salvation of all men without distinction or discrimination.* Each of these might be approved or disapproved separately, but one could not effectively throw them all together into what some would call a statistical middle class. One group might fit into the historic Constitution more easily than others; one group might show more political moderation than others. But it is certain that leadership and primacy of function did not of necessity go to a businessman, a manufacturer, or to another group of any kind just as a matter of course.

One can say, it would seem, that the defense of the mixed constitution and the role assigned to public opinion in it is different from a defense simply considered of the middle class. The mixed Constitution goes far back into history, before the rise of anything like a modern middle-class group. The mixture of the Roman Constitution, moreover, does not resemble the arrangements of the Greek city state, where a balance between oligarchy and the *hoi polloi* was sought. The Greek conception of a middle class was an ideal to be sought, rather than the recognition of a social fact in political organization. The Greek balance in the constitutions of the city states was different from the Roman system, and from the British and American systems of mixture and check and balance, established for the preservation of moderation in politics. Neither is it possible to say that a middle class, noted for its late eighteenth-century revolutionary inclinations, could be relied on to preserve mixture, balance, moderation, or any degree of political serenity. The primary search has been for moderation and competence in public opinion, or rather a virtuous and free

* See Mario Hernández Sanchez-Barba, "Los Fundamentos Sociológicos del Imperialismo Histórico Britanico" (1765-1786), *Revista de Estudios Políticos*, No. 76 (July-August, 1954), 61-113.

public opinion; and the idea that the middle class would provide such opinion was only hypothesis rather than social fact. That public opinion might be restrained by a complicated constitutional arrangement was obvious. But it was not certain that such arrangements accorded with the wishes of a middle class. A mixed Constitution may assist in the expression of restraint, competence, moderation, and order in popular participation. Such qualities, however, must rest finally on the educability of men. They must rest on the assumption that individuals may be taught virtue and reasonableness, as Socrates, Aristotle, the Stoics, and the Christians have believed.

IV

We may say today there is a crisis in the middle class; and if we consider the middle class as an economic group of small businessmen, as is commonly the case in European writings, there is and has been one indeed. We say there is a crisis in government by public opinion; and if we consider dictatorship, or the waning of moderation and democratic techniques in government today, there is indeed. But whether the crisis of public opinion and the crisis of the middle class is the same crisis is another issue. Today's crisis may mean the final separation of the sometimes coinciding evolutions of public opinion and the middle class. A restoration of freedom in government may not restore the idea of a middle-class society as a social ideal, and the restoration of some form of middle class may not in fact restore the mixed or balanced constitution on its historical form.

A revolutionary bourgeoisie once created the symbols of revolutionary progress, and the sovereignty of the class; another revolution by the proletariat, which tried to overthrow the middle class at the moment of its triumph, has now, no doubt destroyed the promise of the middle class theory of society. Revolution today stands against the middle class, and it would destroy the constitutional system that the triumphant bourgeoisie learned to love —the balanced constitution modified by the parliamentary system of responsible government. The crisis raises questions about the liberal free-market system, and the free competition of any kind of ideas, including those of the contemporary conspirators. The revolution suggests a Hobbesian concentration of power, the loss of balance and civil rights, and in turn the frightful loss of moderation shown by the massacres and forced labor of modern dictatorships. Into a new system of political illusion, in which the middle class plays little or no part, has come the principle of equality established by law, and a conformity in idea under a benevolent civil service that goes beyond anything appropriate to an earlier theory of the middle class.*

In retrospect, the defense of the middle class appears a transitional stage which has passed more quickly than many other political ideas that have been put into modern practice. The very defense of the "middle class" implied another class which might seize its political power. If not this, then the substitution of unpolitical functional groups where forceful opinion on other than purely professional matters is difficult to generate. In other words, such groups follow the leadership of the "political class" on the assumption that their own status is recognized.

What, then, can be the relation of the middle class and public opinion, when ideas or symbols have been radically changing during the last fifty years of revolution and war? Public opinion is ceasing to be the rational ideal of reforming liberals or utilitarians; instead, it is becoming a series of symbols directed at the individual by the techniques of mass communication. It is mass communication usually in close agreement with the government, especially if such means of communication are owned by a government in a nation where democracy has been weakened or destroyed. Propaganda is directed at the mass man, the ordinary man, the man of the lonely crowd,† in which control may be highly oligarchical.

* Bertrand de Jouvenel, *The Ethics of Redistribution* (1951).

† David Riesman, Reuel Denny, and Nathan Glazer in *The Lonely Crowd* (1950), have provided a widely influential existential statement of the character of the modern man. The issue is noted in Chapter *XII*.

Moreover, the middle class is ceasing to be the wealth producing class that it was once at the onset of industrialization. Instead of businessmen and owners of property, the middle class is becoming a group of people engaged in the professions, seeking government contracts and employment, and meanwhile in various ways trying to assure themselves of security in old age. The poverty of the broad world is encroaching on the wealthier political systems, and in the process the middle class as a propertied class is finding its position weakened and the future solution of its problems increasingly uncertain. Production and the common man is the symbol of the future, not the rational sovereignty of the middle class.*

If one may say the middle-class theory of public opinion has been given unhealable wounds by the new revolutionary movements which use the techniques of mass communication to establish or to stabilize their own power, we may say also that the political idea which fostered such a theory of public opinion in the last century is now in full decay in most of the world. What is meant is that the idea of balance, of Attic moderation, of restraint in the action of government, and of the mixed constitution, is passing also. The new revolution is against the "parliament" as an ideal of discussion, and against the transmission of the sum of political power on the outcome of a division in the House of Commons. It is commonly said that European intellectuals are against both capitalism and parliamentarism. The parliament itself has represented a multiclass system, in which there was some balance in the divergent interest groups, and some compromise directed under the art and skill of the politicians. There could be no sovereignty of class in the theory of the mixed constitutions and its technical symbols, the check and balance system, and the two-house legislature. Our critical days suggest, then, not only the failure of the middle-class theory, but also the failure of the idealized parliament of the nineteenth century. Socialism as a

* See by way of further analysis, Alfred Sauvy, "On the Relation Between Domination and the Numbers of Men," *Diogenes*, No. 3 (Summer, 1953), pp. 31 ff.

whole has proposed that the power of the middle class be destroyed, and in its stead it has promised the dominance of the workers, under new political leaders.* Here is the end of balanced government as the expression of public opinion, and as the just expression of the mind of the common man.

Thus a new formula of life is emerging against the old theory of a universalized middle class, which was once considered the carrier of intelligence in public opinion and the sustainer of the parliamentary order. Public opinion as the expression of the middle class failed, just as the middle class, with its classical liberalism, failed to retain the loyalty of the masses of men for the new economic order and the parliament. Once the sovereignty of public opinion meant the middle class, the free market economy, and the parliament; but it does not, nor has it since the great revolutions of the West began in August, 1914. Before the emergence of the transitory sovereignty of the middle class, there was an ideal of functional groups which the French revolutionary leaders sought to destroy. The individual was goverened by groups in which he functioned, and the groups were governed in turn by political society. The modern revolution seems to be approaching something like the older feudal system: the individual will be a member of a productive group (not a potential member of a middle class), and the group will govern in some degree, while the state governs the group.

V

There is profound inquiry into the social structures of modern society, but there does not seem to be much certainty in the results. In the form of political ideals, we cling to the middle class principle as the best expression of intelligence, moderation, and democratic procedures. But the surveyors, the sociologists, psychologists, and political scientists and others who are preoccupied by what the public may be thinking are not so certain.

* See G. D. H. Cole, *A History of Socialist Thought* (5 vols., 1953-1960), *passim.*

If we say that the middle class ideal is the best, we also speak of a society which is without classes and which is moving steadily toward equality in the standards of life. But the social scientists seem convinced that a whole system of classes is taking shape in modern industrial society, and these classes have little relation to the nineteenth-century aggregation of people into a middle class. The point seems to be that the upper middle class is based largely on the privileges of university education; it is a diploma elite. The lower class has technical training, but its members do not move into the upper segment. For some, this division is so basic that the very words "middle class" might be stricken from the scientific vocabulary. If there is a rising fixity of class in industry, the individual may be fully conscious of his status in relation to other occupations, ethnic groups, and to his ability to consume the goods which are recognized as affording satisfaction in status. On the one hand, nearly all of the people may say they belong to the middle class; and, on the other hand, the social scientists may say there are at least half a dozen classes in modern America. Status groups and half a dozen classes may carry opinion, but the "middle class" seems to be a failing channel of communication except in times of crisis when there is great consensus about what the government should do.*

In an age of mass communication the ideal of "middle class communication" can be little more than ineffective aspiration. It is an effort to retain a nineteenth-century belief in the rightful rulership of the middle class. Indeed, the whole theory of generalized and democratic education rejects the idea of a monopoly of political intelligence and political sovereignty in the middle ranges of economic society.

The doctrines associated with middle class theories of public opinion are strikingly weakened in the present condition of

* See William Lloyd Warner, *Social Class in America* (1949). There is an impressive sociological literature on the subject. In a more popular vein, Vance Packard, *The Status Seekers* (1959), surveys the literature of the sociologists, the psychologists, the public opinion, and market researchers, which indicates that a new era beyond the middle class system is at hand.

society. With the shadow of fission warfare hanging over whole nations, the principle of progress seems more in question than it has since its formulation 200 years ago. Parliaments have in many cases failed completely, and in others their inability to deal with pressing questions had led to the view that "parliamentarism" is unsuited to the present day.*

The public opinion ideal and objective of the future would seem to be a free mass opinion, rather than a free middle class opinion. It would be the opinion of groups, however, in a reconstructed society, in which the principle of subsidiarity would find significant expression. In the balance of free groups there may be found the "new mixed constitution" of a limited state; here one may, perhaps, find the moderation and sanity in public opinion which it was once thought would be the office of the middle class to provide.

Much hangs in the balance. There is little "moderation at white heat" in our Western world. The middle class in its historic form, and public opinion in its middle-class-liberal version seem to have passed their commanding heights of influence. New social structures, however, are not yet mature in the free world, and hence one awaits as well the newer forms of public opinion and its system of expression. The modern bureaucracy can overwhelm all before it, and military necessity is like a flood that knows neither bank nor dike. The middle class that the Philosophic Radicals thought of as leaders of public opinion is not highly regarded; in its newer forms, it is often almost unpolitical, being interested in security, and a prey to all of the fears of the salaried

* Of course, the idea of material progress is still central in liberal thought. When Henry R. Luce spoke at the fortieth anniversary dinner of the *New Republic* in Washington, D. C., November 17, 1954, he said, among other things: "One thing clearly foreseeable in the future of the Republic of the human race is an immense increase in the world's wealth and standard of living. Even to call it an Age of Plenty may soon seem old-fashioned. Could there be any such thing as the Age of Too Much? . . . As for the rest of the world, most of it is a wretchedly poor place; yet it surely cannot escape the prospering impact of an American Age of Plenty." Reprint from the *New Republic*, December 6, 1954.

classes of the urban commercial and industrial system.* Groups approve of the views of the professions, and we may consider the professional men, the civil servant, and the ranges of management the newer upper middle class—if the term can still be applied with any propriety. Though Tocqueville saw that the American middle class was essentially religious, his strictures on the bourgeoisie in Europe were savage; he could not attribute to it charity or social generosity in any form.† Both the proletarians and the aristocrats have damned the bourgeoisie as unimaginative, harsh and greedy. Charles Dickens in his *A Christmas Carol* had love disappear when "business" entered in, and his middle-class men are surely no model for the rest of us.

* C. Wright Mills, *White Collar* (1951). To make the point more specific for emphasis, the middle class in its historic form has always been a class between two others, an upper and a lower. It has been the middle income and business group between large elements of the poor and the more limited numbers of the rich. This has been the Greek, Roman, medieval, and the modern meaning of the term. See, for example, H. Hill, "The 'Equites' as 'Middle Class,'" *Athenaeum,* XXXIII (1955), 327-332. Instead of such a class society, we are developing a "group interest" society, in which there is a dialectic between groups and group interests, and between groups and those who hold political power. See Samuel H. Beer, "Representation of Interests in British Government," *The American Political Science Review* LI (September, 1957), 613-650; G. A. Schubert, Jr., "The Public Interest in Administrative Decision-Making: Theorem, Theosophy, or Theory," *The American Political Science Review,* LI (June, 1957), 346 ff; C. W. Cassinelli, "Some Reflections on the Concept of the Public Interest," *Ethics,* LXIX (October, 1958), 48 ff.

† See J. P. Mayer, *Alexis de Tocqueville,* trans. by M. M. Bozman and C. Hahn (1940), 14, 134 ff. Tocqueville's judgment on the French middle class was expressed most forcefully in the early pages of the *Souvenirs.* One of the elements in the prophetic quality of Tocqueville's mind was that as a conservative he could yet reject the middle class. Here is the source of fruitful conservatism.

CHAPTER 10

The Proletarian Definition

I

The revolutionary flavor was stronger in the socialism of 1850 than of 1950. Having recognized that democracy was not irretrievably an instrument for the rule of the bourgeoisie, a large segment of the socialist movement was willing to commit itself to the preservation of the Classical ideas about public opinion, to accept parliamentarism, civil rights, party conflict, and the continued existence of free public opinion, in which, indeed, all individuals were to participate, whatever might be their class feelings.* But it had to be a public opinion to which all the means of communication were open, and to which the socialist could address his appeal. Like the Christian, the democratic socialist became confident that he was bound to win the masses to his side by persuasion, rather than by the coercive organization of a revolutionary government. And, though the socialist might, like the conservative, recognize that there is always some sort of class

* See in general G. D. H. Cole, *A History of Socialist Thought* (5 vols., 1953-1960), for a comprehensive treatment of the increasing socialist allegiance to democratic political action. The great new factor in the nineteenth century was the advance of representative government. Vol. I, p. 315: "As voting rights were extended, the possibility of the 'Welfare State,' resting on democratic pressure without violence, came gradually into view." Cole traces the rise of socialist parliamentarism throughout Western Europe.

struggle in progress, such a struggle might be either sharp and violent or more in the vein of friendly argument—somewhat as in a Chamber of Deputies.*

Marxian revolutionary thought, as it came into the twentieth century, was profoundly convinced of the oppressive and class character of parliamentary and democratic government. As the moderate socialists drew away from the stern materialism of Marx and Engels, the revolutionists drew closer, until the contemporary union of the Russian revolution and Marxian materialism was achieved. This new union could make no compromise with the ideology of democracy and constitutionalism, for a new state had to be constructed on dialectical materialism. According to Gray, Marx and Engels retained the then universal Cartesian dualism; they were epiphenomenalists, taking the customary materialist position of the time. The universe and the mind consist of matter in motion, and ideas arise from the conditions of material existence. Social existence, then, determines, consciousness. While these ideas had in part stemmed from Locke through Helvétius, Godwin, Owen, and others, Hegel and Marx were perhaps the first to see the indirect economic and social processes which influence our thinking.† As a participant in the drama of atheistic humanism, religion was for Marx and Engels the first object of attack; and after religious ideas had been destroyed they might begin the construction of a materialistic philosophy through which the economic and political system of both liberalism and conservatism might be destroyed.‡ It was possible, they thought as rationalists, that they might discover an absolute and materialistic truth about man in society. Some of the "truths" they discovered are familiar enough at the midpoint in the twentieth century. They believed, for example, that since capitalist and bourgeois economic interests use force to sustain themselves, only force can destroy

* Cf. Edmund Wilson, *To the Finland Station* (1940).

† J. L. Gray, "Karl Marx and His Social Philosophy," in F. J. C. Hearnshaw's *The Social and Political Ideas of Some Representative Thinkers of the Victorian Age* (1933), 116 ff; Eric Voegelin, "The Formation of the Marxian Revolutionary Idea," *The Review of Politics*, XII (1950), 275-302.

‡ See Henri de Lubac, *Le Drame de l'Humanisms Athée* (1945).

them. As Marx said, "force is the midwife of every old society that is pregnant with the new."

II

Marx was peculiarly concerned with conditions in France, and the influence of French experience on socialist tactics and theory has been profound. Marx was convinced that under Louis Bonaparte in the 1850s it was completely impossible for any general opinion to exist in France.* He described parliamentary government much as it was just before the advent of Hitler to power. Unbridgeable divisions in the bourgeoisie prevented any resistance to Napoleon, and the new dictator got the farmers, the Church, and the army to support him, thus forcing the bourgeoisie into line. But Marx observed that "taxation is the foundation of life to the bureaucracy, the army, the parsons, and the court, in short to the whole apparatus of the Executive power . . . A strong government and heavy taxes are identical." The French government could act as the mediator between classes, but the social and political situation was inherently unstable.† It was experience with the Commune in 1871 that had the greatest influence of all on the Marxian revolutionary attitude toward representative government. Marx's *The Civil War in France* was rewritten in Lenin's *State and Revolution,* and the two together constitute the primary justification of the tactics of Marxism as practiced in the Soviet Union. One point is clear: Marx insisted that the bourgeois state, the parliamentary state, and political democracy had no value for the working class. From this point on, it was clear that Marxian proletarian democracy had to be in its nature something new, different, and in contradiction with "democracy" in the nineteenth century.

Marx was convinced that after every revolution marking a

* See L. M. Case, "French Opinion and Napoleon III's Decision After Sadowa," *The Public Opinion Quarterly,* XIII (1949), 441 ff.

† See Frederick Engels, *Herr Eugen Dühring's Revolution in Science* (first pub. in 1894); Karl Marx, *The Eighteenth Brumaire of Louis Bonaparte,* trans. by Daniel De Leon (3rd ed., 1913).

progressive phase of the class struggle, the purely repressive character of the state power stands out in bolder relief. In France during the nineteenth century, the bourgeoisie had been losing the power to govern, but the proletariat had not yet reached a stage when it might seize the state. Bonapartism, thus, had to fill the gap or vacuum in the structure. The government stood outside and above the struggle between capital and labor. But whether a transitional Bonapartism is involved, a forthright regime of the bourgeoisie, or of the proletariat, two things are clear: the Marxist concept of the state as the agent of class repression limits or destroys both the liberal and conservative idea of public opinion. Proletarian democracy rejects the principle of government by discussion, if that principle includes discussion with or within the bourgeoisie.

Marx rallied his metaphors and similes, his fervor and enthusiasm, for the Commune. He praised the destruction of the old state machinery, he gloried in the new functional representation that the Commune established, he was moved by the excellence of the political virtue of the Parisian working class, and he saw even a new and glorious womanhood rising from the ruins of decadent bourgeois family life. Marx, like many of his followers, turned to a naïve adoration of the primitive crowd as the true foundation of democracy; he believed, it seems, that mass experience can generate useful and true ideas.*

In apology, Bertrand Russell has observed that Marx's ideas were formed when democracy did not yet exist. *Das Kapital* appeared in the year when the urban working class was first given the vote in England, and universal suffrage was granted by Bismarck in northern Germany. Marx, like the orthodox economists of his time, assumed that opinions are guided by class interest or economic self-interest. However, Russell was inclined to the view that both Disraeli and Bismarck were shrewder judges of human nature than either the liberals or the socialists.†

* Henry de Man, *The Psychology of Socialism*, trans. from 2nd German ed. by E. and C. Paul (1928), 36.

† Bertrand Russell, *Proposed Roads to Freedom* (1919), 30.

There are, of course, many sects and groups in the proletarian revolutionary movement, and each illustrates at least a mild ferocity in the condemnation of the other. The *Communist Manifesto* discusses at length the kinds of proletarian or socialist thought that Marx and Engels condemned. Some of these movements relied on political reform, and they were in effect proponents of what we call democracy. Such movements, primarily bourgeois and petty bourgeois socialism, looked to political parties working within the framework of the existing state for the establishment of a new social order. They made an appeal to mass opinion, including all social groups, and they were, it seems, the precursors of late nineteenth- and early twentieth-century democratic socialism. Such groups were composed of neither utopians nor anarchists, nor were they revolutionists; but they were perhaps close to some trends in liberal thought—closer, no doubt, than to the Marxian theory of revolutionary social change. But socialist hostility toward both the still strong forces of the Old Regime and the new and powerful bourgeoisie made it easy to reject the potential value of the historic state in favor of the socialist movement. It was, let us say, easier in the last century for a socialist or revolutionist to reject democracy than at the present time.

III

There are other currents in the revolutionary movement which criticize proletarian participation in politics. The communist will say that the worker can only participate worthily in the new proletarian state, but the anarchist and the syndicalist have doubts about any political participation; that is, they do not think that even a communized version of political democracy can offer anything to the working class. Certainly, they would agree with the communists that the democratic socialists are simon pure betrayers of the proletarian cause. The anarchist, who rejects the state and turns to a voluntary organization of society, would deny in effect the historic theory of public opinion, as the participating opinion of a commonwealth in which some ingredients of social justice may be found. Anarchism might, on the contrary, insist that its theory of public opinion is much purer and more elevated than any society which accepts the principle of coercion. For to the extent that coercion prevails, the freedom of public opinion is denied. Moreover, participation in functional groups formed on a voluntary basis could be argued to be the only possible free public opinion, since opinion would be free from the warping influence of present-day institutions. Such a free opinion would, in turn, be more forceful, perhaps even more coercive. The anarchists have believed, and still do—especially in the Latin countries—that liberty is the best remedy for the excesses of liberty. In this sense, anarchism can be considered a kind of exaltation of public opinion, as the only force needed in the organization of a just society. Participation, however, would be changed fundamentally in character, since whatever public might be conceived to exist would not be political but communitarian, and the individual would participate, not as the historic citizen, but simply as a functioning member of society.

Thus anarchism stands first of all for political abstention; it is non-voting carried to final implications. The state, being uncreative, is pushed aside for the creativeness of the masses in generating freely the proper social regulations. But abstention has not been enough, and therefore the anarchist has been led to formulate alternative political techniques, all based of course on the idea that the people, consciously or unconsciously, really want an anarchist or non-political organization of society. One of the illusions common among anarchists of the last century was belief in the great force of the propaganda of action, propaganda of the fact, or propaganda of the deed. A single individual might set such an example that others would be inspired to accept the new order of freedom. Prolo tells of the small group of Italian anarchists who in 1877 wanted to offer such an example. Early in the morning they seized the local police in a small village and they issued their manifesto to the people. But the people only called in police from outside and had the anarchistic visionaries arrested. It seems that Italian anarchists in particular tended to be taken by the idea of the propaganda of the deed. The socialists condemned these practices, as they condemned also assassinations of outstanding "oppressors" by individuals or small groups of anarchists. One must confess that the effect on the public mind of such "propaganda" was the reverse of what was expected by anarchists. As the Marxians also found, the ordinary man continued to be a citizen and often a patriot, and his attachment to democracy resisted the propaganda for the revolutionary overthrow of capitalism or of the modern state.*

Syndicalism as a proletarian movement has been equally critical of the state, but its emphasis on the organization of the new society has been different from that of the anarchists. French syndicalism in its revolutionary phase, down into World War I, criticized particularly the parliamentary or the democratic process because it was controlled by intellectuals. Syndicalism was anti-intellectual in two senses: it opposed the functioning intellectuals—such as journalists, professional socialist leaders, parliamentarians, bureaucrats, professors, clergy, and technicians—but it was also anti-intellectual in the sense that it rejected the processes of decision-by-discussion, turning instead to the realities of the class struggle led by proletarians. The syndicalists accepted violence as the creative way in which the proletariat might bring into being the new society in which the sovereign group would be those who produce, not those who consume. In detail, it meant that the working class should not have political parties or members of parliaments, that they should abstain from politics, and from general strikes primarily political in purpose.

In France, the pre-World War I General Confederation of Labor represented the syndicalist movement, while syndicalist ideas in the United States were debated in the struggle between the In-

* See Charles Gide and Charles Rist, *A History of Economic Doctrines from the Time of the Physiocrats to the Present Day* (n.d.), 634; F. W. Coker, *Recent Political Thought* (1934), 247. Gide and Rist stress particularly the ideas of Bakunin and Kropotkin. See Peter Kropotkin, *Modern Science and Anarchism* (1908), 48-49; Jacques Prolo, *Les Anarchistes* (1912), 14 ff.

dustrial Workers of the World and the Socialist Labor Party led by Daniel De Leon.* In the United States the issue centered on whether there should be, in addition to unions waging the class struggle, a political party which could organize and present the propaganda of the movement. As the anti-political movement faded in the United States, so World War I made much of syndicalist thought seem unreal. But the underlying anti-democratic trend—that is, the rejection of the traditional and constitutional democracy of the modern state—was clear in both instances. However, theoretical justification varied, since in the United States syndicalism was a clear addition to or interpretation of the Marxian analysis of the state, while in France late nineteenth-century anarchistic thought had been profoundly influential in the establishment of the General Confederation of Labor. After World War I, the French Confederation took an active part in political organization and in parliamentary affairs, while the Socialist Labor Party continued to insist that it was the only true Marxist party in the United States, and it offered to the voters its candidates for public office, including the Presidency.

Intellectually, the French syndicalist movement has been far more systematically hostile to political activity and to any compromise with democracy and parliamentary institutions than the American movement. The name of Georges Sorel, of course, stands out as the primary theorist of violence, and the chief formulator of techniques in non-political but effective struggle against the capitalist order.† According to Pouget, parliamentary life emphasizes a superficial analysis of politics. Such superficial opinions

* P. F. Brissenden, *The I.W.W.; A Study of American Syndicalism* (1919); James B. Stalvey, *Daniel De Leon: A Study of Marxian Orthodoxy in the United States* (Dissertation, University of Illinois, 1946).

† Georges Sorel, *Reflections on Violence*, trans. by T. E. Hulme (1912). See James H. Meisel, "Georges Sorel's Last Myth," *The Journal of Politics*, XII (1950), 52 ff; "A Premature Fascist?—Sorel and Mussolini," *The Western Political Quarterly*, III (1950), 14 ff; *The Genesis of Georges Sorel* (1951). A substantial recent literature on Sorel has developed, both in France and in the United States. One may note Richard D. Humphrey, *Georges Sorel, Prophet Without Honor* (1951); and James Burnham, *The Machiavellians, Defenders of Freedom* (1943).

are subject to change, and have in the long run little significance for the working man. What syndicalism attempts, in its rejection of a democratic theory of public opinion, is to turn to the long-run and permanent interests of the proletariat. According to the views of the syndicalists, these interests are not subject to rapid change, either by reinterpretation or by the counting of votes in elections, and a grouping of people by functional class is the only way to arrive at a realistic view of what public opinion is.* On the other hand, the rejection of the democratic theory of public opinion has implied for syndicalism the condemnation of the intellectuals, that is, syndicalism has been anti-intellectual as well as anti-parliamentary. Sorel observed that he had been struck by the ferocity of idealistic revolutions. The terror in France was the work of stubborn theorists, and it ignored the economic and juridical necessities of a real revolution in the interest of the proletariat. Intellectuals as ideologists, said Sorel, are thirsty for vengeance and power. It is certain that any revolution engineered by intellectuals will be marked by cruelty and ferocity. If a revolution could be achieved without the intellectuals and by the real members of the working class, it might be carried through much more peaceably than has been the case in the past.† In contrast, however, as the proletariat learns the necessity of the class struggle and becomes more willing to resort to violence, the proletariat will become correspondingly less interested in the mechanics of democratic politics. The workers will not vote; they will abstain from parliamentary politics, as the syndicalist movement has urged.

IV

Anarchism and syndicalism failed to become effective movements; they have taken their places along with utopian socialism in the backwash of proletarian ideas. The same can be said of other proletarian movements which have sought to reject the state or the conflicts of practical politics. It is through the state

* Emile Pouget, *La Confédération Générale du Travail* (1912), 27.
† Georges Sorel, *La Ruine du Monde Antique* (3rd ed., 1933), 314-315.

that access to the masses can be obtained, and thus it is through a *public* opinion, as against the social opinion of the community, that proletarianism can have its chance. Two great socialistic movements have taken the field in the twentieth century: the moderate or the democratic socialist movement, and the Bolshevik or communist movement in Russia and its brother communist parties throughout the world. The purpose of the discussion so far has been to show that the acceptance of democracy and the rejection of the class struggle by the socialist movement has been a slow process, and that in the nineteenth century it was uncertain whether those movements that rejected or accepted customary politics would win in the effort to become representative of the proletarian definition of the modern world. What has happened is that one large movement has accepted the techniques of constitutionalism and democracy as the proper way to gain a socialist order, and the other, the revolutionary Marxian movement, has decided to reject the historic state in order to create a new political order on the basis of class struggle, in which consent and democracy would be praised, but in which the principle of discussion, political opposition, and the principle of free elections in any genuine sense of the term would be rejected.

However, both movements which represent Marxism in contemporary politics have been guilty of messianic interpretations of political life under socialist regimes. By 1950 it was clear that at least socialism, whatever its variety, had to stand on the record, and that one of its great problems was to keep alive the myth of the new democracy which both communist and socialist Marxism have used in their appeal to the masses. For both democratic socialism and Bolshevik socialism have preached that public opinion under the new society would be purified, and that it would be animated by the highest ideals of service and self-sacrifice.

Karl Kautsky, the leader of orthodox German socialism, is perhaps as good an example of this issue of idealism in politics as can be found. He seemed to feel that public opinion, even under bourgeois society, was essentially free, and that the socialist problem is primarily to explain socialism to the masses, who will then vote the Marxist program into effect. It seems that he similarly believed the revolution might be a gradual and democratic achievement in which the opposition—that is, the bourgeois state—would wither away, as the workers won the battle for political democracy. In other words, democracy is given a common meaning under both capitalism and socialism. The communist or Leninist movement has been sharply critical on this point, for it has said that Marx taught the bourgeois state had to be destroyed by force, and that it was only the state of the proletarian democracy that would in the end "wither away." In other words, as long as bourgeois opinion is permitted to share in power there can be no realization of socialism, since the bourgeoisie will use the state willy-nilly as an instrument of class oppression.

In any case, the democratic socialist view has seemed to be that a new growth of freedom will occur in a socialist society. "Communism in material production, anarchism in the intellectual," seemed to be the stereotype of the new society. It is believed that such a system will emerge from the socialist productive system, dominated by the proletariat. But the theory seemed to be determinist in nature, since this was the form of society that would necessarily come from the logic of economic facts under socialism. In other words, a purified public opinion is regarded as inevitable under socialist production. Socialist production, however, requires great intelligence, discipline, and talent for organization; these are necessary if the social revolution is to be a fact. Among the petty bourgeoisie and among the agriculturists there is little chance of getting such training, but the proletariat will have it because of the type of social experience they have had under capitalism. Capitalist production, in other words, offers labor the necessary training for the achievement of a new social order. In resisting capitalism, labor has been given the necessary psychological training for organization, and labor will have a high talent for shaping the new society. Yet it is only through the cooperation of the great body of mankind that the proletariat can assert itself against capital and the capitalist state.

The socialist has promised that the achievement of socialism will profoundly alter the conditions of mankind. A new, free man will come from the new, free society. Pessimism, which has been characteristic of past social orders, will be destroyed root and branch; both psychological and social pessimism will disappear. "Socialism will abolish poverty and satiety and unnaturalness, make mankind joyful, appreciative of beauty, capable of happiness, and thereby it will bring freedom in scientific and artistic creation for all." * When these things have been attained, the only issue for public opinion will be the creation of the proper and effective means for its expression; there will be, simply, an issue of the forms of participation.

For the socialist who has been committed to democracy, the future has offered brilliant prospects of a planned utopia, though the present was less bright, for he had to contend with the unwillingness of the mass of average men to trust their futures to him. For the present, it was necessary to build up the party structure, to engage in political campaigns, to organize trade unions and co-operatives, to establish newspapers and journals, and to assist directly or indirectly any social group whose effort would lead toward the overthrow of capitalism. In other words, the socialist movement had to resort to educationl activity on a wide front, hoping that the truth of socialist promises would bring it finally to power. Before the war crises in the West beginning in 1914, the problem might seem simple and solvable in a matter of time. But the war indicated that a profound crisis was sweeping society, a crisis which might make both capitalism and socialism irrelevant, except that the socialists contended, in general, that the wars of the twentieth century were a product of capitalism itself. Thus the Fabian tactics of the British Labor party—or for that matter the democratic socialist parties in any part of the world—were made even more Fabian and remote than before the outbreak of the general military and economic disasters of Western civilization.

* Karl Kautsky, *The Social Revolution,* trans. by A. M. and M. W. Simons (1902), 188, 183 ff.

Socialists were forced more and more to deal with sick societies, they were driven to consider the nature of the Western crisis, and they had to explain as best they could the tyranny of the Soviet Union which was exercised in the name of Marx, Engels, Lenin, and of socialism in general. Moreover, the National Socialist movement in Germany suggested another use of the word that had to be resisted. Instead of having to criticize "capitalists," the democratic socialists were forced to spend an increasing amount of effort in showing that movements calling themselves "socialistic" were not really so in fact. Thus, the nineteenth- and early twentieth-century definitions of socialist aims and tactics were lost in a maze of controversial situations, in which socialist polemics had to be directed against those who claimed to be their brethren. But in this, it might be observed, socialism was not in a markedly different situation than the customary ideological positions which had been defined with some precision during the fifty years before 1917 when the Bolshevik Russian Revolution overthrew the constitutional regime that replaced the Tsar's government.

V

Among the Fabian minds who have considered the modern crisis, we may select for consideration H. G. Wells. He had the conviction "that modern civilization was begotten and nursed in the households of the prosperous, relatively independent people, the minor nobility, the gentry, and the larger bourgeoisie," which became important in the sixteenth century. But this bourgeoisie was remote from the common people who, at the time of World War I, had neither the social nor technical skill to influence their governments. So the old order stayed in power, and, according to Wells, it prolonged the war for two unnecessary years. Though the masses might have doubts about the state and its untouchable ruling class, the other groups, such as the manufacturers of arms and the financiers, could work only through the existing legal machinery. The vote itself was not important.* But as Europe "relapsed" into war in 1914, the vote was flung to women to keep them quiet, without any significant consequences —said Wells—except the further "enfeeblement of the waning powers of democracy." There was no women's movement, for example, that resisted the obliteration of freedom under the fascists and the Nazis. English liberalism had become a "generous indolence" incapable of dealing with the world as it was, and certainly it was unable to preserve the world leadership of the British.

Wells believed the control of the world was beyond the capacity of public opinion. He watched the increasing mechanization of war, the geometrical increase of the power of the few states which had a suitable technological system, and the growing sense among all classes that the movements of world politics were outside of their influence. And Wells believed that education did not go far enough to equip the ordinary man with any adequate sense of what was needed in order properly to direct the future. "This mass of human beings halting in puerility, is the determining factor in most of the alarming political and social processes of today." Most men, Wells thought, hang on to things as they are, and they are so resentful of changes in their habits that they are disposed to resist change even by violence. Wells did not consider the Fabians sufficiently aggressive in their policy of education for the creation of the socialist mind. He believed that there are kinetic people in society, those who would reconstruct social arrangements according to dynamic ideas they may have; and the primary problem was therefore to vest all the executive and administrative power of government in such people, while leaving to the others, the uncreative elements, the right to suggest and criticize, and to advocate legislation. The dull members of society must be given an incentive to kinetic effort.†

The conclusion Wells drew from his observations was that, even in a democratic socialism, there must be a body of competent

* H. G. Wells, *Experiment in Autobiography* (1934), 104-105, 588.
† *Ibid.*, 408, 653, 591-592, 627, 70, 628, 213-214, 562.

receivers of society, an elite, a modern Samurai. In the fascist and communist movements such a solution had been attempted, for the ruling class was educated in the ideology of the movement. Wells believed that some such ruling class is inevitable if the world-state is ever to be realized, but he also contended that the new ruling order should be open to all who are competent. He saw, too, that "sacred texts" are important, and cited Lenin's use of Marx in this way; but Wells thought that Lenin actually "believed in the dogmas of Marx about as much as Balfour believed in the Holy Trinity." What Lenin did was to change a fatalistic doctrine into the basis of a flexible and creative leadership; he emotionalized socialism and subordinated it to the worship of its prophets.*

Critics of socialism did not, of course, look upon its successes in our time as the fulfillment of democracy; it was seen, rather, as the destroyer of the democratic society which had been achieved through the experience of the nineteenth century. James Bryce considered the spread of anti-social doctrines in the United States probably a result of mass immigration, since the unadjusted foreigner was good raw material for demagogues. Still, he was convinced that in the United States we had reached the "highest level, not only of material well-being, but of intelligence and happiness, which the race had yet attained." But the benefits of American society were spread among all the people; they were not just for the few.† At the end of World War I, however, Bryce found his faith in the continuance of democracy shaken. In December, 1919, he wrote to Dr. Charles W. Eliot that "the class war, although preached fifty years ago by Marx, has only lately become really formidable." Bryce saw that society depends on the workers because of modern technology, and that society would be powerless in the hands of the workers if there should be a general strike. "Practically we are now in a position where democracy has been tried and found wanting." In other letters, he declared that the United States had been fortunate in

* *Ibid.*, 563, 664-665, 667.
† James Bryce, *The American Commonwealth* (1891), II, 716, 734.

warding off the growth of a Labor party—which he regarded as a serious menace in England and an enemy of democracy, because it is a "class party." Bryce believed there had been a decline in mass morality in the period immediately after the war, and that socialism was the result of the wide extension of the suffrage; but he did concede that the government had failed to prevent serious exploitation of labor and the mass of people during the war. He was convinced that the younger British people had less sense than those in the United States, since there was a trend toward "Labourism or some form of socialism." He felt that it was up to the educated classes to rise to the occasion and save democracy from these unfortunate trends in public opinion—trends readily demonstrated, he thought, by the general decadence of leadership in Italy, France, England, and in other countries.

But it was the Russian Revolution that caused the deepest disturbance in Bryce's mind, as well as in the postwar world in general. "Never before," said Bryce, "has socialism and anarchism —opposites mixed together—had its chance of governing." One of the great results of the war has been the development of "Labour" and socialism, and the trends in England were simply parallel to those in Russia. Bryce, like many others, caught a glimpse of the complete unsettlement of our time, the complete change in the meaning of democracy, the profound alterations in the public mind, and in the structure of government in Western society.*

As socialism attained greater influence during the present century, it began to stand on its "record." Obviously, the record did not indicate the realization of any of the extreme utopian statements of socialism's advocates, but it could be argued that socialism was spreading the benefits of economic advance to wider groups of people even in sick and war-torn societies. The democratic socialists had turned, long since, to the shaping of public opinion, to Fabian tactics, and to the shaping of opinion through political campaigns, but they had not rejected the principles of

* H. A. L. Fisher, *James Bryce* (2 vols., 1927), II, 234-235, 238-240, 249, 258-259, 164-165.

political democracy as they had been formulated in constitutional government based on a wide suffrage. Where socialism failed to make headway, it was blamed on the propagandist power of interests standing in opposition to socialism.* The socialist answer was to propose a counter-control of the means of mass communication, and an infiltration into the organized forces of society influential in shaping the public mind. Still, as certain of the proposals of socialist reform were used in the increasing centralization of modern industrial society, in order, primarily, to make the state a more effective instrument in warfare, and as government propaganda and control of the means of mass communication became more apparent, the socialist was caught between the resistance of those who did not want a revolutionary change in society and those who urged by governmental propaganda an increase of the social functions of government. In the United States, socialism was caught between the strength and success of neo-capitalism, and the planning of the garrison-state, while in Europe socialist parties were apparently becoming the receivers of war-devastated and economically impoverished nations. Indeed, socialism in practice was finding that it had to fight wars, and that its early propagandist fervor had little relation to the actualities of twentieth-century life.

VI

But beyond this, there was the shadow of the Russian Revolution. For that revolution stood over both democratic socialism, with its conventional ideas of political participation and the education of public opinion, and the defenders of a relatively free economic system. Similarly, the Russian Revolution stood for the rejection of the whole nineteenth-century theory of public opinion. The new Russian rulers would change the structure of power, but retain a formal participation, in which the opposition was not allowed expression. It denied, in effect, the whole theory of

* Scott Nearing, "The Control of Public Opinion in the United States," *School and Society*, XV (1922), 421-423.

democratic society as developed in the West. Naturally, those who defended the conventional freedom of economic and political life in a democracy, could turn with angry criticism toward the Bolshevist government, which both overturned society and retired from the alliance against Germany in World War I. But since the new Russian rulers claimed to be Marxists and socialists, the dilemma of the Western socialists was acute. Bryce, like many others, argued that socialism in England and socialism in Russia had the same roots and would have the same consequences.

At all cost, the Western socialists had to meet this charge. They had to show that Russian socialism was not really either Marxism or socialism; that the capitalist criticism of Russia should not apply to them; and, by paradox, that the Western socialist parties were even more democratic in inspiration than the defenders of the conservative and capitalist order of society. Thus, the Russian system became the great issue of debate, not only for the capitalist and conservative, but also for those who said they wanted a socialist order of society. Because the Russians claimed for themselves the realization in practice of all that socialists elsewhere had claimed, it was easy for the critics of socialism to identify all economic criticism with communism. Socialists, anarchists, and even mild reformers, found themselves charged with being communists. In response communist propaganda insisted that all of the Western movements against the Russian experiment were in common reactionary, and that there was no point in trying to distinguish a Western democratic socialist from a capitalist. Both supported the bourgeois state, that is, political democracy old-style, and the socialist refused to accept the true interpretations of Marx on which the Russian achievements were being based. When the non-communist totalitarian movements got under way in the twenties, it was easy for communist propagandists to insist that all opposition to the Russian system was in nature and ultimately fascist.

It was soon clear that the defense of the Western system of political participation, the freedom of religious and labor associations, the right of opposition political parties to appeal to voters who have the liberty of a free election, and the right of the individual to contribute to public opinion as his education and the use of his reason might indicate, had to be in part a criticism of the Russian system. It entailed an examination of Russian history, showing that in fact the Russians could not understand democracy, since they had never experienced it, and that the despotic socialist system of Russia was not drawn from Marx, so much as from Russian revolutionary experience. This criticism urged that Russian experience has been continuous and unique, and that its socialism is grounded in the peculiarities of the Russian social system. The socialists in the West shared in this argumentative enterprise to the extent that they tried to show that Russian socialism was a complete perversion of Marx and the whole socialist tradition. But the socialists were divided, and it was not until after World War II that efforts at compromise were finally given up, when it was realized that the Russian system would never adjust itself to political freedom in the attainment of its economic goals.* The greatest difficulty of the West was in understanding even the bases on which there could be such a denial of the right of individuals to differ with each other as there has been under the Russian system. In this sense, Russian self-justification offers us the most completely daring and most fundamentally different theory of the function of public opinion that there has been in many centuries of Western discussion of the issue of the freedom of the citizen to participate in the affairs of government.

Sharply diverse opinions have been expressed about the Soviet regime. The Russians themselves insist that their system is based on a science of society, about which there can be no fundamental question, and on which there can be a justifiable suppression of any reactionary and anti-revolutionary opposition. But the criticism of Russia has often minimized the idea that contemporary Russian practice is an outgrowth of dialectical materialism. The Russian refusal to accept at least a moderate version of democ-

* Julius Braunthal, "The Rebirth of Social Democracy," *Foreign Affairs*, XXVII (1949), 586 ff.

racy grows out of the perennial despotism under which the Russian people have been governed. Bolshevism simply continued a situation in which the people had no real share in the government, and it falls squarely inside of the official and orthodox tradition of Russian government. On the other hand, the revolutionary tradition in Russia arrives at the same result. For the Russian revolutionists of the last century turned against the Russian tradition and toward the materialistic and anti-religious theories of the West, but in their borrowings from the West they did not feel that parliamentarism was suitable for their purposes. One might say that the government against which they were struggling made democracy meaningless, and that a revolution is always a real denial of the theory of government by opinion and discussion.

The issue is perhaps deeper than this, however, for the attitudes grouped around the nihilist movement, including various forms of socialist theory, stipulated that force was the proper means of changing society. Particularly is this so if one accepts the idea that in the generation before Lenin the revolutionists believed in an upheaval led by the small, militant minority, and that the *coup d'état* would offer conditions suitable for social change. There was, in this view, no reliance on any "popular genius," and no reliance on the peasantry as a revolutionary force.* Such a view would suggest that among the revolutionists there was little interest in the tentative steps toward the establishment of a Russian parliament. There is likewise a strong but diverse current of opinion that Russia was not a fruitful ground in which to plant the seed of political democracy. Federov notes that the Russian people have resorted to periodic revolts without demonstrating any strong desire to share in the responsibilities of government. It was recognized that the people might get rid of a Tsar, but that they could not constitutionalize his power.† At

* Michael Karpovich, "A Forerunner of Lenin: P. N. Tkachev," *The Review of Politics*, VI (1944), 336 ff.

† G. Federov, "Russia and Freedom," *The Review of Politics*, VIII (1946), 15, 22-23. Konni Zilliacus, *The Revolutionary Movement* (1905),

least, one can say that there was something like a consensus that Russian government had been historically dictatorial or despotic, and that even without the contemporary theory of the Russian Marxists the chances of parliamentary government would have been less in Russia than in a Western society with longer experience in democracy.*

However much the West may debate the policies and moves of the Russian government, the justification of what is done, both internally and externally, is, to the Russians, the Marxist theory of the state. But it is the Marxist theory as it has been interpreted by Lenin and his epigone. To the communist, the philosophy of the state is a science of society which can be neither proved nor disproved by public opinion, by discussion, elections, campaigns, or, finally, by the decisions of parliaments established under the dominance of the bourgeoisie. Civil liberty, indeed, loses much of its value if one drops the rationalistic assumption that man is a reasonable creature endowed with rights—natural rights as in the Declaration of Independence. Alternatively, it is said that man is either a victim or a part of objective circumstances, which

---

Ch. VI, 86-87, 121, 153, has argued that during the last years of Alexander II there was a strong movement for some participation of the people in the government, and nihilist and terrorist activity was justified on this ground. At one point the terrorists said they would lay down their arms if the sovereign would consent to the convocation of a national assembly, and nihilism was theoretically converted to a kind of constitutionalism. The revolutionists declared to Alexander III that there was no government in Russia, since a government exists to give expression to the people's efforts and to execute their will. One proposal for getting at the state of opinion in Russia was to have the governors of the provinces report on opinion in their areas. This idea was used by Alexander III, according to Zilliacus, in place of progress toward a constitutional or parliamentary democracy. During World War I, there was the customary defense of the public opinion of an "ally," that is, of Russia. See George Kennan, "Public Opinion in an Oriental State," *The Outlook,* 109 (1915), 767-770.

* See G. P. Gooch, *Dictatorship in Theory and Practice* (1935), 30-31. For an early analysis of Russian propaganda, see Isaac F. Marcosson, "After Lenin—What?" *The Saturday Evening Post,* 197 (1924), 25 ff, where it is argued that propaganda is the chief enterprise of the Russian system. See Alex Inkeles, *Public Opinion in Soviet Russia; A Study in Mass Persuasion* (1950).

may be discovered by the analytical tools offered through historical materialism, that is, the application of dialectical materialism to specific social situations or historical epochs. Since the Marxist must hold that the theory of a democratic public opinion arose from the historical conditions in which the bourgeoisie was predominant, it is false and oppressive to the masses, or to the proletariat, whether or not any single member of the working class may be conscious of this oppression. Thus, communism will sweep away the false and treacherous demands of capitalistic democracy. Since it is a fraud to assume there will be a peaceful subordination of capitalism to the will of the majority of the toilers, there must be a control of all of the means of communication of opinion, especially of those which run counter to the ultimate, theoretical, and objective will of the proletariat.

Such ideas found in Bukharin's *Course of Political Instruction* (*Politigramota*) are the final and explicit development of the long-sustained criticism of the institutions of bourgeois democracy. Engels spoke with sarcasm of the presumption that in the modern state every citizen is competent to pass judgment on all the issues upon which he has to vote.* The small elite party in charge of the state is the more advanced part of the proletariat, and it must not be subordinated to any mass opinions which go counter to what is held proper by the governing group. The Marxists, in fact, reject in theory the forms of inequality based on wealth, but they accept—like Plato's geometric God—the inequality between the many who must obey and the few who rule. The ruling few are the party and the bureaucracy of the one-party state. As a result, it is little more than the rejection of one form of inequality for the myth of a new order which requires equal acceptance of party "truth." Under the disciplining of workers in the Soviet Union the strike became a form of treason, and the managers, according to Schumpeter, have more power than capitalistic employers. Quite beyond the range of

* Engels, *op. cit.*, 10.

democratic thought on this subject is the fact that in Russia the trade union has become a means of authoritarian discipline, under which there are no free intellectuals who can create and organize opposition as under the capitalist dispensation.*

VII

It is common to speak of the failure of socialism. Many refer to the death of the socialist myth in the democratic countries; but in the West it seems incomprehensible that millions of Asians, Africans, Europeans, and Latin Americans should believe that the goodness of the future rests with a triumph of communism. If the common man in the West takes his socialism in a fit of boredom, the more backward peoples of the world seem to think that every evil thing said about the United States by communist propaganda is a truth to which they can adhere. But it is clear that socialism can offer no utopia, neither the version found in Russia nor any of the weakened Western democratic systems. Without the myth, there is no public opinion to force the forward march of socialism in the democracies.†

In contrast, there is also a resurgence of genuine economic liberalism in Europe—that is, the defense and installation of an increasing freedom of the market. A new swing of opinion has been perceptible in Western Europe, and perhaps a new and restored myth of economic liberalism is in the making. People

* Joseph H. Schumpeter, *Capitalism, Socialism and Democracy* (1942), 216-218. Sigurd Thorn, "Die GPU und ihre Methoden," *Zeitwende*, October, 1934, 45 ff; November, 1934, 76 ff. Communist literature must be considered in relation to its periods—the time of Lenin, then the Stalinist period which was rich in theoretical developments in communist ideology, and finally the period after Stalin. Eras of popular and united front agitation, or co-existence, have different bearings on the theory of public opinion than times when revolutionary efforts are being made. One of the significant books of the mid-twentieth century dealing with communist theory is Karl A. Wittfogel, *Oriental Despotism; a Comparative Study of Total Power* (1957).

† A most important work in this area is Milovan Djilas, *The New Class; Analysis of the Communist System* (1957).

have grown tired of the power of the state; they do not want to be forced to fight in wars; they do not wish to pay confiscatory taxes, and they want to acquire property and to have the right to use it in a manner according to their own wishes. Such a new affirmation of the desire for liberty from state control suggests a number of things. It means class cooperation and the end of the class struggle, except in attenuated forms. It means the formulation of economic purposes through understanding between professional and functional groups. It means, indeed, that the Marxist class analysis is outmoded, if ever it was more than an illusion in the mind of discontented intellectuals like Marx and Engels and their followers. In America we assume there is no proletariat in the nineteenth century sense; we assume, no doubt, that a new system of class identifications is taking shape.

But the failure of socialism suggests, too, that there is no longer any validity in the socialist theory of progress. Optimism comes hard to the socialist outside of the communist orbit, and democracy does not present the smiling, republican face it once did for all the world to see. An alternative theory of progress is found in communism, and a refurbished one in the democracies. It is a chastened belief in the possibility of progress; it suggests that the public may be turning to a more conservative conception of liberty—that is, a liberty in the form of increased freedom from the collective state which, indifferently, either makes war or regulates social behavior.

If a new class system is emerging in Western societies, it will surely merge into the traditional systems by which publics express their opinions. Revolutionary communism obviously repudiated the Western system under which public opinion is both free and is provided with an opportunity to express itself under formal conditions. Democratic socialism has offered no alternative since it has surrendered the active encouragement of class struggle. And many socialists, indeed, have concluded it is more important to prevent the rise of communism or fascism than it is to reorganize the economy.

PART IV

ASSESSMENTS AND CONCLUSIONS

CHAPTER 11

The Situation of the Common Man

I

In intellectual history there is a recurring issue of profound interest to a democracy: when does the common man, the man at the margin of learning, have a right to decide a public question? What issues may be adjudicated by such a man? When has the expert, the man in the house or the office, exceeded his power in preventing a decision by a majority of such people? Much humor, as well as learned philosophical judgment, has been lavished here. At one extreme we recall Joe Miller's eighteenth-century jests which, on occasion, humiliated the Oxford clerk to the advantage of the countryman. And at the other extreme, it may be remembered that Plato in the *Republic* penned one of the most stinging denunciations of the democratic common man that has ever been written. It has been popular to praise common sense at the expense of the abstract knowledge possessed by aristocrats. But in most instances the issue of the right of common ideas to oppose expert opinion has been discussed within the elites, and at the level of sophisticated dialectic. Before the appropriation committees of Congress civil servants expert in budget matters have been locked in combat with inquisitive Congressmen, and throughout society one group of professionals has contended with another for the right to set its sign and seal on policy. Around election time there is suddenly a renewed flurry of affirmation of the democratic right of citizens to make decisions, but at other times most men in office blandly assume that the outsider and the uninformed have no right to share in decision-making. Just as legislators seldom mention "what the people want," so it is in the conflict among intellectuals, and the choice of the expert against the majority is a foregone conclusion.

In form the issue lies between elite groups, who operate within rules of the game, varying from one theater of action to another. In a society of bureaucratic absolutism, as described by Gaetano Mosca in *The Ruling Class,* or Milovan Djilas in *The New Class,* the elements of popular decision have been excluded, except for extreme pressures and explosive action. But in a free society, where any man may speak his piece, and where there are effective means of popular participation, the situation of the official group is changed. It becomes an oligarchy which is open and flexible, and which, short of revolution, can be made responsible for what it has done. In political behavior, then, the issue may resolve itself into this: what groups come closest in their political rapprochement with common men, or with men who function outside of the structures of power? The elected reperesentatives of the people are not necessarily those who are closest in rapprochement with the common man, nor is the bureaucracy, the management of industry, nor the persons who hold power within the organized professions. In a most specific sense, those members of the elite who adhere to the folkways and mores of the society are closest to common men. There is often a regional flavor to the understanding between elites and the workers of the world. The traditions most forceful in the support such members of an elite give to politics are regional, religious, and the emotional or intuitive adherence to the symbols of political parties. One thing, however, seems fairly certain: effective elites are organized and disciplined, as are the professions or the party organizations, while the individuals known as common or mass men do not characteristically form organizations primarily for political purposes, though they may do so in business, union, or fraternal and family associations.

In free society the freedom of the elite consists in part in the right to teach values, policies, ideologies, and skills. Teaching at a technical level is obviously effective. Training in the mechanical skills involves tradition as a system of values that does not have to be discussed. There is generally some willingness to learn a mechanical, a servile art, in groups where under usual circumstances any outside influence would be helpless to reshape the moral tradition.* A general population, concerned with the pragmatic and with what works, easily develops an understanding of the distinction between what is and what ought to be, and soon learns to apply this distinction to issues in times of crisis. A man may have simultaneously a metaphysical vision of life and a concern with its mechanics. The Greek poet, Archilochus of Paros, said, according to a fragment, "The fox knows many things, but the hedgehog knows one big thing." The man of the elite, the intellectual, knows many things, but the common man draws his vision from the tradition in which he lives. Like the hedgehog, he may know one big thing; and he is apt to be suspicious of the intellectual and the technician—and indeed of the whole governing order, which may seem to him like the fox whose claws and teeth he cannot escape.

II

On what ground may the ordinary man, unskilled in the technics of power, resist the technician? May he resist the social scientist? If the course of history is predetermined, then the technician has a narrow range of freedom in which to practice his skills; and his supposed or avowed ends may actually be mere illusions for salving the ego or for deceiving those who are governed. There are few ordinary men who remember what yesterday was said to be the assured goal of political action. If there is, on the contrary, free creation of history, perhaps the men in the street can make it according to their designs, because there is,

* See my article, "Intellectuals and the American Tradition," *Education*, 63 (March, 1943), 391 ff.

according to José Ortega y Gasset, "la rebelión de la masas." History can be shaped, in such contingencies, in accordance with barbarism; it may be predicated on the rejection of culture and science. The new elite can then be little more than the custodians of fools. Here, neither the leaders nor the masses would have any claim to obedience, and the rejection of both would be profitable to the world.

Still, the question may be stated more narrowly, and in such a way that the difference between the determinist conception of history and the theory of its free creation may not seriously affect our discussion. For however limited the capacity to create history, there is still the problem of whether the masses of men may with legitimate right exercise their power to reject the decision of the expert who lives among the small number who control the daily decisions of government. Tolstoy criticized the minority of humanitarians, believers in free will, rationalists, revolutionists, the professors of the science of history and of the science of society, and reformers who because of their blindness are in a practical sense anti-intellectual. The reason he assigned resembled that of de Maistre—the causes at work in the world are beyond the comprehension of men's minds.* But if one rejects the philosophical proofs of religion, thought de Maistre, then all one has left are the incomprehensible "causes" and complexities of the world. Under such conditions, the common man's opinion may be as rational a basis of decision as the considered judgment of the philosopher—"de docta ignorantia," to borrow a phrase from Nicolas of Cusa. In fine, ignorance of how things happen presents the same insecure basis to both the expert and the inexpert; and expert ratiocination becomes clogged by the multiplicity of causes, the smallness of the ultimate units, and the human inability to remember and coordinate what might be known.† Ignorance in the governor is thus inherent, but likewise in the unlettered. It is a condition of existence, and it pervades the qual-

* See in general Isaiah Berlin, *The Hedgehog and the Fox* (1957).

† *Ibid.*, 50-51. Of interest, too, is Tolstoy's contrast between the expert Napoleon and the simple General Kutuzov in *War and Peace*.

ity of decision in a way that is not merely ignorance of a future which has not yet occurred, but is also misjudgment of what is known.

It was to this point that Burke turned his attention. Our trading on a private stock of reason can be a claim to omniscience, a form of megalomania, and part of the system of delusions of Classical rationalism. The liberal reformers of another day, like William Godwin and Robert Owen, were not believers in free will, for they wished to deny human responsibility for sin. They contended that men are as they are made by men; character and the traits of personality are imparted by education, and the individual has no capacity to resist. Only a new philosophy taught to men from infancy will create a new society and dispose of those who, in the corrupted times, have ruled with a pretended knowledge of the secrets of state and consequent capacity for expert political decision. As envisioned by such nineteenth-century optimism as Godwin's, the new intellectuals would have knowledge, just as the new common men would have knowledge, and those who attained reason and information would properly have a right to decide the future of their society.

If, however, we deny free will, as the precursors of socialism and anarchism were disposed to, then the creative freedom of both the intellectual expert and the unlettered men must be restricted, or even denied. And it is out of such discussion that the consciousness of the conservative emerged. For the conservative held that such theories about human nature were destructive, and that there was nothing left in existing society which under this species of revolutionary thought could be considered sacred or preserved by an honorable sense of human duty. But to none was free will so free that the world may be remade by the arbitrary flick of a finger; and to none was human will so negated by determinism that choice had no role to play in the creation of the future.

The dilemma of the conservative is, thus, also the dilemma of the revolutionary. And much the same might be said of both the expert who believes he knows much, and the common man who is not impressed by his own ignorance about the "important" things in his life. How can man determine where the line shall be drawn except by knowledge of the world which only the trained may know? Fixity and free will struggle in the minds of thinking men, and all things seem to have come into being at a given time. A conservative is a theorist of change, and a liberal or revolutionary by paradox is a theorist of that which must endure when it has been achieved. The world may be an accumulation of choices, but they are believed to be choices and in sequence. Normally the human being is conscious of his human situation, and he feels he has some freedom—or could have freedom—to deal with it. But if the conservative would not trade on a supposed omniscience of men, he has proposed two bases according to which choice can be made. It may be made by either the learned or the countryman; and it may be made by either skilled information or by insight into the wisdom of the universal order. To the conservative, cognition may be natural, as the scientist and engineer might contend; but it is intuitive as well, and also subject to an Aristotelian demonstration. Intuition suggests the concept of wisdom as distinguished from knowledge, that is, the poetry of the world, and a sense of the mysterious universe.

III

Let us come to a closer inquiry: how can one defend the choice, the commitment, or the engagement of the man outside of the elite? He is the man with little more than mere technical training or a skill in the performance of a set of industrial duties; he has what may be called a mechanical education. He is the man outside the *artes liberales*—the practitioner of the *artes serviles.* He knows little of the fine arts—painting, poetry, sculpture, music—and the theater is an unknown experience except as it is filtered strangely through the media of mass communication. In a democracy such a man participates in politics. He has some power even when he is not a member of one of the organized massive and arbitrary guilds of our corporate society, but within and through the guild he may feel he has immensely more power. In his function he does not know or use the sciences, nor is he acquainted with mathematics. How then can he make decisions on public questions? Should he not leave such matters to those who are his betters in the science and art of politics? Since his participation in politics must be based on wisdom rather than technics, can he participate at all? Is there in fact even such a thing as wisdom?—for if there is, the common man may have an insight and a moral sense that gives him a profound right to oppose his own decision to those of the elite who form the ruling political class, with its characteristic claim to exclusive expertise.

It is crucial in a democracy to know if Pascal was right when he said: "The heart has its reasons, which reason does not know. We feel it in a thousand things . . ." * Among men there seems to be a continuous experience of the intuition of divine order and the sense of wisdom in the ordering of life. Here we find the difference between those who speak for the intuition of the heart and those who would speak simply of the empirical, countable, aggregate of information. Among those who speak in the Pascalian vein, Isaiah Berlin has listed Blake, Rousseau, Schelling, Goethe, Coleridge, Chateaubriand, and Carlyle. Wisdom is depth, while knowledge sails only the surface.† And Leo Strauss has urged that Rousseau was the first to teach that all the knowledge men need to live virtuously is supplied by the conscience—noting, however, that even when the reasons of the heart have been cited, the need for education has been recognized. In our time we have sought technology in education and the production of the expert in technology, rather than the wisdom obtained from religion and the study of the humanities.‡ In a technical age intellectuality tends to become technical, and its political summit

* Blaise Pascal, *Pensees,* No. 277. Everyman's Library edition.

† Berlin, *op. cit.,* 118-119.

‡ Leo Strauss, "What is Political Philosophy?" *The Journal of Politics,* 19 (August, 1957), 366.

in the midst of the twentieth century is what has been called the behavioral sciences.

Against the technical there is always the beautiful resurgence of the spiritual insight. Did not Albert Schweitzer say that all life is suffering? Can we not look upon the metaphysical poetry of Job and grasp a meaning of life that allows a place even for the technology of the modern age? Or perhaps we contemplate the grandeur of Greek tragedy. There in the midst of sin and evil, where a shallow optimism fades before the assumption of the duties of human charity, man still affirms the right to make his choices, for in every epoch the human situation carries both joy and tragedy. We may sometimes choose only to repent. And if free choice is rejected, there is no duty possible, for there is only law and determinism. If free choice is rejected, the liberal is rejected along with the conservative, and the elite along with the masses. Spiritual insight has affirmed the freedom of man to choose, and if there is freedom it must exist for all. In this we have the existential principle of much of the modern insight, even for those who declare the freedom of the will in the moral vacuum of an icy atheism. The man of free will is the authentic man, while the social and the aggregate may be only destructive or oppressive.

If we think of the free man in the office, or the free man on the job, and if we think of both as making choices, the intuitive principle of metaphysical meaning for life says that the choice made must be moral. It must be just; and it must be defensible in the open and before the public conscience. It must be a moral decision that may be implemented by the technics of whatever science is the foundation of the decision. It may be public administration, economics, biology, or engineering, but the issue is always the same in its ultimate form. And spiritual intuition in its experience with the tragic sense of life has turned to sacred writing and sacred tradition, both of which have offered wisdom, and to education which has been informed by a sacral element. On this basis the common conscience may speak to proclaim the legitimacy of the governance of men. Though wisdom is finally the foundation of legitimacy, it is also the foundation of the intermediate factor: consensus. The consensus involved is precisely that the ruling class is ruling legitimately, and that the inevitable and necessary power or coercion used by the ruling order is paraphrased in turn in the system of consensus. Consent by itself has hardly anything ultimate in it; it is a practical technique of the moment, even though it may serve later in the process by which consensus arises from moral character—that is, the process by which consensus arises from wisdom. Though the philosopher may state these propositions, and though he may argue that the obligation to obey emerges because the state as an instrument of power is radically necessary to the nature of man, one is uneasy and the conscience is troubled.

Machiavellian power is always nearby, and the ancient state as well as the modern democracy has practiced deceit in order to sustain policy or to place the members of society in an irretrievable position. Or a foreign policy may be prosecuted by the ruling order—*i.e.*, to support a secret alliance in a war—while the people are told at the same time that actual engagement in war will not occur. The Treitschkeian "*der Staat ist Macht*" is the eternal enemy of consensus and of wisdom. One can hardly fail to regard as legitimate the refusal of the common conscience to accept the deceits of power, and withal to come to the conclusion that power is deceitful, that is to say, arbitrary. In the generation of agreement to a ruling order, the spirit and not the technics of knowledge must judge. There are, indeed, situations in which the extreme medicine of the constitution must be applied, and in which revolution as well as general disobedience of law is justified. Might not one justify the revolution in Venezuela in January, 1958, on the ground that there had been a brutal denial of civil rights and the curbing of the press; that political leaders had been jailed and exiled; that labor unions had been dominated by the state and formed into instruments of political power; that the political police had been oppressive;

that the nation's great wealth from oil and iron was being misused; that there was widespread unemployment, vice and corruption; and that the regime was materialistic and increasingly hostile to the religion of the people? The conditions for a just revolution were surely fulfilled,* no matter how many intellectuals and experts or technicians of social function might say otherwise.†

IV

Wisdom, and the prudence that it carries, must be balanced by technics and knowledge. All men may have wisdom, but not all are intellectuals—either in function or simply as possessors of knowledge. It is on the basis of their potential in natural wisdom that the masses may express the God-like glory of the poor and that the common man may rightfully refuse to follow a governing minority of technicians and political leaders. It is not always that the common man, by his adherence to tradition or to religion is wise; but neither is it true that the intellectual, or members of the ruling class, have such a technical capacity that it justifies them in their refusal to consider public opinion—though, indeed, the actual and countable majority may be prevented from forming. If the first ground on which the citizen may refuse to follow the intellectual and the expert is the acceptance of wisdom and the tradition of morality, the second is the existential weaknesses of the intellectuals as a class which vitiate the claim that they must always be followed by those who make decisions on public policy.

* See *America*, February 8, 1958, p. 532. The "fact" of popular resistance and revolution is not involved here, but rather the justification of revolution against a ruling class. Though revolution is an extreme measure, it has been common in the modern age of the mass. And, of course, new forms of control over the mass—"the hidden persuaders"—seem to be emerging. These new means of control may put an end to popular resistance in the realization of Orwell's *1984*.

† See Guglielmo Ferrero, *The Principles of Power; The Great Political Crises of History*, trans. by T. R. Jaeckel (1942); Robert C. Angell, *Free Society and Moral Crisis* (1958).

One must ask: what are the existential weaknesses of the intellectual? There is, first of all, the search for power—the power that determines public policy, not that which gains wealth. The power of business property is dispersed and weak against the formal decision-making power of the modern Leviathan. The Marxists have succeeded in persuading a goodly portion of the world that the greatest power is that of "business," whereas in fact the greatest concentration of power is the state. And by "state" one means those who actually determine the impact of sovereignty on the individual. But the search for power (political position, security, prestige, money—all are involved) becomes an expression of ego, and often in a ruthless, inauthentic isolation from the generality of the public. One may say that in this setting the labor of the ego toward its triumph involves a savage rejection of any outside criticism and the unbending determination to reshape society. Reform is one of the high symbols of power, and its process is the persuasion of masses that they do in fact want a given reform. Unhappily, the rejection of the expert must often involve contempt for the reformer and the humanitarian. Berlin has reminded us that both de Maistre and Tolstoy spoke "of intellectuals with scorn and hostility." Maistre regarded them as "grotesque casualties of the historical process" and "a pestilential sect of questioners and corrupters." * This sentiment was expressed against the intellectuals and world-improvers of the French Revolution; but in many revolutions since, the terror continues and the "reform" of the world, which once required the guillotine, now requires the forced labor camp, as well as the heartless and disloyal international conspiracy. The critic will say that those who pretend to analyze, classify, and reduce to science "the social, moral, political, spiritual worlds," are hoaxing the trusting and the innocent. In the pretense of power, it will be charged, science is distended beyond any normal claim of what it can do in reality.† Cannot one say that those philosophies which wash the personality of its

* Berlin, *op. cit.*, 87-88.
† *Ibid.*, 106-107.

humility, are what Aron recently called "the opium of the intellectuals?" *

Though the criticism of the "outsider" may be rejected with fierce pride, it is probably true that the intellectual of the elite reflects more the admitted weakness of human intelligence than the strength of the science he professes. The geneticist insists on the importance of suitable grandparents, and while inequality is a biological law, it does not follow that the inequalities of inherited and native endowment are precisely the same as inherited inequalities in any particular social structure. But the more important modern development concerns inquiry into the personality. It is a study that has come in part from Freudian ideas, but it is pervasive and it runs through various ideological and scientific attitudes from left to right. Nor does it involve exactly the older issue of whether human nature can be changed, because it recognizes that personality traits may change both during the longer years of life and from the shortened experience of trauma. The point very much at stake is that the intellectual, the scientist, or the member of the functioning elite, is always a personality with all of the issues that confront the person in private or public life. The intellectual is, then, really just a common man with a special vocabulary, ideas, skills, or training in a profession or a discipline useful in government. A study of personality has thrown light on the structure of the governing class, as well as on the reactions of common men in facing the political decision. One must, presumably, look at the governing man under the dual headings of his personality structure and the science or technique he professes.

The search for the superior men whose rule will take the place of the rule of majorities is not limited to the so-called "reactionaries," for it has been true of liberal forms of political thinking. On the theory that personality traits are fixed, and that they do not change upon the transition from private life to the possession of power, it has been urged that tests might be devised to pick

* Raymond Aron, *L'Opium des Intellectuels* (1955).

the right kind of people for the governing elite. The appeal to "the man of the hour" or to the man of a particular situation is nothing new, but the kind of man who is fit for the job varies, indeed, with the political values of the group which is seeking to govern. Qualification finally depends, not so much on the traits of the personality, as on the metaphysical conception of public order.* One might agree that the right man for a leadership role in a democracy is one whose personality is not authoritarian (this is a notion most difficult to define) and who has gained power by democratic means. Though the contemporary effort to define the superior man is through psychological inquiry into the personality, such has not always been the case. John Stuart Mill was seeking superior men for Parliament in his *Representative Government,* and F. H. Bradley in *My Station and Its Duties* pleads for the *phronimoi,* the persons who have understanding, "persons with a will to do right," who have identified themselves with the "moral spirit of the community," and who judge accordingly. Moreover, many social scientists have, in effect, proposed themselves as the new elite, the practitioners of "the policy sciences," and as persons who should have the right to direct the stream of public decision.

If one probes a bit, there are two values which seem most prominent. The first is that the governing personality should be accredited with the values which are part of what has come to be called a non-authoritarian personality. These values are loosely defined, but they seem to be those of secular ideologists in their interpretation of democracy. Liberals would deny that the ordinary man is free to create a society in which racism is present, and they might even include censorship to prevent the spread of ideas of which the authoritarian personality approves. But in the second place it seems there must be a strong intellectual com-

* Cf. David Spitz, "Power and Personality: The Appeal to the 'Right Man' in Democratic States," *The American Political Science Review* LII (March, 1958), 84 ff, for his criticism of H. D. Lasswell, *Power and Personality* (1948), and Karl Mannheim, *Freedom, Power, and Democratic Planning* (1950). See Spitz, *Democracy and the Challenge of Power* (1958).

mitment to method—that is, to the social science equivalent of scientific method. Governing is to be the role of the scientist, not of the person whose judgment rests upon training in the humanities. On neither ground would the majority of ordinary men have the right to resist the small group invested with the right to govern.*

The natural scientist, like the social scientist, is perturbed by the fact that disagreement is comomn among scientists, and that the weakness of personality, specialization, and the imperfect state of the sciences vitiate some of its claims to possess a right to stand against public opinion. There are immediate social consequences for the natural scientist. Who shall decide, when the scientists disagree amidst the clash of personalities? But even so it is held for both the natural and the social scientist, that disagreement does not give the masses the right to decide; for a scientific dispute, or one claimed to be so by social scientists, is complex in a special way. As the editors of *Science* have said:

> In broadest outline, a scientific dispute differs from other disputes in that it involves only one kind of disagreement, a disagreement in belief. The attitude accepted by both parties is the scientific attitude, which finds that the way to answer a question, if it can be answered at all, is by an appeal to experiment, not by an appeal to force, to a vote to authority, or to personal revelation. Further, the appeal to experiment must be conducted according to those principles that sometimes are collectively referred to as scientific method . . . Nevertheless, when there is disagreement in belief, but agreement in scientific attitude, there is at least some assurance that the dispute is only temporary, because further application of the same method, a method accepted by both sides, may decide the question.†

The thinker inclined to the humanistic and spiritual perception would say immediately that not all questions are to be answered by scientific method, and that it is extremely and fatally broad

* Cf. *The New American Right*, ed. by Daniel Bell (1955). The study of the elite has, of course, become respectable among American social scientists, as in C. Wright Mills, *The Power Elite* (1956).

† *Science*, 126 (September 13, 1957), 483.

to say that if a question can be answered at all it must be answered by the experimental method. The alternative is surely to say that while scientific issues are to be answered scientifically and in accordance with suitable scientific methods, questions of value and those involving metaphysics must be answered by philosophical inquiry.

If the issue may be stated in this way, then the tone of the inquiry is shifted. Values, goals, purposes, and the sense of significance in living are hardly to be proved by what is called a "scientific experiment." A philosopher might say that only an intellectual who affirms values which can be proved by logical and intelligent demonstration can have the right to reject the ideas of common men, for it is in the field of values, as true, that the common man affirms his right to be. It is here that he affirms his right to defend the "tribe," or the institutions to which he is committed, against the outsider who has no love for these institutional values. Even the liberal intellectual sometimes approves, as in the case of the Jacksonian revolt against the enlightened classes, or against the financial elite and opponents of reform whom the Jacksonians considered their enemy.* In other words, the philosophy of tradition might assert that there is no duty in society to protect the intellectuals from the consequences of their folly, or to spare them any loss of public esteem.†

In the social sciences there are further difficulties, for at times a special language or "jargon" may be substituted for the actual scientific solution; the results are sometimes unimpressive or obvious; and insights gained from statistics seldom suggest a plausible solution, simply because there must be an anterior choice of value which is organic with fact. Or the proposal from an

* Cf. Marvin Meyers, *The Jacksonian Persuasion: Politics and Belief* (1957).

† One of the books which is said to have influenced the progressive intellectuals in the United States is J. E. T. Rogers, *Six Centuries of Work and Wages* (first ed., 1884; 10th edition, 1909), p. 13. Rogers declared that labor would do better still when the peasant is allowed to express his judgment on the policy of government. He noted Aristotle's commendation of the judgment of the crowd.

elite of a "scientific" solution may represent a clash of fact-value situations in which the solution offered is hypothetical. It has been said that reforms seldom attain the ends toward which they are directed, and in more extreme words it has been urged that seldom, if ever, has the human race, elite or otherwise, actually known what it was doing. There appears to be a statistical limitation on the potential of state action, which means limits on elites and scientific bureaucracies. A "situation" is usually multi-factored, while political action is unifactored. But even more so, a decision on policy is usually a prudential judgment, quite difficult of proof, rather than a scientific proposition. Most public policies are chosen, indeed, as the result of prudential judgment.

V

It should be said that the common, traditional, and relatively fixed standards of public opinion are often in conflict with the decisions of men in power, either in government or in areas of highly specialized function, such as finance or the professions. Ideological positions often begin in a small group, but when that group seeks to change society rapidly and against the wishes of the majority, it is bound to meet justified resistance. In the establishment of a pluralistic society, one may suggest the following situations in which the masses, the people, or the majority may turn against the experts who are making judgments which in the strict meaning of the terms are prudential and not scientific. 1) When reform violates generally held views and reformers refuse to heed the principle of gradualism in social change, the elite may be rejected by the majority. 2) When self-conscious and formally trained elites are defending generally held views, the critics, however pretentious in their scientific achievement, may be brushed aside. The highly organized, oligarchic, professional pressure group must often be dealt with in this way. 3) It is generally prudent to be critical of the elite group without a mass following, whenever that group would in fact restrict (in the name of protecting civil rights) the general liberties of the citizen or his political representative. 4) In the end, the ordinary democrat believes in values as true or proved. Metaphysical inquiry for the democratic philosopher extends beyond the facts-values which the intellectual foxes and lions are willing to gather. When the intellectual pragmatists are isolated from the standards of an on-going community, the majority may in good faith refuse to listen or even attack them politically. 5) In an on-going society, in which lasting differences have been generally accepted, any attempt to impose standards in a doctrinaire manner against long-standing traditions may be rejected by majorities acting against the few.

Each professional group is, however, the adherent of a code of ethics; it presumes to represent in a formal sense the morality and the wisdom of historical experience, such as the tradition of a Hippocratic oath for medical men as a symbol of the ethics of their profession, or the Christian moral tradition for businessmen or lawyers. The consent of all members to the code—the basic public opinion of the fraternity—is presumed to have been given. It is assumed that the profession or the functional order is a kind of moral teacher, which each member must respect simply to be a member. The existence of a morality which extends to all men, however, implies that a man who speaks from within the controlling group must attain his right to speak, even on science, by being a person of inner moral stature. To operate a society in a traditional manner means that much imperfection or inefficiency is preserved by customs. Inevitably the intellectual revolutionary feels called upon to condemn it. But while cultural issues cross-grain the "reasons of the heart," the loyalties of cultural areas within a nation must be accepted for the extending vistas of a common history. It is in the technical area of government however, when decisions impinge on the traditional and the cultural that the majority refuses to follow the technological mind which is governed by the norms of efficiency. For society to be a going concern, must not Protestants, Catholics, and Jews defend themselves? May not conservatives repudiate liberals, and Southerners struggle against Yankees? Does not a traditional nationalist have a right to criticize the internationalist? The Anglo-Saxon dream is gone, but must one cease to be proud of religion and culture, and to strive to maintain the marks of differentiation? Must the effete and the cultivated be held to have all rights against the straight-eyed honesty of the unrefined? These are contexts of life for both the common man and the intellectuals. Shall one deny the common man the right in a democracy to make his judgment if he will?

In an age of continuously emerging conflicts, the intellectuals become organized more effectively, and the representative of the people turns to them for technical and scientific solutions that will work. In 1953 the House Committee on Interstate and Foreign Commerce asked the National Academy of Sciences to assemble a panel of scientific experts on major diseases. The experts were given a free hand to discuss the specific aspects of their special knowledge, without interference from Congressmen. As a result, any possibility of Congress doing other than what the experts wanted and any possible criticism from public opinion were both eliminated. The time may come when the radiologists, geneticists, pathologists, biochemists, meteorologists, physicists, chemists, and all the rest of the organized scientists can tell the common man in a democracy to hold his peace; while they themselves speak with firmness to presidents, senators, congressmen, and judges on what must be a proper political decision. It is possible for scientists and technicians to attain a virtually impregnable position in a democracy, and it is possible that the techniques for hearing the scientists will make it impossible to go against their advice on policies. Certainly, this situation can prevail as long as the scientific sovereignty of the nation does not go counter to the articulate value judgments, the religion, and the morality of the common man. The technicians and scientists cannot pretend that their science gives them the right to be philosophers, theologians, or moralists.

CHAPTER 12

Theory for Tomorrow *

I

Public opinion has been studied in a variety of ways, and the method adopted in each case is dictated in large measure by the kind of results the student may seek. One may ask: what is public opinion at a given time, in a given area, on a particular issue of public policy? The characteristic method of such an inquiry is to make a survey, or take a poll, of a number of people, who by some definition may be regarded as a representative sampling of the public. Statistical analysis, mathematical calculations, and just plain judgment, all play their part in such an inquiry. Even the more complicated tabulating and projection machines may be used to reach final conclusions long before complete statistical data have been assembled. Public officials may dream of a time when a competent civil service can use such investigations to determine either what public policy must be, or to what extent it retains the confidence of the general and open public. All over the world such devices for studying popular reaction have come into use, and in spite of some failures they are sufficiently attractive to have a brilliant future.

But one may also ask: what does public opinion mean to any particular individual? In other words, if we start with the self-

* Republished from *The Journal of Politics,* 16 (November, 1954), 601 ff.

conscious existence of a person, we can see him project his consciousness to something "other" than himself. We can see him judging something which may be called "public opinion" solely in accordance with its meaning in his own existence. Little work has been done in this area, and probably not even the most adept pollster can get very far in such an inquiry. Yet any single person must see himself as an organic part of the environment of attitude, judgment, and feeling in which he lives. He must estimate to what extent he lives in harmony with public opinion, and to what extent he is in rebellion against it. He must calculate the pressure it can bring to bear upon him, and the penalty it may exact from him if he openly flouts what the community insists should be done or not done. In a philosophical sense, this is the real public opinion; for the collective judgment, however it is made, must be a product of the individual's conception of the significance of public opinion. Some may escape public opinion to a varying extent, while others live in a disciplined society, such as the army or a business organization, in which the penalty of resistance is exclusion from the society itself.

In another sense, but closely related to the position just stated, one may ask: what do philosophers, students of society, or, in general, intellectuals think public opinion is? Our inquiry has behind it the issue of the sociology of the intellectuals, just as one might inquire into the social role of any identifiable social class. For the intellectual, of course, the conclusions drawn by the more refined students will have a greater validity or force than the ideas of those who operate with a less complex system of concepts or techniques of investigation. On the other hand, those who are committed to quantitative and positivistic techniques of study might argue that the philosopher or the speculative mind in general has little to contribute to the subject. Here is an issue that will not be resolved quickly between those who believe that public opinion is capable of exhaustive theoretical treatment, and those who are concerned primarily with the measured fact—fact according to a pre-arranged statistical conception of the subject.

II

The issue of public opinion has been related perennially to the tension between those who govern and the general community, or the "open" population. In the large sense, a "public" has been always an issue of public law, or of the organization of power and its distribution among those who hold political office. But the recognition or formalization of the role of the community in which government is "public," or generally known or discussed, is merely a beginning. Immediately the question arises of the value of the "opinions" of those outside the decision-making or governing group. The quality of opinion has been the constant object of generalization, and through most of Western history the philosopher has regarded the opinions of ordinary people as of less value than the more critical or elaborate propositions of the civil servant, the philosopher, or the theologian. Much of the uneasiness in the study of democracy arises from this enduring tension, projected from the study of democracy in the ancient world into the Armageddons of political thought in our own time. Even the most complicated and abstruse of theoretical judgments must coincide at times with what may be generally believed by those outside of government. Is such a coincidence mere accident, which may be all but ignored, or does it arise from a more profound epistemological truth, that social and political validity itself in some degree is what "publicity-sharing" individuals may think?

Thus, the method of judging acceptable and unacceptable opinion becomes of transcending importance. In general, one may say that any such judgment must arise in the mind of the judge from his generalizations about the world in which he exists. The inarticulate premise is often the most conclusive factor in any theory of public opinion. One common principle is that public opinion is at times intelligent and well-founded, and sometimes it is not. According to the ancient cyclical theory of the forms of government, public sentiment runs a gamut from high justice to the most abject corruption. However, from the time Christian thinkers rejected the cyclical theory of the universe, the test of corruption or purity, or authoritative or anarchic opinion, has been judgment about correct social policy which is accepted by those who share most intimately in governing the large mass of society.

The growth of technical propaganda, the administrative control and censorship of mass communication, the expanding fiscal and social efficiency of the state, and the necessities of modern war, are present in the democracies as well as in dictatorships. Political invention has strengthened the power of the governing class, and it has at the same time weakened the capacity of public opinion to control the government. Naturally, the independence of mass opinion in the modern autocracy has been destroyed, but the power of censorship, propaganda, and suppression in the democracies has also restricted the influence of public sentiment. Few new devices to make public opinion stronger have made their appearance since before World War I, and such invention as there has been has worked toward the greater power of government in the manufacture of opinion, or toward the neutralization of opposition from the opinion of the general public.

The unhappy conclusion is thus reached that for our time the power and influence of public opinion on government has attained its height, and that it is, considering the general political experience of the recent generation, receding in its ability to control government. Correlative to this proposition is the fact that the denial of the rationality of public opinion has also reached its height in the modern totalitarian regimes. The trend of modern skeptical philosophy in democracies has, moreover, supported the view that the opinions of those who stand outside of government are either irrational or ill-founded. The issue of a free public opinion—that is, democratic public opinion in even a moderately ideal sense—hangs in the balance. Mass communication and government propaganda are immensely powerful in any case.

It is apparently true that in the United States the naturalization of the idea of public opinion has gone farther than in most

European states. The American tradition of equality, of individual rights, of a religious freedom which does not mean in fact the negation of corporate religious life, the belief in the right to an education, and to economic opportunity which in the aggregate is significantly wider than in most democracies, have all aided the acceptance of the principle of public opinion in American life. Respect for public opinion is based on the continuing belief that the American tradition is valid, and that its validities are a context for the right of the citizen to speak back to the state and, indeed, a context for the work of the scientists as the servant of progress. We recognize that much opinion is irrational or superstitious, but the principle of a permanent revolution toward equality, the idea of a great mass-oriented culture, the rejection in principle of class or of status or privilege associated with class, all point toward a charitable society of free individuals. It means that no citizen need mute his voice in the presence of the intellectual, and that the contribution of each citizen to public opinion is part of the democratic process. When the editors of *Fortune* studied the relations of the United States with Europe, they were impressed with our failure to speak the language of the European intellectual. "We have been so unaware of basic differences that we have persisted in talking to the Europeans in terms for which there is no foreign equivalent: *participation, community relations, incentive, public relations, productivity, man-in-the-street, public opinion*—the very listing itself produces a syllabus of the American philosophy. And a glossary of misunderstanding." *

III

It is probably impossible, and perhaps unnecessary, to put into words a precise definition of public opinion. But it is likewise true that discrimination in the analysis of public opinion is a significant step toward understanding it. Definition must reach

* "Have We Any Friends?" *Fortune* (February, 1951), 118.

in two directions. It must seek to clarify the nature of the public as an organ of political society. But definition must also seek, in the second place, to state some of the formal and philosophical conditions of a free public opinion. It is the examination of these two radii of definition that will occupy most of the remainder of this chapter.

If one speaks of the public as *a general and common idea,* it has been defined as the people at large, or every member of a defined community, or more particularly of a political society. The public is spoken of as that which is open or general, or, let us say, a single publicity; it has been defined as a large group, as those among whom there is general communication, as those who pay attention to the matter of mass communication; it is contrasted with private life, as those who speak openly to anyone, and, relatedly, to those who engage in the open discussion of controversial issues. Sometimes the public is defined as the majority, without qualification, meaning unconditional relativism as to values and an absolute power of the majority. It has been thought of as all those who are outside of the group making immediate decisions; that is, the public consists of spectators concerned more with the rules of the game than with its outcome. And, finally, the general public has been defined as those who accept inarticulately the decisions of majorities or pluralities.

It is common, moreover, to speak of the public in *a specialized or functional sense*—that is, the publics of specialization. Thus a public, as distinguished from the mass, becomes a functional group or minority of competence, such as a race, a party, the civil service, the lawyers, those who follow a particular sport, and so on. More particularly, it has been assumed that the public is the middle class, or it is the urban groups who enjoy specialized functions and internal communication. Related to this idea is the definition of the public as a kind of "representative" social class of intelligence and information. The leadership of a society has sometimes been defined as the public, such as some preponderant elite which may in fact be outside of the formal or parliamentary means of decision. In the larger sense, however, this concept of publics relates to groups of people who pay attention, for whatever reason, to special types of communication.

Another approach to the public is to identify it with *some sort of analysis of community life.* The most impressive and withal monistic approach to the community in modern political thought is that of philosophical idealism. One might say here that the public consists of all who are members of a moral organism or society, or all of those who are equal in such a community. Shading away slightly from idealism is the pragmatic or instrumental concept of the public, in which the public consists of all those who are affected by the indirect consequences of behavior. As to direct consequences of conduct, the public consists of spectators; but as to indirect consequences those affected become participants in community experience. Similarly, the public has been defined as all those who have either consciously or unconsciously a common interest. The emphasis on psychological unity is sometimes related to idealism and sometimes it is not, but psychological study has suggested that the public consists of people who share a unity based on communication, such as a crowd, a mob, or a group united without direct physical contact. In the extreme, such a view may identify the public with those who share membership in a group mind.

Lastly, the public has been defined in various ways as *an organ of political society,* and this view is related ultimately to a decisional theory of the state. Here, one may say that the public is simply all those who are subject to a government, who presumably have a common allegiance and some degree of common loyalty. But this affirmation makes the public essentially the object of decision rather than its subject. The public as subject may be spoken of as those who generate public power by the mechanical force of opinion, whether such opinion or consent may be true or false. Public opinion is, then, identified with ruling or effective opinions. The public has also been defined as an attention-for-power group, or a group that will accept the decisions of a constitutional majority on commonly recognized political issues. In turn, the public has been defined as all who share in political decisions, though only in extreme and perhaps revolutionary theory has the public as the people been identified with the government itself. More common, however, is the view that the public consists of those who share in or affect certain types of political decisions under conditions of control—that is, under a public law which assures participation in a specific sense, or the recognized forms of political behavior which receive the protection or acceptance of public law.

Under these conditions of diversity in definitions of the public, it is reasonable to try to state the problematic quality of public opinion simply as "the public opinion situation." Public opinion, then, arises in the dynamics of a society, one phase of which is, of course, the government or the political aspect of a functioning society. For a public or a public opinion to exist, there must be a division between those who rule and those who are ruled; in other words, there must be a recognition of the political distinction. But in addition there must be some body of norms of governmental conduct, which may be traditional or of more immediate provenance. That is to say, the political distinction itself implies some form of constitution or system of public law, whether it is written or customary. It is these circumstances that define the pre-conditions of the existence and action of the public.

Most significant of the implications involved here is that the public consists of those who in some identifiable way are outside the decision-making group, the government, the political class—or, let us say, outside the group of those who at least announce the sovereign or final decision. Public opinion, thus, always comes from the outside in, from the least influential to the most, from those who have least to do with political decision toward those who have the most to do with it. Public opinion must be finally a body of opinions on political or policy decision, but it is more than just this, for it is that opinion which shares more or less in influencing decision. Depending on the details of the public code, the public may make some decisions, such as the election of public officials, and it may have only an ultimate and indirect share, as, for example, in the course of judicial interpretation of the fundamental law. Participation, then, in the public opinion situation is both a legal arrangement and a sociology of power. The primary public opinion situation is concerned with notions of constitutional law, perhaps in the Aristotelian sense of the arrangements of office and power, and it is to be distinguished from the decision-maker and the "public" in the voluntary social group. Such a group would at best have a quasi-public and social opinion rather than actual public opinion.

IV

Such an analysis of the public opinion situation is applicable in theory to any society, though it would, of course, be more relevant to the mature political community. But it answers none of the qualitative issues which arise in the modern theory of public opinion. In a modern democracy it is admitted, broadly, that a free public opinion carries with it the obligation of deference from the ruling order. That is to say, a public opinion of proper moral and intellectual quality carries with it the right to direct to a degree the course of political decision. Philosophies of social life and obligation are, finally, the basis of judgment as to the obligatory character of public opinion.

Democratic theory states this proposition in a rather formal manner without specifying in detail the circumstances in which a free public opinion exists. It is said, for example, that we must abide by the majority decision if such a decision is made with a full knowledge of the facts, but in a different vein it appears to some that a full knowledge of the facts will be attained only if the conscience of most members of the public is inspired enough to seek it.* Otherwise, what we may have is simply "confused public thought." † It has been said, also, that "public opinion should be the final judge on matters of policy only when

* See Owen J. Roberts, "Wanted: Public Opinion," *The Public Opinion Quarterly*, IX (1945), 261 ff.

† *Ibid.*, 85, for the opinion of the editors.

all the pertinent facts have been widely discussed, so that it can be reasonably certain that interrogator and respondent are talking about the same thing." * And it is recognized that democracy is not merely applying the will of the people, for "it is the whole long process by which the people and their agents inform themselves, discuss, make compromises, and finally arrive at a decision." Moreover, such theories imply that the executive and administrative agencies are best able to see a public policy as a whole, while the legislature becomes rather a forum for the criticism of executive and administrative proposals,† more or less as in Hegelian or Wilhelmian Germany.

Aside from the issue of the power of any body of public opinion, democratic theory must be concerned with the conditions under which the proper action of the public creates political obligation. In general, the answer is that only a mature public opinion creates such obligation. Consent in an original sense may make a government legitimate, but such consent does not answer the issue as to any specific and subsequent political decision. The maturity of opinion is, therefore, the pre-condition of any majority rule at all. If in policy one value, or one set of facts, is more intelligent than another, leadership, in democratic theory, must offer the choice and urge the rational decision.‡

An issue which has disturbed many sensitive students of our times, however, is that of the "mass man." Here the student is concerned with the utter and abject corruption of the general public, and he shrinks with horror from the political participation of such masses in the operations of the modern state. What does one do if a preponderant number of people with the modern right of political participation turn to fascism or communism,

* See *The Public Opinion Quarterly*, XIV (Winter 1950-51), 686, citing H. Field and P. F. Lazarsfeld, *The People Look at Radio* (1946), 76.

† John C. Ranney, "Do the Polls Serve Democracy?" *The Public Opinion Quarterly*, X (1946), 349-360. The elitist bias is always just below the surface, even in the most enthusiastic of democratic thought.

‡ Cf. Lester Markel and others, *Public Opinion and Foreign Policy* (1949). A judgment of the "ignorance" of public opinion is offered in this volume.

or some variety of totalitarian society? What if public opinion expands the area of irreconcilable conflict in politics so that the customary and long-established pluralities of society are denied with violence, or with whatever denials of rights may be necessary? It is not sufficient to claim that then there is no public opinion—as A. L. Lowell might—for there is still the right of participation and a public "opinion" which sustains these views. Under these conditions the "social" becomes the terrible and implacable enemy of man. A philosophy of values is inescapable, if for no other reason than that such revolutionary and divergent regimes can and do resort to war to overthrow those who disagree. It seems best to admit that the mass man represents a kind of public opinion, but that in the light of Western philosophy the corrupted reality of this opinion denies it the capacity to create political obligation. And, implicitly, obligation may then arise from some source which is not public opinion.

For tomorrow, then, one of the great issues for the student of public opinion is what to do about the mass man and his leaders, who exemplify "the treason of the intellectuals." The mass man is not a member of a mere mob or a crowd, for these form and reform, passing as the symbols of unity wane in their power. The mass man has fled from freedom and responsibility, and his political life is a selfless loyalty to a political system. He admits no personal responsibility for his opinions and his escape from freedom seems perfect. He does not care for accuracy in political communication, for he is willing to accept what his leaders tell him, and his hates and loves move with the symbolism of mass communication. Perhaps he has fallen into this condition because his leaders have discovered that power can be gained through his willingness to surrender his right to personality in the political process. Ours is the age, said Benda, of the intellectual organization of political hatreds; it is also the time of mass passion directed at government. Politics has been divinized with a new amoralism, beyond Machiavellian conceptions, which makes "good" anything the state may do. And the "soul of Greece has given place to the soul of Prussia among the educators of mankind." * The really new thing in politics, argued Benda, is that both intellectuals and mass men claim the right to feel publicly their political passions.

What can be done? Hope, patience, and even war may be the answer to the totalitarian regime, but the answer within democratic and constitutional society is to face again some of the seemingly outworn issues. Technique is not sufficient and philosophy for freedom may not be. And the fine point of discrimination is probably the point at which techniques in the democratic management of opinion become in fact harmonious with the further techniques and theories which have assisted in the destruction of the freedom of the personality. Admittedly, this is a difficult issue, for the contrast at the extreme produces agreement and a common recognition that all are really on the side of the angels. It is appropriate that the theory of democracy should be re-examined constantly, but the re-examination must, in an age of technics, consider the narrowing range between the democratic management or manufacture of opinion and the totalitarians who carry techniques a step further in order to proclaim a new freedom for their selfless followers. It is clear, thus, that the background consideration of the quality of free opinion is a consideration of philosophies that state and evaluate the norms of social existence. On these matters perhaps little agreement can be expected in our time.

V

The analysis of free public opinion coincides frequently with the discussion of democracy. In the late eighteenth century consent to government meant some procedure by which the people knowingly agreed to constitutions and the revised codes of civil law. Consent was first of all constituent, which was the formal context in which all other immediate consent to public officials

* Julien Benda, *The Treason of the Intellectuals* (*La Trahison des Clercs*), trans. by Richard Aldington (1928). Also, Hannah Arendt, *The Origins of Totalitarianism* (1950).

or measures might be given. With the decline of confidence in the written fundamental law, consent has increasingly become an immediate issue. That is to say, the question is whether the day-to-day actions of a government command the assent of the thinking and functioning part of the political community. To say that since there is no revolution the people have given their consent has for a democracy, or for a believer in a free public opinion, only a negative meaning—if, indeed, it is not an actual absurdity. Free opinion expresses itself in the public as an organ of the state, but it is an organ that by its pressure or influence shapes to some degree the course of governmental decision. But the quality of consent is determined in no small degree by the effectiveness of the methods of participation, for these are part of the conditions of participation. It seems clear that the means of mass communication, the art of propaganda, the existence of massive psychological factors in leadership, and the increasing functions and effectiveness of political administration, all suggest that the tide is running against the freedom of public opinion. In other words, in order to preserve or stimulate free public opinion there must be a sustained effort in social invention which will increase the power of opinion outside of government. Methods to balance the power of mass communication and the secrecy of public decision must be invented, if public opinion as a democratic power is to hold the political balance. At least the machinery must be there for use in normal political matters, and not merely in extreme situations in which public opinion may and does act with explosive force.

Democratic and republican theory has held that general, popular opinion should to some extent control the government. It has held especially that fundamental decisions should be an expression of the people as sovereign, though it has not held with equal conviction the belief that the immediate decisions of a government agency should express such opinions or ideas. Thus democratic inventiveness was fostered during the great days of democratic and republican enthusiasm in the nineteenth century. The extension of the suffrage, the election of more public officials, and the rise of the political party system clearly worked for greater popular control. On the contrary, historic monarchic theory believed that public opinion had a duty to support the government, that its criticisms should be restrained, and that the bodies which represented public opinion should be critics of policy rather than its formulators. Such an attitude, of course, stimulated the invention of devices for the organization and control of popular sentiment in favor of the government. Had the techniques of mass communication and propaganda been as well known before the rise of democracy as they are known today, democracy might never have come into being. For these techniques clearly support the government against the freedom of public opinion; they are extremely effective; and they no doubt explain in part the success of the modern authoritarian regimes.

A continued search for a meaningful participation is needed in the increasingly centralized societies of the present day. Such a search is difficult at best. When citizens are resentful, they may disobey the law and prevent any enforcement at all. They may explode in revolution or support a *coup d'état* among the elite; or free opinion may at best be confined to the ideas commonly held by underground movements. There is then no commitment from anyone that the democratic processes of political society will be observed. The study of the democratic process, while obviously important, lags behind the study of how to make the state more efficient in its administration, or how to discover the latent trends of opinion in order that administrative policy may either retreat or all the more vigorously create new sentiment. The areas of society in which elements of the democratic process are present can, no doubt, be increased; but the large functional organization, such as the army or trade union, removes increasingly the control of government from the rank and file. Free public opinion retreats before the confirmation of the iron law of oligarchy.

A free public opinion is more than an opinion which has at its disposal the means of participation sufficient to balance the perennial force of those in power who want to shape opinion to fit their own interest. A free public opinion involves, finally, philosophical views of what justice in a society may be. We can say that a just government is one which arises somehow or other from the consent of the governed, but we can also say that the state exists for the realization of justice, and that the idea of justice involves social theory. If it is admitted that some values are better or more true than others, that justice as well as consent is necessary to a free public opinion, then majority rule or any system of participation has its pre-conditions of legitimacy.

VI

The pre-conditions of majority rule are, indeed, more important than majority rule itself. The issue perhaps may be phrased as follows: what are the conditions under which majority rule is an agency of freedom? A majority in democratic public law is an organ of the body politic, and it is a permanent one, since even the dictatorships have preserved the formality of majority decision, however drained the process may be of any implications of free opinion. However, there must be a consensus in a body politic on what majorities will and will not do; even an agreement in a state to disagree on certain fundamentals implies that the majority is limited. The statement or understanding of consensus within the public is the first and the most important of all the pre-conditions of consent, of the governmental power of public opinion, and of the peaceful existence of any type of majority rule. Moreover, the formulation of consensus is the formulation of a part of the content of a free public opinion; it is the public rather than the private system of rationality and morality in an orderly society. In a formal sense at least, a majority based on consensus is an agency of freedom. Consensus is the essential pre-condition of a free public opinion.

One of the persistent and traditional means according to which consensus can be stated is the bill of rights. Civil liberty implies that the rights of the person are more fundamental in ordering the state than are the rights of any organ of the body politic, and that the rights of the minority are as fundamental as those of a majority. Civil liberty is the formal eighteenth-century answer to the issue of consensus. But the statement of a national social philosophy in a bill of rights is a common device which has developed since bills of rights were first placed in our revolutionary American state constitutions. The effort has reached the international stage with the United Nations Declaration of Human Rights. Here we have, without agreement on essential philosophical views, the broadest existing statement of consensus among modern political leaders. A modern democracy, then, affirms both the inalienable rights of the person and the right of a majority to make decisions within the pre-conditions laid down. Free public opinion is, therefore, one that has the capacity to resist the the projection of governmental influence, to thrust its own power back at the government through its means of participation, and it is one which is guided by the morality and the reasonableness of consensus.

The bill of rights, however, is hardly a completely satisfactory means of stating the pre-conditions of the majority rule of free public opinion. Declarations of rights seldom state the philosophical views on which consensus stands or falls. As instruments of democracy, they seek to reach agreement on a particular right between diverse and fundamentally hostile theories of obligation. The reluctance of democracy to insist on uniformity in philosophical view, and its great effort to attain agreement on things that can be done, is one of its powerful attractions as a system of government. Part of the search, then, for a free public opinion is the perduring examination of the nature of the community and the nature of man. If we deny the truth of all values, we deny that man has a nature, and we assume that the community is such a limitless experimental process that there can be no criticism of anything it does. We may well agree that there is little chance that all the Western world will ever agree on one set of theories of man's nature or of the nature of the community. A free public opinion must rest in practice on the consensus of such documents as the United Nations statement of rights, and on the strength of philosophies which affirm those rights as rational or valid.

Implicit in such a view is the defense of some sort of pluralistic society. We can say that democracy rests on certain fundamental agreements, but it is equally true that it rests on the peaceful ordering of fundamental disagreements. In a practical sense, freedom is granted the fundamentally divergent view as a matter of public law, though it does not imply that the fundamentally diverging views are accepted as true. If one believes his own philosophy is true, he must fight for it, but he can also accept the formal democratic consensus and instruct his philosophy to support that program. The pluralist notion of a free community suggests that ultimate distinction in the New Testament: render therefore unto Caesar the things which are Caesar's, and unto God the things that are God's. The state, then, can be a condition of right; it may be will and not force. An arbitrary political will is by definition the denial of the rights of the person and the destruction by government of such rights. Pluralism affirms against individualism the existence of *corps intermédiaires,* that fiercely resented relic of the Old Regime. It does not suggest that the freedom of the person can be expressed only in the individual; rather, it implies that freedom may be found in traditional and voluntary social groupings, which by implication carry with them the inalienable rights of the United Nations Declaration; it may be found in the family, in the religious body, in the economic group, or in loyalty to the professional society. It means, withal, that a democracy may have a program, but not uniformity in its theory of the nature of man and society. It implies speech for freedom more than it implies freedom of speech; the legitimate majority is the creature of civil liberty, but civil right is not the philosophical creature of the majority.

On government and on citizen rests the most serious obligation to create a free public opinion and the conditions of legitimate majority rule, for we have here the elements of democratic public order for our time. But there can be no perfection in any political procedure; the achievement of free public opinion is, therefore, always short of what may be considered ideal. The sovereignty of a free public opinion as an abstract idea, for instance, is different from the modalities of majority rule, for the latter implies a formal expression under carefully defined conditions, such as election laws and existing political party activity, which may and often do in fact deviate from what might be called public opinion. The public, on the other hand, is to be discovered through the voluntary social group and through the organization of the compulsory political community. For it is from the social group, which is the functional aspect of an idea, that public opinion through the channels of participation in public law arises to the area of actual decision.*

VII

Diversity in the creation of the conditions of a free public is harder to reach than might be thought at first glance. The dominant political ideologies of our time are locked in conflict, and strength in such conflict is greater as uniformity within the ideology is reached. Freedom of opinion in such a conflict is an evidence of weakness—at least to the opponent. Independent corporate opinion means internal conflict in philosophy, in public policy, and in regard to the men who are granted power. Associations, once free, tend to become compulsory in times of social struggle, their governing orders widen the distance between themselves and the common members, and dissent may be regarded as treason to the recognized common cause.

But more subtle tendencies than this are involved, since liberalism has a strongly individualistic background which has resented from the time of the French Revolution the formation of corporate thought. Liberalism has stood for freedom, but the expression of that freedom has increasingly become the unitary policy of the collective state. Tolerance is no easy matter. Can

* See Herbert McClosky, "The Fallacy of Absolute Majority Rule," *The Journal of Politics*, XI (November, 1949), 637 ff; Willmoore Kendall, "Prolegomena to Any Future Work on Majority Rule," *ibid.*, XII (November, 1950), 694 ff.

secular scientists really tolerate a public opinion which is not guided by the postulates of science? Can it accept with generosity a public opinion guided, for example, by religious values? Can it stop short of accepting the Bismarckian state, a species of German *Rechtsstaat* with its characteristic bureaucratic control, its concern with military affairs, its theory of a directed public opinion, its "idea-planners," and its belief that good citizenship means support of the government? In such a society, whatever diversity in group organization there may be is sanctioned or approved by the state, while group life which runs counter to the principles of the government may be controlled by censorship and suppression. Must not the media of mass communication become increasingly the means by which public opinion is organized, rather than the means by which a vital group life imposes its wishes on those who rule? And the theory of communication in such a situation becomes more technical, mathematical, and scientific, and correspondingly less concerned with the values being expressed in communication.*

Liberalism in more recent times has become committed to a complex group or corporate life. Against the totalitarian regimes, liberalism stands for free communication, the emergence of the content of that communication from associative life, and diversity in policy and in basic philosophical theories of man and society. And the consensus which is accepted as the precondition of free communication closely resembles the ideas in the United Nations Declaration of Rights. The problem may be stated like this: how can any ideological movement adhering to freedom nevertheless insist that some issues must not be discussed in mass communication? How can we keep the so-called "lower levels" of opinion from the area of "outloud" opinion and discussion, and yet preserve freedom at a higher level of agreement? Can we not say that the expression of opinion in

* Cf. C. E. Shannon and Warren Weaver, *The Mathematical Theory of Communication* (1949). These authors believe, apparently, that a purely mathematical theory of communication can have some import for the content of communication.

favor of race riots, race discrimination, the denial of religious freedom, and the rejection of democratic processes, may be restricted within the context of free public opinion? It is only when these things are restricted to private opinion that a free public opinion is possible.

Such a conception implies no uniformity in public opinion, nor any right of a government to insist upon it. Such a restriction on public opinion is to be based on social theory; on views of the common good and of justice in the relations of men and groups. Neither the revolutionary elite nor the degenerate group can be permitted to take over politics in the name of another form of freedom. Logically, there should be no general, popular vote, and no majority action on whether the human person is entitled to freedom, on whether the process of democratic lawmaking and decision should be kept or rejected, and none on a multitude of issues concerning the religious, moral, philosophical, familial, and other freedoms of the individual. Assuming all of these things, however, the customary range of democratic political controversy remains hardly changed, for the consensus and diversity of a free public opinion in a free society has not been attacked.

Even a free society does not have to idealize public opinion, or to say that the common man has all wisdom, as sometimes seems implied in the contemporary cult of the common man, who appears to have no family or economic associations and certainly no roots in his own history. Perhaps extreme idealism is out of place until something approximating a Greek excellence has been realized. And a democracy does not need to assume that all men must understand all things political. For there are levels of appreciation both in principle or morality and in political technics. We can admit the complexity and the danger in human motivation, but we can say that the criticism of principle goes beyond the analysis of motive. A democracy must seek through its public consensus to achieve popular support above the level of average opinion on technical and administrative matters, while it remembers it is of the greatest importance that the common man understand there is a common good and political justice, however imperfectly governments may realize them. If a free public opinion is to exist, all this must be done short of political tyranny; it must be done within the framework of constitutional society. In this way, the means accepted by public opinion may fall short of violence, except as violence is used by the state for war and the repression of the criminal. But the education of public opinion is free in the sense that it is not dominated by the views alone of those who have power, and education itself is shared by the state and private, voluntary associations or functioning groups of citizens.

Moreover, the import of this discussion is that there must be a continuous search for a common good, for social justice, or indeed for a general will. The general will is to be found in history and experience, in philosophy and religion, and in science and scientific advance. It is not to be found alone in economic satisfaction, nor alone in personal creativeness, nor in an uncriticized tradition or custom of the popular mind. It is not to be found in a surrender to the state in the name of freedom and welfare, or in the rise of a supreme legal coerciveness. When political power rather than the disinterested general will is stressed, there is, it is true, an exaltation of the prerogatives of the sovereign people. Majorities are sought rather than the common good; intransigence becomes a corroding way of life, and tyranny may arise from what was once the protection of the presumed rights of the people. And "the way is prepared for the sophistries of modern political management, for manipulating electoral bodies, for influencing elected bodies, for procuring plebiscites." *

In our own day the issue of what is a free public opinion has become curiously and bitterly precise. One group asserts that such an opinion can be based entirely on a modern, scientific view which affirms the nominalistic and empirical theory of rationalism. The other group of thinkers affirms that a free public

* See Thomas Hill Green, *Lectures on the Principles of Political Obligation,* Sec. 69.

opinion can come only from an adherence to the moral and religious values of Western tradition, in which the truth and the permanence of social values are affirmed. On the one hand, it is said that democracy arose from the denial of the moral traditions of Christian thought, from the rejection of any discussion about ends, and from the emergence of social relativism. On the other hand, it is said that democracy emerged from the evolution of Christian philosophy as it has been increasingly applied to the creation of free governments, that democracy has been produced by the affirmation of ends which have a rational foundation, and has developed from the rejection of those philosophies which postulated a relativism of values. On the one hand, a free public opinion is held to be one which accepts its ends as suitable myths, being more concerned with its immediate political techniques; on the other, free opinion is said to be grounded in a philosophy of a common good which is subject to rational defense. On the one hand, all public opinion is to be judged in terms of organization, complexity, or social pattern applied with the coolness and scientific dispassion of anthropology; on the other hand, public opinion, while it may exhibit some of these characteristics, is free because it has had a glimpse of legitimate government through consent, and of a social justice which can be the goal of political authority.

One may reach a theory of free public opinion, therefore, either by saying that nobody's opinion is any good, or by saying that the opinion of everyone on a question of values is likely to be worth listening to. In a time of prosperity one may avoid the ultimate question of whether public opinion can be a vehicle for the expression of the more profound values of the human spirit. But this is hardly a view of the procedures of democracy, such as majority rule and civil liberty, that can be defended when great injustice is sensed by public opinion; when there is an external issue such as war; or some objective crisis rises in the life of the state, such as the shortage of a vital raw material. There are times when a citizen must be prepared to say that a government or a majority is wrong, and to stick by that decision.

VIII

What method can be used to evaluate the philosophical basis of a free public opinion? One of the useful types of inquiry is to look at the history of democracy. Does the actual development of the democracies of our time give proof of cultural relativism, moral nihilism, and skepticism as to the attainment of truth? The great defenders of rights, of a tradition of constitutional government, and of the rise of the people toward intelligence in opinion, have believed in principles of moral judgment. Democracy in its historical emergence, its defense, and in its expansion has not been an adventure in skepticism; rather, it has been an adventure in faith. It has been, historically, very close to religious ideas.

It is not feasible in the American or in any other Western tradition to exclude the idea of a law of nature from the magistral conceptions which have served in the emergence of the preconditions of a free public opinion. Under that law, as variously interpreted, there seems to be agreement that the human personality is worthy of respect, that government should serve its moral and rational needs, and that each man in turn has a right in some degree to consent to the government that rules him. Much modern history has been written with a tendency to underestimate the force and creativeness of moral judgment in shaping historical events. Yet who can deny that in our opposition to fascism and communism, it is the keen sense of injustice we recognize that has led us to take positions which may put us into war? When we get a glimpse behind the iron curtain, we see that more than a fortuitous agreement exists on what the rights are which men demand.

If we can say that the historical development of democracy has been related to a principle holding that by reason and knowledge we are to arrive at some defensible social values, we can also say that on purely logical grounds democracy is compatible with the standards of Western political ethics. By democracy is meant, of course, some system by which the participation of the people in politics is real, and in which such participation becomes the basis of public decision. In addition, democratic theory suggests that the quality of the judgment of the citizens is or can be worth consulting.

Here we have the issue of a theory of public opinion, the analysis of which weaves back and forth between the idea of participation and the idea of the worth of public judgment. We have developed a variety of means of public expression under constitutional government, but the confusion of current democratic theory is fully apparent in the way we judge the opinions which are expressed in politics. In the extreme, it is said that the values of public judgment are myths, that they are to be evaluated purely and simply under the canon of cultural relativism, and that the only judgment worth considering is one which condemns itself to moral skepticism. The issue of political ethics is twofold: on the one hand, we apply legal and ethical standards to those who hold the reins of power, but, on the other, the great issue in our time is what kind of ethics we should apply to the judgments of men in their corporate life. The issue is, indeed, whether any ethical knowledge is possible in the assessment of public opinion. In the past, writers from the Greeks through St. Augustine, to Thomas Jefferson and on to the present, have said there are times when public judgment is corrupted. If this view has any meaning at all, it is that mass judgment can lose its ethical hallmarks, and that politics can become a naked struggle for power, in which money is commonly used to purchase favor and to neutralize opposition. We find this idea among the Romans, in the Middle Ages, in such a man as John of Salisbury, and among the muckrakers of our own Progressive era.

Let it be added quickly, however, that if all judgments are hypothetical, if public opinion consists solely of current myths, if participation and consent are only a phase of the technics of politics, or if all ethical values are relative to cultural accumulation and evolution, there is no basis for saying that any opinion in its political expression can be corrupted. An honest democracy is no better on rational grounds, in this view, than one dominated by bribery, demagogy, and assassination. Even the most ardent advocates of democracy have seldom held that any public has been a paragon of virtue, but it has been held that a public opinion which reflects the standards of Western ethics is more worthy of consideration than one which does not. In a practical sense, resistance to modern tyranny must be based on the idea that a corrupted opinion does not preserve a decent respect for the rest of mankind. How could a Greek or anybody else resist tyranny if all views and judgments of behavior were purely hypothetical? *

If we affirm the moral foundations of democracy, we make the same affirmation for the rights and evaluation of public opinion. We may then say with *The Nation* that "The voice of the people is neither the voice of God nor the utterance of Belial—it is simply the cry of man." †

* For a brilliant discussion of the issue of Socrates against the Assembly which condemned him, see Willmoore Kendall, "The People Versus Socrates Revisited," *Modern Age*, III (Winter, 1958-1959), 98 ff. Kendall offers a criticism of the "liberals" who denounce the Athenian Assembly as acting without reason.

† "Vox Populi," *The Nation*, 91, No. 2361 (September 29, 1910), 283.

INDEX

CPSIA information can be obtained at www.ICGtesting.com
Printed in the USA
BVOW08s0434260713

326872BV00010B/161/P

9 781412 815017